Earth First!

Religion and Politics
Michael Barkun, *Series Editor*

Syracuse University Press is pleased to introduce a new series, *Religion and Politics,* with the publication of *Earth First!* by Martha F. Lee.

Contemporary religious movements constitute a wide spectrum of energetic responses to the conditions of life in the modern world. Whether fundamentalist or liberal, apocalyptic or millenarian, world-renouncing or world-embracing, such movements often become enmeshed in politics—either by participating directly in the political process or by challenging existing regimes outside of normal political channels.

The series will provide readers with critical and interdisciplinary studies of the entire range of politically involved religious movements—and, as this first volume suggests, religiously oriented political movements—in the United States and throughout the world. The series will be of interest to scholars in the fields of religious studies, politics, history, the social sciences, and contemporary affairs. The editor, Michael Barkun of the Maxwell School, Syracuse University, is advised by a panel of distinguished scholars from a variety of disciplinary and topical specialties.

EARTH FIRST!

Environmental Apocalypse

Martha F. Lee

SYRACUSE UNIVERSITY PRESS

Title page: Earth First! demonstrates against the timber industry, Ft. Bragg, Calif. Photography by Michael Schumann/SABA.

The paper used in this publication meets the minimum requirements of American National Standard for Information Sciences—Permanence of Paper for Printed Library Materials, ANSI Z39.48-1984. ∞™

Library of Congress Cataloging-in-Publication Data
Lee, Martha F. (Martha Frances), 1962–
    Earth first! : environmental apocalypse / Martha F. Lee.
        p.   cm. — (Religion and politics series)
    Includes bibliographical references and index.
    ISBN 0-8156-2677-0 (cloth : alk. paper). — ISBN 0-8156-0365-7
(paper : alk. paper)
        1. Environmentalism—United States.   2. Social ecology—United
States.   3. Deep ecology—United States.   I. Title.   II. Series.
GE197.L44   1995
363.7'00973—dc20   95-309

For my mother, Margaret Lee

Martha Lee is an assistant professor in the Department of Political Science at the University of Windsor. She is the author of *The Nation of Islam: An American Millenarian Movement.*

Contents

Preface

During the final decades of the twentieth century, profound political changes have occurred. One of the most critical of these changes has been the rise to power and prominence of environmental ideologies. Environmentalism is particularly significant because it addresses a fundamental fact of our existence: the relationship between human beings and the natural world. In the words of political philosopher Hannah Arendt, the fact that we are earthbound creatures is "the very quintessence of the human condition."[1] Our relationship with this planet is critical to our political identity.

It is therefore not surprising that environmentalism has spread across the traditional left-right spectrum. In so doing, it has accumulated significant political weight. Once the purview of interest groups such as the Sierra Club and the Wilderness Society, concern for such issues as acid rain, global warming, and toxic waste disposal has permeated the discourse of both citizens and politicians. It is now part of the political mainstream.

In all its forms, environmentalism is—at least marginally—apocalyptic. It is the wellbeing of this planet that most fundamentally supports human life; threats to the health of the earth are therefore threats to human life itself. It is the power of that connection that drives environmentalism. Confronting pollution and extinction is in a very real way confronting the source and limits of human power.

Among environmental movements, Earth First! is unique because it makes this connection explicit in its doctrine and in its activities. For Earth First!ers, ultimate political meaning is found in wilderness, and Earth First!ers are willing to protect that wilderness by any means necessary. Their creation of a standard of good that lies outside traditional political life, coupled with their willingness to use illegal and potentially violent tactics to defend that good, makes their story compelling.

ix

This book focuses on the evolution of the Earth First! movement, which began as a result of the direct political experience of Dave Foreman and a number of likeminded environmentalist colleagues. Over time, the movement split into two factions, one that emphasized biocentrism, and one that emphasized the interrelated nature of biodiversity and social justice. It is Earth First!'s original doctrine, rather than subsequent developments, however, that most clearly raises the issues of why individuals might anticipate an apocalyptic event, and choose not to compromise in their defense of the earth. For this reason, it is this initial conformation of Earth First! that is held as a measure of the movement's later evolution.

Throughout Earth First!'s history, its adherents grappled with issues such as the nature of political community, the definition of justice, and the degree to which human life is meaningful. For these reasons, the movement's development illustrates in compact form the tensions inherent in all political communities that anticipate the end of civilization. In this way, it tells us much about our own lives and politics. If we take environmentalism seriously, and follow it to its logical conclusion, we must confront many of the issues that have been (and are) confronted by Earth First!ers.

This book began as a doctoral dissertation, and I have been fortunate in the help I received during the more than four years of research and writing that it consumed. I am most indebted to Michael Barkun. His own work inspired my interest in millenarianism, and his insightful comments and great patience were a boon to me at all stages of this project. I am also grateful for the advice and criticism of Ralph Ketcham, Amanda Porterfield, Margaret Shannon, Tom Patterson, and Joe Cammarano. As the dissertation became a book, the comments of Mike Cummings of the University of Colorado at Denver helped me clarify many of my arguments, and Cynthia Maude-Gembler of Syracuse University Press was an enthusiastic and supportive editor.

I learned a great deal from my discussions with the many Earth First!ers whom I interviewed for this project. They were more than kind to me, and I appreciate their trust during a time when they had every reason to be hostile to strangers. I am particularly grateful for the aid of Dave Foreman, Mitch Friedman, George Draffan, and John Davis. The staff of the Earth First! journal was also extremely helpful. While I worked in Tucson, Roxanne Pacheco graciously gave me the use of the office facilities at Ned Ludd Books. The office staff at the Greater Ecosystem Alliance in Bellingham, Washington, was likewise obliging.

I must also thank those individuals who, in the course of my research, helped me in other ways, particularly Paula Shimp, Janine Weir, Tracy Hamill, Gillian MacKay, Nina Rupprecht, Andrew Beh, and the Ross family.

This research would not have been possible without the financial support provided by the Roscoe Martin Fund of the Maxwell School of Citizenship and Public Affairs, and by a Doctoral Fellowship from the Social Sciences and Humanities Research Council of Canada. Its completion would not have been possible without the further encouragement of my patient colleagues at the University of Windsor. I owe a great debt to our secretary, Barbara Faria, who cheerfully and tirelessly helped me in the last stages of this project.

Last but not least, I could not have finished this work without the support of my family, Frank, Carol, David, and Lisa, and the help of John Sutcliffe, who is a veritable master at finding humor and joy in the most difficult of circumstances.

Windsor, Ontario   Martha F. Lee
March 1995

Acknowledgments

Permission to reprint the following material is gratefully acknowledged:

From the University Press of Virginia for lines of poetry from *The Black Riders and Other Lines*. Volume 10. *Poems and Literary Remains* from *The Works of Stephen Crane,* edited by Fredson Bower. Used with permission from the University Press of Virginia.

From Gibbs, Smith, Publisher, for material from *Deep Ecology: Living as if Nature Mattered,* by Bill Devall and George Sessions.

From Dave Foreman for material from his "Memorandum Regarding Earth First! Statement of Principles and Membership Brochure," September 1980.

From Bart Koehler for material from his song "Were You There When They Built Glen Canyon Damn?"

From Mike Roselle for material from his song "The Ballad of the Lonesome Treespiker."

Earth First!

1

Millenarianism in the American Context

Our forefathers, inhabitants of the island of Great Britain ..., left their native land to seek on these shores a residence for civil & religious freedom. [A]t the expense of their blood, to the ruin of their fortunes, with the relinquishment of everything quiet & comfortable in life, they effected settlements in the inhospitable wilds of America.[1]

—Thomas Jefferson

Social protest movements do not appear, fully formed, on barren soil; they are instead deeply rooted in the culture from which they emerge. From their genesis, they bear the mark of that culture's assumptions about political life, and their development likewise depends upon the way in which that soil nourishes them. Earth First!, a modern American millenarian movement, thus reflects the assumptions that are peculiar to its context.

We can turn to both theoretical and historical frameworks for initial help in understanding Earth First!'s origins, its millenarian character, and its development. I therefore begin this introductory chapter by reviewing the underlying philosophical assumptions of the American state and by examining the difficulties that emerge from that context, as discussed in modern critiques of American liberalism. Because the United States Forest Service illustrates the substance of those critiques so well and moreover is of particular relevance to the emergence of Earth First!, it receives special mention. I continue with a brief examination of other radical environmental groups and an initial consideration of deep ecology, the doctrine that underlies Earth First!'s belief system. Finally, I conclude with a survey of the relevant literature concerning millenarian movements and apocalyptic doctrines.

The American Context

The founding of the American republic embodied two distinct but interrelated projects: the creation of a nation "conceived in liberty"[2] and the establishment of European civilization in the center of a vast and threatening wilderness. The formation of the American state was an attempt to create what John Winthrop termed a "city upon a hill,"[3] while its subsequent development encouraged the growth of cities and industries that made the encounter with the wilderness a "battle of subjugation."[4] The emergence of a political community on this continent was thus a deliberate act of creation that allowed Americans to believe that they had made the land their own.

In his classic essay "In Defence of North America," George Grant summarizes the founding experience as "the meeting of the alien and yet conquerable land with English-speaking Protestants,"[5] and he claims that this primal experience continues to shape American thought and action. It is part of a mythic consciousness that Richard Rubenstein argues is expressed in "the myth of the American as the New Adam and the North American continent as a New Eden."[6] Within the American state, this mythic primal found expression in the hopes of the Puritans, the actions of the revolutionaries, and the creation of a government by the American founders. Such a vision reflects, in part, the desire to make a perfect world, and in this respect carries with it millenarian overtones.

The term "millenarian" has its origins in the Latin words *mille*, one thousand, and *annus*, year. It evokes the specter of an imminent apocalypse, and the promise of a thousand year period of glory for the community of believers.[7] Norman Cohn, however, in his classic work *The Pursuit of the Millennium*, uses the term more liberally. He argues that millenarian movements are a particular type of salvationism, and his work creates a framework of analysis useful for characterizing such groups.[8] Cohn identifies five elements common to all millennial ideologies and millenarian movements: they envision a salvation that is imminent, ultimate, collective, this-worldly, and miraculous.[9] Cohn argues that poor and politically marginalized groups are most likely to adopt this type of belief system. They have little to lose from the apocalyptic destruction of the present order, and millennialism's myth of the elect holds only promise for them. In millenarian belief systems, the transformation of the community is of central importance.

In *Visionary Republic,* Ruth Bloch traces the millenarian themes in early American political thought. Although it is incorrect to say that millennialism *caused* the American Revolution, "it can illuminate how many Americans understood the ultimate meaning of the . . . birth of the American nation."[10]

According to Ernest Tuveson, that meaning is clear: Americans believed that they were founding a nation that would set an example for all the world. In *Redeemer Nation,* he identifies the millenarian themes present in that founding as a faith that Americans were a race chosen by God, that their state constituted a chosen nation, and that all subsequent history could be understood as a battle between good and evil, where good was defined as progress and evil as reaction.[11] Tuveson outlines the evolution of these themes from the arrival of the Puritans on American soil to the conclusion of the Second World War, and he convincingly argues that they continue to dominate American political thought. His book closes with the suggestion that Americans' extreme reaction to "Bolshevism" (as perhaps a "new and powerful strategy of [the] Antichrist"[12]) might in part be due to the fact that it emerged after they believed their apocalyptic battle had been won. Thus, Tuveson shows that millenarian theory not only provides insight into the early years of the republic but also helps to explain modern American society. The millenarian symbols that were part of the revolution still form an element of the American political identity.

In *Sons of the Fathers,* Catherine Albanese further discusses these symbols and the belief system that links them, which she refers to as a civil religion. On her view, the revolution and its civil religion still resonate with meaning for contemporary American political life. They provide a way for one to "orient oneself in the world, with reference to both the transcendent and the ordinary,"[13] and they are testament to the religiosity of the American public.[14] Albanese also suggests that Americans, as a "new and rootless" people, must expend tremendous amounts of energy to maintain their identity.[15] As Grant has pointed out, North Americans are not autochthonous: they do not live "undivided from [their] own earth," and therefore they must continually struggle to define their identity.[16] Albanese argues that in such situations, millennial expectations are likely to re-emerge, and she highlights the fact that Americans have often channeled those hopes towards "the redemptive powers of nature."[17] Albanese explains this by noting that culture depends upon nature to remain alive, and that as American culture has moved further away from this sustenance, there has emerged a need for its artificial re-creation. She cites Daniel Boone, Davy Crockett, and the conservation and ecological movements as examples of this tendency.

In *Nature Religion in America,* Albanese traces these themes in more detail, following them from early Native American spirituality through to late twentieth century authors such as Starhawk. In her analysis of "Republican Nature," she notes that nature functioned in republican religion in three interrelated ways. It meant "the purity and wholesomeness of clean country living," the "transcendent reality of heavenly bodies . . . and the universal law that grounded human rights and duties with the body politic," and "the quality of the sublime as it was discovered in republican terrain."[18] In subsequent millenarian movements (particularly nineteenth century evangelism), "nature moves from the settled past to the active pull of the time to come. Significantly, the innocence and perfection of the first creation are posited in a future time."[19]

In her work, Albanese thus links political symbolism with religion, and millenarianism with nature. She mentions only briefly, however, the irony that emerges from this situation. As the polity was strengthened, the governmental apparatus grew in size and scope, cities expanded, and industries flourished, Americans—partly out of necessity—attempted to master nature. In the words of George Grant, "Even when we fear General Motors or ridicule our immersion in the means of mobility, we must not forget that the gasoline engine was a needfilled fate for those who had to live in such winters and across such distances."[20] Cecelia Tichi argues that this confrontation with nature was fueled by a vision of America as the site of a utopian "New Earth," which resulted in a situation wherein "[t]he American spirit and the American continent were bonded ideologically."[21] That development also embodied a spirit of triumphalism; in David Brower's words, "Wilderness was the Frontier and Progress celebrated its retreat. As we destroyed wilderness, it built us."[22]

In *Virgin Land,* Henry Nash Smith directly links the mythic western wilderness to the American system of government. His work supports Frederick Turner's assertion that "American democracy was born of no theorist's dream; it was not carried in the *Susan Constant* to Virginia, nor in the *Mayflower* to Plymouth. It came stark and strong and full of life out of the American forest, and it gained new strength each time it touched a new frontier."[23] These arguments are in part economic, but they also highlight the importance of wilderness and frontier as part of American political identity. Americans' perception of themselves as a society "shaped by the pull of a vacant continent" still defines "what Americans think of their past, and therefore what they propose to make of themselves in the future."[24]

Earth First!'s founders created a movement that was in part a reflection of these historical influences. They emphasized the preservation of wilderness, but that emphasis was also understood as a way to rejuvenate the political community. Many of the original Earth First!ers adopted a critique of the American state that stemmed from their analysis of the American founding. Although their analysis was (and is) radical, it shares many themes with other, more mainstream critical evaluations of the American polity.

In the early battle to shape the character of the United States, the Federalists prevailed over the Anti-Federalists, and Hamilton's vision triumphed over that of Jefferson. The new nation became a large and powerful industrial state rather than a small and inward-looking agricultural community. Those victories, however, also occasioned a loss. The Federalists understood the freedom obtained by the Revolution as the freedom to pursue individual interest. Dave Foreman, Earth First!'s most influential founder, believes that this emphasis meant that "the business of America became business."[25] The government became a mechanism for promoting rapid economic growth and balancing competing interests. As Madison wrote in Federalist 14, "We have seen the necessity of the Union as our bulwark against foreign danger, as the conservator of peace among ourselves, as the guardian of our commerce and other common interests, as the only substitute for those military establishments which have subverted the liberties of the old world, and as the proper antidote for faction."[26]

This type of vision created an economically powerful state, but it carried with it a particular set of difficulties. Where individuals pursue only self-interest, political community is difficult to maintain; where government is only management, it can do little to rectify the problem. Jefferson predicted such difficulties in the early nineteenth century, when he wrote that self-love or self-interest is ultimately destructive of republican virtue: "Self-love . . . is no part of morality. Indeed, it is exactly its counterpart. It is the sole antagonist of virtue, leading us constantly by our propensities to self-gratification in violation of our moral duties to others."[27] The accuracy of his judgement is evidenced in several major twentieth century critiques of American liberal democracy.

Benjamin Barber, for example, argues in *Strong Democracy* that while American liberal democracy is certainly liberal, it is not necessarily democratic: "Its conception of the individual and of individual interest undermines the democratic practices upon which both individuals and their interests depend."[28] Liberalism does not necessarily support a democratic conception of political community. It cannot provide a theoretical foundation for citizenship, public participation, and public goods, and most importantly, it does not support civic virtue. The Federalist vision assumes that human beings are only "solitary seeker[s] of material happiness and bodily security" and thus fundamentally unable to live in peace with one another.[29] Barber terms this type of government "zookeeping" and "thin democracy" and argues that it discourages participation, citizenship, and political activity. Ultimately, on his view, such a situation will destroy the polity.

A related critique is made by Theodore Lowi in *The End of Liberalism*. Lowi argues that growth in the size and scope of government and the lack of meaningful political alternatives have yielded "interest group liberalism," wherein the "policy agenda and the public interest [are] defined in terms of the organized interests of society."[30] In such a situation, government has no real substance; it is comprised only of process.[31] Rather than governors, we have, in George Grant's words, "ruling managers."[32]

The United States Forest Service

The critiques of Barber, Lowi, and Grant are applicable to many branches of the American government, but they are perhaps nowhere more appropriate than in the history of the Department of Agriculture's Bureau of Forestry, which in 1905 became the United States Forest Service. In the attitudes and activities of the Forest Service, the technical rationality of the modern state meets the undisciplined American wilderness.

In *Timber and the Forest Service,* David Clary (a former Forest Service historian) writes that from its origins, the Forest Service understood its mission to be the management of national forests as "instruments of social reform" that could "promote community stability, institute sustained-yield harvesting to stave off a timber famine, improve the lot of the lumberjack, [and] fight monopolies."[33] Its foresters believed themselves to be experts whose "principles were wholly technical and free from self-interest"; their goal, in the words of Gifford Pinchot, was to look after the national forests for "the greatest good of the greatest number in the long run."[34] For most of the twentieth century, that goal was interpreted as emphasizing the need for regional economic development. From such a perspective, the role of foresters is the management of timber, not the conservation of forests.[35] The Forest Service thus became a technocracy convinced that "only it could make the correct decisions for the national forests."[36] Its manner of action thus reflected Lowi's interest group liberalism: change within the agency and its policies occurred only after "vicious" controversy, restrictive legislation, and "a growing volume of criticism from the forestry community at large."[37]

Clary concludes optimistically by implying that the Forest Service will evolve over time to become less concerned with timber production and more responsive to the public.[38] His evidence, however, does not justify such optimism. Rather, it supports Barber's contention that the American political system has become a "thin democracy." Clary's own analysis finds that the agency acts in its own self-interest and is resistant to change, and that its employees still hold the belief that "any opponent [is] perforce in the wrong."[39]

Thus, it is in bureaucratic agencies responsible for the protection of natural resources (such as the Forest Service and the Bureau of Land Management [BLM]) that the peculiar development of American government and the erosion of North American wilderness intersect. In such institutions, a government charged with promoting freedom has imposed bureaucratic limits that undermine that freedom. A citizenry whose identity was, in part, forged by its experience of the wilderness now encounters managed forests.

Given the history and civil religion that underpin the American state, it is not surprising that it was at this convergence that a radical environmental movement emerged. Its adherents, linked by their belief in an imminent environmental apocalypse, sought to recreate political meaning and community through their attempts to preserve American wilderness.

Radical Environmentalism and Earth First!

Although Earth First! developed in a specific historical context, it shares certain commonalities with other radical environmental groups. In *The Greenpeace Story,* Michael Brown and John May outline the history of one such organization, which began in 1970 as the three member "Don't Make a Wave Committee" and then developed into an international lobbying network with a multimillion dollar budget.[40]

Like the radical environmentalists who followed them, Greenpeace's founders came together because they were frustrated by the moderate tactics and goals of mainstream environmental organizations; in particular, they were angered by the Sierra Club, which refused to protest against nuclear weapons testing. As a result, they decided to act against such tests themselves. The original group rented a boat and traveled to the site of a nuclear test at Amchitka, Alaska, hoping that their actions would both raise public awareness of the issue and prevent the test itself. During the journey, those aboard the ship read a book of Indian legends and adopted one of its prophecies as particularly meaningful for their own mission. According to the legend, "[t]here would come a time, predicted an old Cree woman named Eyes of Fire, when the earth would be ravaged of its resources, the sea blackened, the streams poisoned, the deer dropping dead in their tracks. Just before it was too late, the Indian would regain his spirit and teach the white man reverence for the earth, banding together with him to become Warriors of the Rainbow."[41] Greenpeacers thus became the Warriors of the Rainbow (and their ship the *Rainbow Warrior*) and in so doing added a millenarian element to their mission. They believed that humankind's destruction of the environment was leading to an imminent apocalypse and that they could help prevent it. They hoped to remake society in the image of their vision: a nuclear-free, ecologically sensitive community.

Over time, however, as Greenpeace grew in size and wealth, it adopted the more moderate tactics of the environmental mainstream. It now engages in lobbying and press conferences more often than in environmental campaigns, a transformation which has left it open to criticism by more radical environmental groups. Indeed, members of such groups consistently deride Greenpeace as "an empire-building fund-raising establishment" whose primary goal has become gaining credibility among lawmakers, not preserving the environment.[42]

In *Eco-Warriors*, Rik Scarce discusses the emergence of other, more radical environmental groups, specifically Earth First!, the Sea Shepherd Conservation Society, and the animal liberation movement, which includes such groups as the American Animal Liberation Front (ALF) and People for the Ethical Treatment of Animals (PETA). Scarce's account contains limited analysis, being for the most part a sympathetic journalistic discussion of the means and aims of radical environmental groups; it is worth noting, however, because it stands as the first attempt to gather such information together to facilitate comparative analysis. It also provides sufficient richness of detail concerning its subjects' illegal activities to have resulted in the arrest of its author. In May 1993, Scarce was jailed for refusing to reveal the identity of his sources to a grand jury.[43]

Scarce argues that these environmental groups are "radical" by both definitions of that word. On the one hand, they wish to fight for the most basic fact or root of human existence, "the lifegiver Earth";[44] on the other hand, their doctrines and tactics are often described as extreme. Such groups share five basic characteristics that distinguish them from their counterparts in the political mainstream. Most often, they confront environmental problems through direct action (and might willingly destroy private property); the goal of their protests is the preservation of biological diversity; they act without direction from an organizational hierarchy; they are poor; and they have little hope of actually ending the practices against which they protest.[45] They believe that they are in a war and that it is their responsibility to "rise, fight back against the onslaught of technomania sweeping every corner of the world . . . from the high seas to the highest mountain that holds an ounce of silver or gold."[46] Finally, they believe that the earth's capacity to withstand such devastation is almost at its end.

Scarce argues that such radical movements began in the 1970s with the emergence of Greenpeace, which he believes was a watershed in the history of the North American environmental movement. In the context of that decade, it was radical: "[Greenpeace] was unlike anything the mainstream of the movement had ever seen. Greenpeacers were *active* activists. They not only sailed, climbed, and hiked to the sources of environmental problems, but they became daredevils who constantly created new tactics."[47] Greenpeacers were willing to "[bolt] shut effluent pipes leading from chemical plants and [skydive] off power plant smokestacks to publicize pollution."[48] The tactics they used were not intended to stop an environmental problem in and of themselves; instead, they were intended to draw the attention of the media and mobilize the population at large.[49]

As noted above, Greenpeace enjoyed rapid and widespread political and financial success, and Scarce claims that with this growth in size, the organization has approached the mainstream of the environmental movement.[50] It is now more appropriately described as a "bridge to radicalism," existing somewhere between mainstream and radical environmentalism. Like the mainstream, Greenpeace possesses an hierarchical organizational structure, a "longing for political legitimacy," a registered membership, and a "concern for human well-being."[51] At the same time, it shares with radical movements "direct action, support for grassroots activists, emphasis on attracting the news media's attention, and an adherence to an ecocentric philosophy on many issues."[52]

According to Scarce, what ultimately distinguishes radical movements from mainstream groups is the former's willingness to destroy private property.[53] Earth First!, the Sea Shepherds, and animal liberation groups believe sabotage is a legitimate tactic, while Greenpeace does not. In proposing this rather startling conclusion, Scarce briefly acknowledges the fundamental differences between the philosophy of anthropocentrism, which includes only humans in its conception of moral subjects, and that of biocentrism, which includes all elements of the ecosystem in its moral calculus. In his overall neglect of such conceptual issues, however, Scarce errs.[54] The differences between the two philosophies are critical; they are the means by which radical movements distinguish themselves and determine their motives, tactics, and goals.

Christopher Manes's *Green Rage*, the first book to deal specifically with the Earth First! movement, highlights the distinction between anthropocentrism and biocentrism. Manes gives a sympathetic account of the early history and development of Earth First!. He begins by stating that he "does not pretend to be objective or dispassionate about the radical environmental movement";[55] he is an Earth First!er and writes from that perspective. His affinity with the movement is evident from his definition of radical environmentalism, which in his view has an apocalyptic theme: "The understanding of radical environmentalism . . . begins at the end, the end of the world as we know it, the meltdown of biological diversity that our industrial culture has recklessly set in motion."[56] Radical environmentalism argues that human beings' care of the environment (or lack of it) has set in motion historical processes that will end in the culmination of history. Manes, like many Earth First!ers, believes that the earth's biological diversity is a fundamental good and that humanity's role is to ensure that after the apocalypse, diversity remains. He expresses that belief through the philosophy known as deep ecology.

Deep ecology, a philosophical perspective initially developed by Arne Naess, rejects "the man-in-environment image in favour of the *relational, total-field image.*"[57] Thus, it abandons anthropocentrism for biocentrism and assumes that all nature has intrinsic worth. For Manes, it is only deep ecology's emphasis on biocentrism[58] that can allow individuals to fully reevaluate their relationship with the natural environment. He argues that its focus on the community of all species makes it part of a minority tradition that includes both Henry David Thoreau and Thomas Jefferson.[59]

Manes is careful to distinguish deep ecology from the New Age movement, citing a 1987 article by George Sessions in the journal *Earth First!*. Sessions, along with Naess a principle theorist of deep ecology, writes that "the New Age movement often characterizes the world as sacred and criticizes the approach of industrial society. . . . But to New Age thinkers humans occupy a special place in the world because we possess consciousness, reason, morality, and any number of privileged traits that make us fit to be stewards over the natural processes of the planet."[60] According to Manes and many Earth First!ers, the New Age movement is anthropocentric.

Applying the distinction within the environmental movement itself, Manes believes groups such as Greenpeace act from anthropocentric premises and advocate only "reform environmentalism."[61] Reform environmentalists aim to preserve the environment in order that the earth can continue to support human life and that humans may continue to enjoy wilderness areas. In that respect, they act for the wrong reasons and pursue the wrong goals. Manes admits, however, that in terms of saving the environment, such groups serve a tactical function: they can pursue court battles that might save wilderness, and they can educate the general public.[62] For Manes, these types of activities are useful only because they might succeed in preserving wilderness, not because they might benefit humankind. For similar reasons, Manes argues against Scarce's inclusion of animal rights groups in the panoply of truly radical environmental movements. Those groups, he points out, are only willing to extend ethical and moral standing to animals; they do not include nonsentient entities such as rivers and mountains in their privileged circle.[63] Manes insists that all species are equal, a philosophy (known as "biocentric equality") shared by many Earth First!ers, but one that has brought him a particular notoriety. As I shall discuss more fully in chapter 6, Manes is known within the movement as the pseudonymous author "Miss Ann Thropy" who, in mid–1987, wrote two articles concerning overpopulation. His infamy is largely due to the second of these articles, "Population and AIDS," which suggested that the spread of AIDS might provide a viable solution to the world's population crisis.[64]

While many Earth First!ers were highly critical of Manes's articles, one very important Earth First!er was not. Dave Foreman, the most important of the movement's founders, agreed with Manes's controversial argument. This perspective dominates Foreman's only publication in the mainstream press that directly concerns his reflections on radical environmentalism, *Confessions of an Eco-Warrior,* in which he reprinted a list of Earth First! principles earlier published in the movement's journal. First among them was the belief that the earth had to be placed first in all human decisions, "even ahead of human welfare if necessary."[65] The majority of *Confessions* utilizes this philosophy to explain Foreman's actions "in defence of wilderness." The book does, however, illustrate one very important point: by illuminating Foreman's philosophy after his 1990 departure from Earth First!, it makes clear that the movement's development and Foreman's arrest and subsequent trial did not much change his temperament or ideology. If anything, *Confessions of an Eco-Warrior* indicates that he became even more emphatically biocentrist during the course of Earth First!'s history.[66]

Another perspective on Earth First! is presented in Susan Zakin's *Coyotes and Town Dogs,* a journalistic account of the movement. Zakin comes closer than any previous observer to providing a complete history, but even her work lacks objectivity. Zakin is a friend of Dave Foreman, and she sympathizes with the movement's goals.[67]

As a journalist, Zakin is interested in recording the movement's history in a compelling manner; she therefore provides little analysis of Earth First!ers' philosophical motivations and focuses instead on its most colorful characters.[68] Such a focus, while useful for dramatic purposes, causes two major problems. First, it leaves the work open to criticisms that the character portrayals are inaccurate. If there is no objective standard of judgement, such depictions are only a matter of opinion. Indeed, many individuals have objected to the way they have been characterized by Zakin.[69] Second, such an emphasis skews Zakin's perspective on Earth First!'s development. Those persons without dramatic credentials are virtually ignored. One example of this neglect is the fact that Zakin does not fully attend to the role of women in the movement's history. Foreman has stated that for much of Earth First!'s early history, women played a critical but unobtrusive role; indeed, he credits their organizing skills and financial support with ensuring the movement's continued existence.[70] This role is not analyzed by Zakin. As one obvious example, Susan Morgan—the first editor of the movement's newsletter, and one of the original members of the Circle, its first coordinating body—is only briefly mentioned.[71]

Zakin's focus on the movement's most dramatic personalities and actions also yields another, similar problem: she is selective in her coverage of environmental campaigns. This selectivity is not, in and of itself, problematic. It would be impossible for any one book to cover the multitude of campaigns that the movement has undertaken during its long history. However, Zakin does not make clear the bases for her choices in stressing some actions at the expense of others. As a result, her book is once more left open to charges of bias, and again, those in the movement's social justice faction have found problems in her work.[72]

Coyotes and Town Dogs, written by a journalist and aimed at the mass market, thus provides an uneven picture of Earth First!. It focuses on the movement's personalities at the expense of its philosophy and ideology, and it does not make explicit its own biases. Its usefulness for my analysis therefore lies, first, in the insights that can be gleaned from the anecdotes that Zakin recounts (most of which were obtained from primary sources), and, second, in her description of the events surrounding the trial of the 'Arizona Five,' the Arizonan Earth First!ers accused of conspiring to sabotage nuclear facilities in Arizona, California, and Colorado.[73] At the time I undertook my research, this historical material was unavailable elsewhere.

Two articles from the 1990s began the analysis of different aspects of the Earth First! movement from a more scholarly perspective. In June 1994, David Peerla, a former Greenpeace campaigner, presented a draft of his paper "The Moral Optic of Earth First!" at the annual meeting of the Canadian Political Science Association. In it, he argues that Earth First!'s reliance on direct action campaigns means that social scientists who wish to understand the movement must look to the character of the media events that it stages. However, much of Peerla's paper is inapplicable here; it is for the most part a post-modern analysis of environmental campaigning and the media. With respect to Earth First!, for example, he writes that the movement "made old growth forest and wild rivers appear in a media space."[74] At the same time, his analysis does help to explain how the decentralized Earth First! movement retained its sense of community, with his observation that Earth First!ers were linked "through the exchange of words, images and information throughout the electronic media."[75]

Bron Taylor's "The Religion and Politics of Earth First!" provides a more immediately relevant analysis. Taylor examines Earth First!'s doctrine and argues that it contains both religious and political themes.[76] While most Earth First!ers reject organized religion, the foundation of the movement lies in "a radical 'ecological consciousness' that intuitively, affectively, and deeply experiences a sense of the sacredness and interconnection of all life."[77] Taylor does not provide a specific definition of religion, but he implies that Earth First! links this "sacredness of all life" with its own cosmogony, cosmology, moral anthropology, and eschatology.

By implication, Taylor is adopting Clifford Geertz's definition of religion, wherein religious faith is interpreted as a means of ordering the events of this world. Geertz defines religion as "a system of symbols which acts to establish powerful, pervasive and long-lasting moods and motivations in men by formulating conceptions of a general order of existence."[78] Variations of this basic definition can be found in the work of Mary Douglas and Peter Berger.[79] In all of these definitions, religion is understood as a faith in a transcendent reality that gives meaning and purpose to existence in the profane world.

These theorists of religion define their subject in a way very similar to that of political philosophers, who see political life as rooted in "basic assumptions concerning the human condition, the purposes of society, the meaning of nature, the direction of history, and the structure of being itself."[80] These assumptions are thus ordering principles which determine the way in which politics is undertaken in a given age. (Eric Voegelin, for example, argues that reason was the transcendent ordering principle in the political thought of the Greek philosophers and in Greek society as a whole.[81]) Theology and political philosophy are thus parallel endeavors, a fact that helps to explain why they so often conflict. Mark Juergensmeyer, in his examination of modern religious nationalism and its battles against secular states, summarizes this situation well. He writes that because religion and politics are competing "ideologies of order," they are always potential rivals: "Either can claim to be the guarantor of orderliness within a society; either can claim to be the ultimate authority for social order."[82] This coincidence of purpose also helps to illuminate why religious beliefs may so easily enter the political sphere, and why there are often political implications to specific religious doctrines. (As will be discussed below, this interconnection is most clearly evidenced in millenarian movements.)

Taylor's analysis of the religious nature of Earth First!'s beliefs is convincing in many respects. He emphasizes the spiritual nature of Earth First!ers' connection with the wilderness and outlines the explicitly religious themes that emerge from this relationship. Taylor notes that Taoism, Buddhism, Hinduism, witchcraft, and pagan earth-worship are "diverse tributaries" to the movement[83] but argues that the most important of these influences is "American Indian Spirituality."[84] Taylor uses Porterfield's definition of that phenomenon, which stresses that it is primarily an invention of Euro-Americans, and a means by which "proponents define themselves against American society."[85] Later, however, he states that a better term for his purposes would be "primal spirituality," because "Earth First!ers believe we should emulate the indigenous ways of life of most primal peoples, not just those in North America."[86]

Taylor's discussion of politics is more limited. Again, he does not provide a definition of the term, but he implies that it consists only of that which is specifically related to government. He therefore considers Earth First!'s genesis as political in nature. Specifically, in discussing its origins he claims that the founders were "disgruntled conservationists, who were licking their wounds after losing an important legislative battle over the Federal Government's 1980 Roadless Area Review and Evaluation process."[87] Likewise, he assumes that its tactics are political only to the extent that they influence mainstream environmental groups' lobbying positions. In political terms, its success can be measured by the degree to which it popularizes biocentrism and "extends the range" of the environmental debate in the United States.[88]

While many of Taylor's points are well taken, a more thorough definition of the term "political" would add depth to his analysis. For example, he identifies deep ecology as the primary cosmogony of Earth First!, but he does not attempt to link its precepts to the Jeffersonian philosophy that dominated many Earth First!ers' interpretation of that doctrine. Such a link provides insight into the movement's definition of community and helps to explain why July 4 was chosen as the date of its annual meeting, and why the burning of the American flag at one of those meetings became one of the pivotal events in the movement's fragmentation. Many of the movement's early adherents believed that American government had developed in such a way as to betray the fundamental principles of the Revolution and that their efforts were in part an attempt to redefine and recreate the political community. In the words of Edward Abbey (cited by Taylor in another context), "Representative democracy in the United States has broken down. Our legislators do not represent those who elected them. . . . Representative government in the USA represents money not people and therefore has forfeited our allegiance and moral support."[89]

Taylor makes two arguments with respect to the cause of the schism that eventually developed within Earth First!. He says first that it was caused "more by disagreements about strategy and tactics than in fundamental moral differences"[90] but later contradicts himself by arguing that it resulted from "small but significant differences in beliefs about human nature and eschatology."[91] Differences in conceptions of human nature and eschatology can neither be characterized as small nor can they be reduced to squabbles concerning tactics. Indeed, such assumptions are critical to the foundation of any millenarian belief system. Because individuals are the building blocks of the state, one's conception of human nature determines what kind of political community one believes to be the ideal state. In the case of Earth First!, the social justice faction's belief that human nature is perfectible contrasts markedly with the biodiversity faction's assumption that human nature is unchanging. That divergence yields marked differences in each faction's tactics and goals. The first group believes education and reform are possible, while the second does not; the first group aims for a post-apocalyptic millennial community, while the second hopes simply for an imminent apocalypse.

Taylor's article thus sheds valuable but limited light on the political and religious nature of the Earth First! movement, as well as on the importance of its eschatological vision. By default, it also indicates that in order to more completely understand the Earth First! movement, it is necessary to examine the literature of millenarian theory.

Millenarian and Apocalyptic Doctrines

Taylor's article illustrates well the difficulty of classifying any millenarian movement as either "religious" or "political." Although such a distinction might be made in very general terms (for example, National Socialism was predominantly a political ideology, but early Christianity was predominantly a religious movement), in most cases such classifications are unsatisfactory. As noted, religion and politics both provide systems of order; when they appear in millenarian movements, a transformation occurs that makes them even more difficult to distinguish in terms of both theoretical and practical analyses. Millennial expectations transform the meaning of their adherents' existence in history. Their believers become a chosen people and the bearers of a truth that dictates the order of the world. A belief that is primarily religious will therefore have distinctly political implications; followers may make formal preparations for the end of the world or attempt to remake the world in the image of their hope. Similarly, a political movement may have religious overtones when adherents possess a moral justification for committing any actions that they perceive as necessary to achieve salvation.

Thus, as Michael Barkun writes, millenarian movements are both religious and political; real life does not come "neatly packaged."[92] Earth First!'s genesis, tactics, and goals were all rooted in the immediate material world, but its adherents at all times believed that a more transcendent and ultimate measure of worth existed.

As noted above, <u>Earth First!'s belief system</u> was rooted in a philosophy <u>known as deep ecology.</u> Although many Earth First!ers claim that
reading and studying this philosophy is unnecessary (they "were not
dependent on books to explain their own views of things"[93]), the movement's founders and most of its adherents are familiar with its precepts.
In its most basic form, deep ecology demands that human beings reevaluate their relationship with the environment in such a way as to
acknowledge that both human and non-human life have an intrinsic
moral worth.[94] In adopting a deep ecology perspective, one moves from
the anthropocentrism of industrialized society to what is believed to be
an ecologically responsible biocentrism. The philosophy also predicts
that if things continue as they presently are, a crisis will result, and thus
includes an imperative to action. The final element in Bill Devall and
George Sessions's influential summation of deep ecology's basic principles is that "[t]hose who subscribe to the foregoing points have an obligation directly or indirectly to try to implement the necessary changes."[95]
They argue that adopting the principles of deep ecology will not yield a
personal deprivation; rather, it will provide a vision of a new society
and way of living that is "joyous and enlivening" and a "more satisfy-
ing way of being fully human."[96] With its assertion of an impending
crisis, its demand for action, and its vision of a new society, deep ecology thus provides the basic elements of a millenarian movement.

In its specifically Christian form, millenarianism has been marked
by a division between premillennialism and postmillennialism. The distinction is based upon when the believers anticipate the return of Christ
will occur: postmillennialists believe that Christ will return after the
church has established the millennium; premillennialists expect Christ
to return to establish the millennium by his own power.[97] Although certain parallels might be drawn between Earth First!'s social justice faction and postmillennialism, and between its biodiversity faction and
premillennialism, these terms are too closely tied to their religious context to be meaningful here. Rather, I have found more helpful another
distinction, one which provides greater insight into the development of
environmental millenarianism in general and the Earth First! movement
in particular.

In this distinction, millenarianism is contrasted with apocalypticism. Apocalyptics are concerned only with the events and earthly conditions leading up to the apocalypse, the climactic and dramatic event

that they believe will soon bring about the end of human history. They are not interested in a millennial future for a chosen race or people; indeed, they may or may not anticipate that human life will continue after the apocalyptic event. Apocalyptics may, however, be concerned with their role in the pre-apocalyptic world. They might, for example, understand themselves to be responsible for ensuring particular conditions are met in order that the apocalypse may occur. They believe that their community's importance lies in its pivotal role in the culmination of history. Thus, where millenarian belief systems focus on the transformation of the community, apocalyptic belief systems focus primarily on the imminence and meaning of the apocalyptic event.

For these reasons, apocalyptic movements do not embody the same potential for political mobilization as millenarian beliefs. They do, however, pose a significant threat to the social order. Like millenarians, apocalyptics are often prepared to commit any action that they believe is necessary to prepare for the end of the world. They are not, however, necessarily concerned with the preservation of their communities or of their own lives. A belief system with little conception of a future involving human beings would, under normal circumstances, have little mass appeal; indeed, taken at face value, such a doctrine would appear to be more a psychopathology than a political ideology. Apocalypticism does, however, fit well with a biocentric philosophy. For a believer in biocentrism, human beings are not the most important historical actors; rather, the future health of the ecosystem is of primary importance. In the case of Earth First!, both its apocalyptic and its millenarian belief systems developed from the fertile ground of deep ecology.

There are a number of major theoretical frameworks that are most commonly used to explain the origins of millenarian movements. Although none of these theories alone can provide a complete explanation for the emergence of Earth First!, all provide some insight into the genesis of that movement.

Norman Cohn's definition of millenarianism (outlined above) characterizes such movements as anticipating an imminent, ultimate, collective, this-worldly, and miraculous salvation.[98] Later scholars have liberalized the term by removing the requirement that the salvation occur miraculously (that is, with the help of "supernatural agencies").[99] With this change, the term has come to be used more frequently in the analysis of political movements.[100] Following Cohn's work, many schol-

ars of millenarianism have found that such movements most often develop amongst the politically powerless and rootless poor. Those individuals lack a variety of social and political goods; they suffer "multiple
deprivation." Among such groups, however, it is a particular kind of
deprivation that has seemed most conducive to eschatological belief systems: relative deprivation.[101] Perhaps the most often used framework of
analysis, relative deprivation theory was explicitly tied to the development of millenarian movements by David Aberle.[102] He defines relative
deprivation as "a negative discrepancy between legitimate expectation
and actuality"[103] and is careful to emphasize that this discrepancy is
relative, not absolute. In fact, there is (in Barkun's words) no " 'objective' yardstick with which an outside observer might measure conditions in a society."[104] What is important is that the individual or
individuals concerned perceive a condition where their circumstances do
not meet their expectations.

Aberle notes three specific conditions wherein such deprivation
might occur: "(1) one's past versus one's present circumstances; (2)
one's present versus one's future circumstances; (3) one's own versus
someone else's present circumstances."[105] A single individual's experience of such deprivation is insufficient to produce a social movement;
what is required is that a number of people share a similar perception of
deprivation. Only then is it possible that the experience of relative deprivation will yield political or religious action. In such a situation, Aberle argues, a millenarian movement becomes a way "to overcome the
discrepancy between actuality and legitimate aspiration."[106]

Although deprivation theory does help to explain the development
of millenarian movements, its central concepts are difficult to opera-
tionalize. It is, for example, difficult to measure the concept of subjec-
tive comparison that is at the core of relative deprivation theory.
Additionally, deprivation theory implies that individuals will realize
their lack and pursue its resolution with a kind of instrumental rationality. However, this emphasis discounts religious and/or political action that is not instrumental.

A second explanation for the emergence of millenarian movements
can be found in Anthony Wallace's influential article "Revitalization
Movements."[107] Wallace argues that societies function like biological organisms in that they prefer to maintain homeostasis, or a "steady
state." By their very nature, however, societies must confront continued

challenges. Thus, they are always involved in a process of adaptation and adjustment; much like living organisms, they follow a kind of life-cycle. When the stress upon them becomes too great, social movements may emerge to address the particular problem. Wallace terms these groups "revitalization movements" and places millenarian and nativistic movements, as well as cargo cults, in this category.[108] Such movements allow a society to readjust its method of dealing with problems (its "mazeway") and to return to a new steady state. Thus, society is "revitalized." Wallace outlines this cycle as follows: existence in a steady state, increased individual stress, cultural distortion, and finally, revitalization.[109]

As Barkun points out, however, revitalization theory (like relative deprivation theory) suffers from a lack of specificity and quantifiability: "We wonder but are not told precisely what kind of stress must be involved, over how long a period of time, involving what proportion of the population."[110] Although Wallace's theory does not offer a reliable means of accurately predicting when such movements will develop, his work does provide insight into the kind of function that millenarian movements perform. They are a means for societies under stress to adapt to new conditions.

This line of reasoning is taken further by Yonina Talmon in her article "Millenarism." Talmon does not discount either relative deprivation or functional theories, but she suggests a related, more specific cause of millenarianism: the search for a "coherent value system" and a "regained sense of dignity and self-respect."[111] Talmon states that the disintegration of traditional values often causes a loss of personal identity. This loss is magnified when individuals are no longer "firmly embedded in well-integrated kinship groupings."[112] As evidence, she cites the clash of cultures that occurred during colonization as well as referring to medieval religious movements. These arguments, however, could well apply to the development of many modern, politically marginalized groups (for example, the Nation of Islam).[113] Indeed, Talmon goes on to argue that one of the most important contributions to the study of millenarian movements has been identification of the fact that they are usually prepolitical, nonpolitical, or postpolitical phenomena.[114] Prepolitical millenarianism occurs in primitive cultures where there are few if any political institutions; nonpolitical millenarianism emerges among populations which, although living in developed states, are "politically passive and have no experience of political organization and no access to political power."[115] Postpolitical millenarianism, however, occurs after the collapse of a developed political system. While Talmon argues this point in sweeping terms, suggesting that these postpolitical beliefs might occur after "a crushing defeat and the shattering of tribal or national hopes," she also states that they can emerge when individuals believe that they have no effective institutionalized way of voicing their political grievances or making political claims.[116]

As has been noted, each of these explanations for the development of millenarian ideologies outlines conditions that are generally conducive to their development, but offers no specific means to predict when such movements will develop. In *Disaster and the Millennium,* Michael Barkun addresses this issue. Barkun argues that societies may well be primed for the development of millenarianism through an experience of relative deprivation or mazeway failure, but those conditions, in and of themselves, are not sufficient for the development of a millenarian movement. In addition to these circumstances, "highly focused and intense" changes must directly threaten an individual's "true society," or meaningful community.[117] Such severe changes, he argues, constitute disasters; they are disruptions of "normal structural arrangements within a social system."[118] In a society that has suffered a particularly drastic event, or a number of these disasters, "disaster syndrome" results: "[I]ndividuals attempt to interpret the unfamiliar in terms of the familiar and, when that fails, lapse into behavior patterns that are nonrational and reflexive."[119] Millenarian movements are one possible response to this disaster syndrome.[120]

Although this type of analysis would most typically be applied to the development of millenarian movements in areas where natural disasters have occurred, it is also useful in examining the origins of Earth First!. At the conclusion of his book, Barkun argues that in the modern era, disasters might occur in unusual and unanticipated forms, for example in the televised assassination of a president.[121] It is indeed conceivable that such an experience might also occur as a result of governmental processes themselves. During the late 1970s, the founders of Earth First! experienced increasing discomfort with the changes that had occurred in traditional conservation groups. Their goals and tactics made it seem as if they had been "co-opted" by "the system." It can be argued that those individuals experienced a "disaster," the situation brought about in the late 1970s by the actions and decisions of government and traditional conservation groups. It shattered Dave Foreman's faith in American government, and his faith in traditional conservation groups; in so doing, it rendered his early political activity meaningless, and his work in the Wilderness Society virtually useless. A large number of his colleagues shared that experience, and thus their "true society" was shattered. Rather than lapsing into apathy, they founded a new movement.

However, such an approach does have its limitations. It is more difficult to argue that the resurgence of millenarianism in Earth First!'s social justice faction was caused by disaster syndrome. While Californian Earth First!ers had experienced many setbacks in their efforts to save the northern wilderness and redwoods, the decisive moment in that faction's formation is more closely related to the dynamics of the larger Earth First! movement than to specific environmental disasters.

The social and political environment from which Earth First! emerged thus caused the movement's formation and marked its development. Earth First!'s birth represents the conjunction of the crisis in American liberal democracy with the conflict between the resource needs of industrialized society and the governmental agencies charged with protecting American wilderness. Wallace's argument that millenarian movements may serve as revitalization movements suggests that Earth First! might function to help alleviate that crisis. The group has raised public awareness of the problems linked to "big government" and has brought increased public attention to the state of the American wilderness. It also has embodied the search to redefine political identity in that context. In practical terms, it has succeeded in directly preserving some wilderness areas and indirectly has helped mainstream environmental groups preserve wilderness. Earth First!'s tactics and goals made those organizations and their demands appear moderate, and that comparison strengthened the latter's bargaining positions.[122]

At the same time, however, Earth First! also suffered the same characteristics that have led many scholars to identify such movements as pathological. Cohn, for example, argues that millenarian ideologies always involve the myth of a chosen elite fighting "a final, exterminatory struggle."[123] The millenarian movement thus becomes the final arbiter of history, and in this role, its adherents believe they possess sufficient justification to impose their will on the outside world. In this way, millenarianism can itself become a form of oppression.[124] Likewise, Voegelin states that any ideology that attempts to posit meaning in history is dangerous. All such belief systems represent attempts to bring a spiritual faith into the immanent world.[125]

Although Earth First! emerged in response to what its adherents felt was the oppressive and coercive nature of the American state, these themes can also be seen in its own tactics. Earth First!ers often used illegal means to preserve the environment. They imposed their will on the state and other citizens by violating private property. Ironically, however, these themes also influenced the movement's internal development. For much of Earth First!'s history, its leaders struggled to maintain ideological purity, while at the same time welcoming heterogeneity amongst Earth First!ers.

2

The Founding of a Movement

Many workmen
Built a huge ball of masonry
Upon a mountaintop
Then they went to the valley below,
and turned to behold their work.
"It is grand," they said;
They loved the thing.

Of a sudden, it moved:
It came upon them swiftly;
It crushed them all to blood.
But some had opportunity to squeal.[1]

—Stephen Crane

The constellation of environmental lobbying groups in Washington, D.C., functions to influence and educate members of Congress with respect to environmental issues. Groups such as the Sierra Club and the Wilderness Society have a long history, but it is only since the mid-1950s that they have been important political actors. Since that time, their membership has changed markedly, echoing the changes in American society as a whole.

The American conservation movement began in the late 1800s as a fraternity of the upper-middle class, "an elite band—sportsmen of the Teddy Roosevelt variety, naturalists like John Burroughs, outdoorsmen in the mold of John Muir, pioneer foresters and ecologists on the order of Aldo Leopold, and wealthy social reformers like Gifford Pinchot and Robert Marshall."[2] The character of this membership changed little during the next fifty years. At the 1954 hearings of the House Committee on Interior and Insular Affairs, David Brower, the executive director of the Sierra Club, noted that the group's membership included the chief executive officers of large corporations, as well as an assistant United States attorney general.[3]

During the 1950s, two major events initiated the increased involvement of these lobbying groups in political decisionmaking: the preservation of Dinosaur Monument's Echo Canyon (1954) and, subsequently, the loss of Glen Canyon through the construction of Glen Canyon Dam and the creation of Lake Powell (1956). Brower argues that until the flooding of Glen Canyon, citizens and environmental groups had trusted the Bureau of Reclamation not to violate the national park system.[4] For many, the dam's construction symbolized the "technological ravishment of the West,"[5] and it caused widespread disillusionment within the environmental movement. As a result, environmental groups refined their lobbying efforts and became more disciplined and directed. This development of a more politically professional lobbying effort coincided with the political upheaval of the 1960s, an era that brought about increased political involvement at all levels of American society. Environmental organizations such as the Sierra Club and the Wilderness Society experienced a remarkable increase in local or "grassroots" activity during this period. Between 1960 and 1970, their combined membership tripled.[6] This trend soon created a far more diverse membership and encouraged the upward mobility of grassroots activists to the movement's lobbying elite.

These two trends, the growing importance of effective lobbying coupled with the development of a more militant lobbying elite, eventually came into conflict. Successful lobbying requires considerable financial resources, specialized knowledge of governmental functioning, and an active presence in government; the practical success of such efforts also requires compromise with other interest groups and with Congress. While some grassroots activists who came to Washington as lobbyists were content with this process, many were not. In every compromise made, they saw wilderness lost, and by their participation in those compromises, they felt they were betraying their cause.

The publication of Edward Abbey's 1975 novel *The Monkey Wrench Gang* coincided with this increasing tension. Abbey based his book on a group known as the Eco-Raiders, who in the early 1970s had used unconventional and illegal tactics to slow the growth of the suburbs of Tucson, Arizona.[7] Their tactics ranged from burning billboards to "decommissioning" bulldozers, and their vandalism thwarted several major development projects. They caused over one-half million dollars' damage to private property, and in the process became local folk heroes.[8] Abbey's fictional story concerns four individuals (one woman and three men) who likewise decide to defend the wilderness by any means necessary. The book opens with brief citations of Whitman and Thoreau ("Resist much. Obey little" and "Now. Or never"), followed immediately by the dictionary definition of sabotage.[9] The Monkey Wrench Gang (Bonnie Abbzug, Doc Sarvis, Seldom Seen Smith, and George Washington Hayduke) travel across the American Southwest pulling survey stakes, destroying heavy machinery, and plotting to explode several bridges, but their ultimate goal is the demolition of Glen Canyon Dam. Abbey's characters shared a passion for wilderness and a contempt for authority that many Washington environmental lobbyists wistfully admired from afar; for some, however, it also became a model for action.

During the late 1970s, the Wilderness Society's chief lobbyist was Dave Foreman. In background and perspective, he was closely tied to the grassroots conservation movement. Foreman had been interested in the environment since childhood. His family was not one of environmental activists, but he avidly read wildlife books; in his childhood he witnessed a shark attack, an occasion that did not repulse him but left him in awe of wilderness.[10]

Foreman's political history, much like the movement he founded, belies the traditional dichotomy of right/left politics in the United States. His family background was conservative: his father was a senior master sergeant in the United States Air Force,[11] and the women in his family are members of the Daughters of the American Revolution.[12] During his youth, the family attended a fundamentalist Protestant church, and at one point he considered becoming a preacher.[13] Foreman was a registered Republican, supported the Vietnam War, and for most of the 1960s was an ardent anticommunist. In college he campaigned for Barry Goldwater and was the New Mexico state chairman of the ultra-conservative Young Americans for Freedom. After graduating with a B.A. in history in 1968, Foreman briefly attended the Marine Corps Officers' Candidate School. His tenure there was a mere sixty-one days, thirty-one of which were spent in the brig.[14] He later described the experience as "a Jeffersonian running head on into the military state,"[15] and it prompted him to abandon Republican politics.[16]

Foreman's experience with the regulated character of modern politics and the military contrasted markedly with his appreciation of wilderness and the wild. In 1969, Foreman's leisure interest in hiking and backpacking prompted his first visit to the Sierra Club's Albuquerque office; two years later, he became politically active in the environmental movement. He had faith in the just character of the political system and initially chose to address his environmental concerns in a traditional way. A poster he had produced for the Gila Primitive Area Reclassification Campaign caught the attention of the Wilderness Society, and he began working for them in January 1973, first as their Southwestern issues consultant and later as their Southwestern representative.[17] In 1976, he was New Mexico state chairman of Conservationists for Carter,[18] and late the next year he moved to Washington as the Wilderness Society's chief Congressional lobbyist.

Foreman's certainty of an imminent environmental crisis and his disillusionment with traditional politics began during the Carter administration. The two forces that fostered his millenarian tendencies were his general dissatisfaction with the "professionalization" of the environmental movement, and the second United States Forest Service Roadless Area Review and Evaluation (RARE II).

Foreman observed the environmental movement's transformation during the late 1970s and interpreted it as the replacement of conservation activists with environmental lobbyists who were "less part of a cause than members of a profession."[19] At first he was uncritical of this change and of the moderate demands and tactics that it engendered. He believed that President Carter was a "great friend of wilderness,"[20] and his faith seemed justified by Carter's appointment of M. Rupert Cutler (a former Assistant Executive Director of the Wilderness Society) to the position of Assistant Secretary of Agriculture, with jurisdiction over the Forest Service. However, although Carter's presidency appeared to provide the ideal opportunity for great advances in wilderness conservation, the environmental lobby enjoyed no such success. Foreman placed the blame for this failure on "the system." Jimmy Carter, the man he identified as "the most decent man to have become President in this century . . . [and] at heart the strongest conservationist,"[21] was corrupted by the system through his desire to be reelected. His appointees were likewise seduced, and Foreman's fellow lobbyists were drawn into a cycle where salary and prestige became more important than protecting the environment. Foreman later succinctly described this transformation in *Confessions of an Eco-Warrior:* "Perrier and brie replaced

Bud and beans at meetings."[22] The movement's corruption and its increasingly moderate tactics were confirmed by an event that he identifies as the primary impetus for the creation of Earth First!: RARE II.

The Forest Service's Roadless Area Review and Evaluation II, which began in 1977 and continued through 1979, reviewed the sixty-two million acres of national forest that were eligible for federal wilderness designation, a status that would protect them from commercial development. The Washington environmental lobbyists were committed to achieving a consensus among the organizations they represented, and they were unwilling to jeopardize their Congressional support by making large demands. As a result, they demanded what many environmentalists deemed "the lowest common denominator," requesting that only close to one-half of the eligible land receive wilderness designation.[23] The resource industry lobbied to have as little area as possible given protected status. In the end, the Forest Service concluded that thirty-six million acres should be immediately opened to development, eleven million be considered for future planning, and fifteen million be protected. RARE II was a tremendous disappointment to the environmental movement, and compounding the dissatisfaction of many, Foreman included, was the conviction that another eighteen million acres should have been considered for protection but were not, owing to sloppy inventory procedures and political pressure.[24]

For Foreman, RARE II's diminution of the American wilderness was devastating; it symbolized the inability of the traditional political system to effectively address the environmental crisis. First, the system was biased in such a way as to favor the very actors who were destroying the wilderness: wealthy corporations and large government agencies such as the Forest Service and the Bureau of Land Management. In promoting corporate wealth at the expense of wilderness, government had allied itself with evil and denied the public good. This evil was magnified by the fact that in this essentially self-serving activity, the people were denied true self-government: "Ronald Reagan had become King George III."[25] Second, and more important, the government's decision denied the immediacy and severity of the environmental crisis. The ravages of the industrial system had left only a few remaining areas of pristine wilderness in the United States. The government and the mainstream lobbying groups had used tactics of compromise that resulted in the loss of much of this land.

Foreman's concern over the direction of the environmental movement thus came to a head in January 1979 with the conclusion of RARE II. This was the first major turning point in his career as an environmentalist. He left Washington convinced of the system's perversion and its inability to protect the wilderness and returned to New Mexico as the Wilderness Society's Southwestern representative. Foreman left not only the Washington environmentalists behind, but also his first marriage; he arrived back in the West ready to begin both his personal and professional life anew.[26]

Foreman's return to New Mexico was a return to his origins. Although his father had been in the Air Force and the family had lived in many locales, it was in the Southwest that he felt most at home. The move also brought him back to the wilderness. His attempt to rebuild, however, was marked by further events that increased his despair of human civilization. Although by most accounts the Wilderness Society (and therefore Dave Foreman) had taken a relatively moderate stance in the RARE II negotiations, upon his return to New Mexico Foreman was the victim of several death threats issued by ranchers concerned over the economic consequences of wilderness designations.[27] This response surprised Foreman, because he had spent many of his early years in the Wilderness Society building alliances between ranchers and environmentalists, and he had assumed many of the area ranchers to be his friends. Moreover, during RARE II, he had in fact convinced New Mexico conservation groups to demand that less acreage of the Gila Forest be designated wilderness than they had originally wanted. Foreman found this paradox writ large in the Sagebrush Rebellion, an event he identifies as the second major turning point in his reevaluation of the American political community and the environmental crisis.[28]

In mid-1980, a coalition of what Foreman characterized as "chambers of commerce, ranchers, and right-wing fanatics,"[29] demanded that federal public lands be transferred to the states and then to private hands. The "Sagebrush Rebellion," as it came to be known, began on July 4, 1980, when the county commission in Moab, Utah, began development of an area that the Bureau of Land Management had identified as a possible area for wilderness designation. For Foreman, the Sagebrush Rebellion was a personal and political betrayal. A group of people of his social circle, whom he understood to be his political allies, had turned against him. Where Foreman had first become disenchanted with the environmental movement, then with the political system itself, the Sagebrush Rebellion provided clear evidence that the people who would be his true political allies were those who, like him, held wilderness to be the fundamental good and derived their morality and actions from that principle.

The roots of Earth First! are closely linked to Dave Foreman's political history and his experience in the environmental movement. However, these experiences were not unique to him. Many grassroots environmentalists who had shared his tenure in Washington were similarly disillusioned with the political process. During the RARE II negotiations, many had talked about forming a group that would take strong stands and refuse to compromise.[30] Foreman identifies the support of these individuals as critical to the development of Earth First!, but the movement was directly the creation of Foreman himself and four of his Southwestern colleagues.

In April 1980, Foreman was ready to leave the Wilderness Society permanently. Together with four of his friends, he spent a week hiking and camping in Mexico's Pinacate Desert. It is this journey that Earth First! folklore identifies as giving birth to the movement. The men who traveled with Foreman had similar backgrounds: Ron Kezar had long been a member of the Sierra Club, as well as a seasonal worker for the National Park Service; Bart Koehler had worked for the Wilderness Society in Wyoming, and had left after RARE II; Mike Roselle was a veteran of many radical, left wing groups, among them the Yippies and the Zippies;[31] and Howie Wolke had been the Wyoming representative for the Friends of the Earth.[32] All but Roselle had devoted their lives to protecting the wilderness and had a significant amount of experience working with mainstream environmental groups.[33] Like Foreman, each of these men was convinced that the earth was in imminent danger and that the traditional political system was incapable of effectively remedying that crisis.

The founding of Earth First! has become part of the movement's mythology. Many variants of this story exist, all of which emphasize spontaneity and rebelliousness against a technological order perceived to be destroying the wilderness. These stories stress attention to a higher law and to the importance of a community of shared beliefs in the fight against industrial civilization. In all versions, the founding occurs after a week spent wandering in the Pinacate Desert, apart from the evils of technological society, and discussing the necessity of preserving wilderness. The social controls and mores of American society are of no relevance; in all variations, the "group of five" are also drunk. Rik Scarce writes:

> Earth First! got started in Foreman's VW bus on the [return] to Albuquerque. . . . Emulating *The Monkey Wrench Gang*'s wild-eyed leader, Wolke and Foreman were in the front seats polishing off a case of Budweiser, Roselle sprawled out in the rear . . . ranting and raving about the emasculated mainstream and fantastic talk of a group that would fight to set aside multi-million acre ecological preserves. . . . Suddenly, Foreman called out, "Earth first!" . . . Roselle drew a clenched-fist logo, passed it up to the front of the van, and there was Earth First!.[34]

Other variants of this story are not as benign. Roselle, for example, recalls that the movement's founding occurred in a Mexican whorehouse,[35] and critics have questioned the integrity of a radical movement that originated in what was a "proudly redneck" milieu. Regardless of the meaning placed upon these events by outsiders, those within Earth First! understand the most important components of this trip to be a leave-taking from traditional society, a journey into an unknown and difficult wilderness, and a return to society with knowledge of the political good. Foreman's simple declaration "Earth First!" is all that is required to become part of the movement.

On April 28, approximately three weeks after the Mexican journey, the group committed its first public act. Foreman and approximately eight others hiked into New Mexico's Gila Wilderness. At Cooney, a ghost town, they erected a plaque in honor of Victorio, an Apache warrior who had destroyed a mining camp to protect the mountains "from mining and other destructive activities of the white race."[36] This action expressed clearly the movement's delimitation of good and evil in the battle to save the environment. A female member of the group interviewed by the press stated, "We think the Sierra Club and other groups have sold out to the system. We further believe that the enemy is not capitalism, communism, or socialism. It is corporate industrialism whether it is in the United States, the Soviet Union, China, or Mexico."[37] In other comments, members drew attention to the movement's biocentric perspective and the character of the tactics it would use. "The Gila Monster" declared, "We will take pure, hard-line, pro-Earth positions. No nukes, no strip mining, no pollution, no more development of our wilderness. We are concerned about people, but it's Earth first."[38] It should be noted that press coverage of this action also remarked upon the lighthearted nature of the participants.

Despite their rich symbolism, the journey to Mexico and the action in the Gila Wilderness did not yield a comprehensive statement of the new group's doctrine. Earth First!'s central concerns, an impending ecological crisis and the necessity of immediate wilderness preservation, became more fully developed and clearly articulated through meetings and correspondence later that year.

The creation of Earth First! was in part a rational and strategic act. The traditional political system, as exemplified by RARE II, had failed, and another means of preserving the remaining wilderness was needed. An important part of the movement's platform was, and continues to be, specific political demands for wilderness preservations. At the same time, however, Earth First! differed from other interest groups in important ways. Embedded in the founding myth is an implied statement concerning the freedom and simplicity of the wilderness, and its provision of a standard of good and evil that exists prior to political society. In this way, Earth First! resembles Albanese's nature religions, wherein the freedom of nature is understood to be intrinsically good.[39] Earth First!'s doctrine embodies issues of meaning and identity that lie outside the boundaries of traditional politics.

It is important that two points be clarified here. First, it is now often asserted that Earth First! is a "movement," not an "organization," and that its adherents are "Earth First!ers," not "members." While this position is assumed by many Earth First!ers to have always been the case, at its founding Earth First! was well-organized, and adherents were formally termed members. The historically appropriate terminology will be utilized here. Second, and following the above, it is often asserted that Earth First! has no set doctrine. There was, in fact, a set of core tenets to which all Earth First!ers adhered, and which I will examine in more detail below. (Doctrinal changes will be examined in their historical context in subsequent chapters.)

The "group of five" who traveled to Mexico were not the sole architects of the movement's doctrine. An early Earth First! memo suggests that a number of their close friends and associates were also influential in its creation. These individuals were similar in background to "the group of five." Included among them were: Mike Comola, former president of the Montana Wilderness Association; Randall Gloege, former Northern Rockies representative for the Friends of the Earth; Sandy Marvinney, past editor of the *Wilderness Report;* and Susan Morgan, a former education coordinator for the Wilderness Society (who later became editor of the group's newsletter).[40] The leadership of the movement, as it existed prior to the autumn of 1980, also welcomed another influence, the wider audience of individuals who were to become the bulk of the group's membership.

The movement's first general meeting, or "Round River Rendezvous," was held on the Fourth of July weekend of 1980 at the T-Cross Ranch in DuBois, Wyoming. The Rendezvous gatherings, which became an annual event, were named to recall Aldo Leopold's essay "The Round River—A Parable."[41] The legends of Paul Bunyan told of a river in Wisconsin that "flowed into itself, and thus sped around and around in a never-ending circuit,"[42] but for Leopold, Wisconsin was itself a round river: "The current is the stream of energy which flows out of the soil into plants, thence into animals, thence back into the soil in a never-ending circuit of life."[43] For those in Earth First!, the term "Round River" symbolized the interconnectedness and equality of all elements of the ecological cycle; "Rendezvous" was chosen by Foreman, and referred to the "get-togethers that the Indians and the mountain men of the Old West used to have."[44]

Over sixty people attended the first Rendezvous; most were from the western states or Washington, D.C.[45] Organizational details were clarified, as were the movement's ideological parameters. Following the gathering, Foreman issued "Vol. O, Number O" of the movement's newsletter, which reported on the decisions of the meeting. He tentatively called the journal *Nature More,* after Lord Byron's poem "Childe Harold's Pilgrimmage":

> There is pleasure in the pathless woods,
> There is a rapture on the lonely shore,
> There is society where none intrudes . . .
> I love not man the less, but nature more.[46]

(The title was quickly changed to the *Earth First! Newsletter,* and later simply *Earth First!*.) In this first document, which Foreman requested remain confidential, he outlined the movement's organizational structure. The founders of Earth First! had identified the corruption of the political system to be in part a result of its monolithic character. They were therefore determined to avoid its hierarchical and authoritarian structure and to create a movement with as little structure as possible: "[W]hen you take on the structure of the corporate state, you develop the ideology and the bottom line of the corporate state. So what is the one kind of human organization that's really worked? The hunter/gatherer tribe, so we tried to model ourselves structurally after that."[47] The decision to adopt a tribal structure accorded with the movement's ideology; such institutions were not, however, entirely practicable. During its first years, the movement struggled to resolve the tension between a central authority entrusted with considerable power and a doctrine that rejected hierarchy and organization. The 1980 Round River Rendezvous instituted two formal governing structures: the Circle of Darkness and *La Manta Mojada* ("the wet blanket").

The Circle of Darkness was to be Earth First!'s "national co-ordinating committee," a group of individuals whose role was to determine policy, approve memberships and state and local groups, select new members of the Circle, and generally "run the outfit." Members of the Circle had to be willing to be publicly identified with Earth First!, and they could not be employees or officers of "straight" conservation groups.[48] Twelve individuals were selected as members; among them were the original "group of five," and Susan Morgan.[49] In the newsletter, Foreman emphasized that while it was desirable to keep the Circle as small as possible, it was open to new members (subject to approval by a three-quarters majority of the current Circle membership). Later, women and East or West Coast representatives were directly solicited in order to fill representational gaps.[50]

It is interesting to note that while Foreman left open the question of whether the Circle should have officers (suggesting the possibility that it could be anarchistic in nature), he emphasized that a treasurer was immediately necessary.[51] From the movement's inception, its leaders insisted that anyone who believed that the earth should be first should be able to join, regardless of their financial status. Often, newsletter subscriptions were extended without renewal fees. This idealistic approach was, however, countered by the group's commercial endeavors. From its beginnings, Earth First! was financially self-supporting. This was due in part to various money-raising ventures such as the sale of t-shirts and calendars (which came to be known as the sale of "snake oil and trinkets"), and in part to financial contributions from well-off individuals. Financial campaigns were always successful; when the movement or its newsletter needed extra funds, there were always individuals prepared to donate that money. The movement's financial operations illustrate its ideological origins, which were firmly situated in the fabric of American liberalism. The movement never advocated the overthrow of the capitalist economic system, but instead argued that the return to small-scale economic ventures and agriculture would yield the good society. Its financial operations also reveal much about the movement's sense of itself as a group. Its commercial endeavours were successful because members purchased memorabilia that identified them as part of the Earth First! movement. In the words of Foreman, "We created a community . . . and you need that . . . [but] you don't have that in your family anymore, and you don't have that in your neighbourhood anymore. . . . To a lot of people in Earth First!, the tribal belonging became the main thing."[52] Its open membership policy was financially supported because the movement's cause was of greater importance than "the concerns of Babylon."[53]

The group's other original governing structure, *La Manta Mojada*, was "an official and secret group of advisors to the Circle."[54] The newsletter did not list its members, stating only that it "currently consists of eight people who are involved with moderate conservation groups."[55] *La Manta Mojada* was not mentioned again in later newsletters; its secret status makes any analysis of its evolution impossible. In later interviews, however, Foreman stated that its existence was short-lived and implied that it was also ineffectual; Earth First!'s doctrine and actions were independent in both spirit and practice.[56] Given the character of later Earth First! activities, there is no reason to dispute this claim.

The 1980 Round River Rendezvous also saw the first delineation of the movement's doctrine. No formal decisions were made there, but two months after its conclusion, in September, Howie Wolke and Foreman sent out a memo that summarized the issues that had been raised in Wyoming. It was mailed to all those who had expressed a commitment to Earth First!, and it encouraged comments and revisions.

The first members of Earth First! were unusually similar in terms of their age, education, and occupational backgrounds. Their experience in the world had led them to a shared belief that modern society and its destruction of the natural world could only end in an apocalyptic crisis. The immediate political imperative was therefore to save as much remaining wilderness as possible, in order to allow continued life and evolution on the planet. These beliefs were rooted in practical experience, and required of their adherents a new perspective on humankind's role in the ecosystem. Earth First!'s membership adopted this perspective almost intuitively; they did not need to read philosophy to have their lives explained to them: "Most people in Earth First! are not dependent on books to explain their own views of things. I don't think it has much effect. We have a pretty simple philosophy and very simple feelings about things, and the fact that environmental problems are complicated . . . doesn't mean that we don't know what we're about. It's pretty simple, what we're trying to do."[57] Indeed, many Earth First!ers are uncomfortable with identifying a philosophical source for their beliefs. They believe that evidence for their beliefs appears in the world around them and in scientific documents that identify elements of the environmental crisis. However, despite this general aversion to philosophy and the written word (which also reflects a predilection for acting over thinking, and a fear that written doctrines yield dogma),[58] many of these "intuitive feelings" surfaced in the foundations of the philosophy known as deep ecology. Indeed, deep ecology became an integral part of the movement's discourse in mid-1984. Thus, for analytical purposes at least, a consideration of deep ecology can be useful in illumining many facets of Earth First!'s doctrine.

Deep Ecology

Arne Naess first used the term "deep ecology" to distinguish between "reform environmentalism" (an approach to environmental issues that remains within traditional political parameters) and a perspective that recognizes the need for a reevaluation of humankind's role in the world.[59] Deep ecologists argue that the Copernican revolution taught human beings to approach the world "anthropocentrically," that is, with a vision narrowly defined by their own needs and desires. This perspective is ultimately destructive, for human beings are not properly nature's master, nor are they separate from it. There is "no firm ontological divide in the field of existence . . . there is no bifurcation in reality between the human and the non-human realms."[60] Human beings have a prepolitical link with nature that is both physical and spiritual. As Paul Shepard writes, "The epidermis of the skin is ecologically like a pond surface or a forest soil, not a shell so much as a delicate interpenetration. It reveals the self ennobled and extended rather than threatened as part of the landscape and ecosystem because the beauty and complexity of nature are continuous with ourselves."[61] Nature is therefore part of the moral community.

Deep ecology demands that individuals understand the world in biocentric terms. This perspective advocates a respect for all species and a dedication to maintaining the full biodiversity of the earth: "[A]ll things in the biosphere have an equal right to live and blossom and to reach their own individual forms of unfolding and self-realization."[62] A biocentric perspective requires that important changes be made in the way societies are organized and what individuals demand from the environment. Deep ecology rejects centralized, bureaucratic authority and technological society and advocates the simplicity of a "natural life." A return to preindustrial social organization is understood as desirable and necessary. The ideal is the "primitive" society, because it fulfills the needs of individuals and communities and preserves the integrity of the natural world. In such societies, human beings are organized in small, decentralized, nonhierarchical and democratic communities. Devall and Sessions imply that this tradition allows for a morally upright population; individuals in such a society help each other and regulate their own actions, and their relations are communal rather than competitive. They do not revere secular authority but instead respect "spiritual mentors," and the entire community participates in rituals. Individuals in such a community live in harmony with nature, for their needs are "elegantly simple"; they preserve natural resources and practice a "nondominating science."[63]

The Ideology of Earth First!

The founders of Earth First! were moved to action by the conclusions of RARE II, a crisis that, in Foreman's words, constituted "the greatest single act of wilderness destruction in American history."[64] In Earth First!'s early documents, Wolke and Foreman defined wilderness as areas that are large enough to support a complete ecosystem and that are free from human influence.[65] A September 1980 memo written by Foreman contains the following "Statement of Principles":

—Wilderness has a right to exist for its own sake
—All life forms, from virus to the great whales, have an inherent and equal right to existence
—Humankind is no greater than any other form of life and has no legitimate claim to dominate Earth
—Humankind, through overpopulation, anthropocentrism, industrialization, excessive energy consumption/resource extraction, state capitalism, father-figure hierarchies, imperialism, pollution, and natural area destruction, threatens the basic life processes of EARTH
—All human decisions should consider Earth first, humankind second
—The only true test of morality is whether an action, individual, social or political, benefits Earth
—Humankind will be happier, healthier, more secure, and more comfortable in a society that recognizes humankind's true biological nature and which is in dynamic harmony with the total biosphere
—Political compromise has no place in the defense of Earth
—Earth is Goddess and the proper object of human worship[66]

(This final item was abandoned almost immediately. Foreman claims the clause was a result of his temporary fascination with the writings of Starhawk, a feminist theologian.)[67]

These principles reflect both a biocentric perspective and an emphasis on biodiversity. Wilderness is identified as an absolute good, against which all actions should be judged, and all species are recognized as being equal and of intrinsic value. With the political good so defined, all actions in support of wilderness are justifiable, and any compromise becomes an act against good, that is, evil. While biocentrism requires an understanding of the environment that recognizes the intrinsic good of all species, the belief in biocentric equality is a belief that all species are intrinsically equal. This principle is well illustrated in Foreman's remark that "[a] Goodding's Onion . . . has a history, has a pedigree on this planet just as long as mine is, and who's to say I have a right to be here, and it doesn't?"[68]

These principles form the basis for a radical critique of the traditional way environmental questions are addressed in western society.

They demand that human beings look beyond their own needs and wants to determine what is best for all species and for the ecology of the earth itself. Earth First!ers transplanted these ideas from the realm of philosophical speculation to political action; in so doing, they added to them the urgency of a belief in an imminent apocalypse.

For Foreman and those individuals who were originally drawn to Earth First!, the political landscape was well defined. The American government and the corporate infrastructure embodied the evil of human greed, and were destroying the ecosystems that sustained the planet. Western culture utilized excessive resources, and in a vicious cycle had become materially dependent on that excessive consumption. It was overextended in terms of its resource use, and was spiritually sick: "If we take the tenets of civilization, psychic, social, sexual and spiritual, and stand them on their head, then we would have a decent basis for a respectable and creative existence."[69]

The end of civilization could only be prevented by a complete change in government, industry, and cultural values. At the minimum there would need to be an immediate halt to industry, a ban on the use of automobiles, elimination of range cattle, and the restoration of major wilderness areas. The sweeping nature of these changes, however, rendered them impossible. The government, industry, and even conservation groups were unwilling to initiate the necessary restrictions:

> America's and humankind's assault on Mother Earth continues unabated—indeed at an increasingly feverish pace as our junkie technological order seeks quick fixes . . . national conservation groups have become more and more lethargic and moderate, seduced by promises of establishment respectability. *Earth is being raped—and those who claim to speak for Her are afraid to open their mouths!* . . . The juggernaut of modern corporate technology must be stopped![70]

The early issues of the Earth First! newsletter are notable for their lack of philosophical discussion, but their contributors' language is clear. Earth First!'s call for action was not a call to reform the system; it was a call for its demise.

While Earth First! demanded the end of the political and economic order, it also evinced a faith that the "corporate industrial monolith" would destroy itself. Earth First!ers believed that industrial capitalism was becoming increasingly corrupt and dangerous, a fact best expressed by Ronald Reagan's administration. In an editorial entitled "The Hounds of Hell are Howling High," Foreman compared the federal government's environmental policies to the Holocaust, a comparison that later became common in the Earth First! newsletter. "With the taste of blood in their yapping maws, the mad dog political toadies of the Earth-raping corporations are closing in for the kill. Witness Sam Hayakawa's big anti-wilderness bill that makes Tom Foley's of last year look like a Sierra Club project. Or how about Jim Santini's bill to 'liberalize' the 1872 Mining Law? (That's like Himmler loosening up the restrictions on sending Jews to the Nazi death camps.)"[71] The system would, however, collapse owing to its own corruption.

The inevitability of the impending crisis is a certainty, but its specifics and the exact date of its occurrence are unknown. The nature of the coming disaster will, however, reflect society's abuse of the environment, and it is understood to be imminent. For example, one Washington Earth First!er declared,

> I don't have any specific number of years that I would set, but I think it's pretty clear from recent events that total economic collapse, the cessation of the infrastructure of our current civilization is only a heartbeat away. It could happen next week, or it could take longer than that. . . . I'm not sure which event will actually be the breaking point, but it's certain that things cannot continue as they are.[72]

"The sooner the system collapses, the better,"[73] because each day its destruction continues, more irreplaceable wilderness is lost.

Coeval with the building crisis in the corporate industrial monolith was an impending ecological crisis: "[T]he destruction of the natural life of the American Continent is only the beginning of the dynamics of industrial civilization. Its continuing, exponential increase of biocide that reaches toward the fallacy of materialist salvation, that of power and wealth, is rapidly reaching its conclusion, biological entropy."[74] Earth First! members therefore understood the adoption of a biocentric perspective to be an immediate imperative, for they anticipated and feared the occurrence of a "biological meltdown."[75] This meltdown would see the disappearance of one-third to one-half of the earth's species and result in an ecocatastrophe that would threaten all life forms. Although extinctions have occurred in the past, this would be far worse than any that preceded it, for it differs in two important ways. First, past extinctions occurred amongst higher order species and did not significantly disrupt evolution. The current crisis, however, is destroying plant species and entire habitats. Because plants are the foundation of life, a mass species extinction carries with it the probable extinction of an "exponentially greater number of animal species."[76] The very origin and foundation of species life is therefore threatened. Additionally, the demise of so many plant species would hinder the restoration of biodiversity for thousands of years. Second, this crisis is ultimately most dangerous because it has been created by the will of human beings, not by the "inevitable" forces of nature. Human beings have taken upon themselves the task of governing evolution. It is this crisis that Earth First!ers are most concerned with: the unsustainability of western civilization is destroying what little remains of the natural world.[77]

The evil of the system and the inevitability of its imminent collapse were understood to be the cause of Earth First!'s emergence and evidence of its important role in sustaining the earth's biodiversity. After Reagan's election, an anonymous author from Colorado wrote to the newsletter that "the process now taking place under Reagan is more hopeful even as it appears more bleak,"[78] implying both that the increasing evils of the system would hasten its demise and that individuals who recognized its character would be more likely to act.

The converging industrial and environmental crises make it an immediate imperative that as much wilderness as possible be saved from human intervention and commercial exploitation. Early issues of the Earth First! newsletter focused on the necessity of saving what remained of the North American wilderness, and re-creating greater wilderness.[79] The movement's first platform demanded forty-one wilderness areas, totalling over 137 million acres. It also demanded the entire island of Hawaii, the end to all development in Alaska, RARE II's "Alternative J (see note 30 above)," and that all Bureau of Land Management roadless areas be designated as wilderness.[80] Much of this land was already in commercial use, and therefore "[w]ithin each reserve, all existing developments (roads, towns, . . . etc.) will be obliterated by the same implements of technology that put them there. We intend to help nature reclaim the earth."[81] The platform concludes with further demands for "reasonable land management":

> —No nukes, dismantle all existing nukes.
> —No uranium mining.
> —No more stripmining.
> —No more power plants (fossil fuel, nuke, hydroelectric).
> —No more dams. . . .
> —No more roads on public lands.
> —A complete ban on the recreation use of ORV's [outdoor recreational vehicles].[82]

In their demand for the preservation and re-creation of wilderness, Earth First! adherents did not understand themselves to be radicals. Indeed, they said that it was the earth destroyers who were radicals and that the destruction of the corporate/industrial monolith was an opportunity for the rejuvenation of true American political community: "Wilderness is America. What can be more patriotic than the love of the land? We will be Americans only as long as there is wilderness. Wilderness is our true Bill of Rights, the true repository of our freedoms, the true home of liberty."[83]

Earth First!'s ideology evolved over time to become more refined and complex; in these early stages, adherents clearly understood themselves to be actors whose role was pivotal in the history of the world. Tir Eriaur Aldaron, a member of the Circle, emphasized the importance of the group as well as its role in history in a lengthy newsletter article:

> The Earth is our first love, our first concern. Our children must be imbued with an unswerving sense of responsibility and respect for Her, and a recognition of the significance of *our* role leads to even greater dedication. Grant understanding to our fellows but show no compromise. . . . Earth first! . . . . [She] must live Her healthy, tumbling life, free from a dread of infestation and misdeed. As Her seed, we become embassadors [*sic*], emissaries in the final drama, and our mission is indeed grand![84]

The salvation that Earth First!ers envisioned therefore reflected the characteristics that scholars of millenarianism have identified as critical to such belief systems. It was anticipated as imminent, ultimate, collective, and this-worldly.

The Earth First! movement chose as its first target the Glen Canyon Dam. As has been noted, the dam was a symbol of the environmental movement's first disillusionment with traditional politics. It was physical proof of "government officials motivated by a quasireligious zeal to industrialize the natural world, and a diffident bureaucratic leadership in the mainstream environmental organizations that more or less willingly collaborated."[85] That symbolism was important, but it was not the sole reason that Earth First! chose the dam as its first protest site. Edward Abbey's Monkey Wrench Gang sabotaged bulldozers and billboards, but its members dreamed of exploding Glen Canyon Dam. In its war with the industrial monolith, Earth First!ers had adopted monkeywrenching tactics as their own.

3

The Cracking of Glen Canyon Dam

To have a deep blue lake
Where no lake was before
Seems to bring man
A little closer to God.[1]

—Floyd Dominy,
Commissioner, Bureau of Reclamation

Were you there when they built Glen Canyon Damn [*sic*]? . . .
Were you there when they killed this river dead? . . .
Spirit come and tear this dam away . . .
People stand and roll away these stones
People stand and roll away these stones
Oh, you know this Earth is going to tremble, tremble
People stand and roll away these stones.[2]

—Bart Koehler

On the morning of the spring equinox, 1981, seventy-five members of Earth First! gathered at the Colorado Bridge, near Glen Canyon Dam. Their demonstration began as a "traditional" political protest, and their placards and speeches successfully occupied the dam's security force. During the disturbance, however, a small group approached the dam from an access road. Unnoticed, four men and one woman, carrying with them a one hundred pound bundle of plastic, scaled the dam's guard fence and ran towards the center of the dam.[3] As the Earth First! demonstrators on the bridge yelled "Free the Colorado," the "monkeywrenchers" unfurled a three-hundred-foot black plastic wedge, ta-

45

pered from twelve to two feet in width, and held together with seven hundred feet of rope and one thousand feet of duct tape. The large plastic wedge that rolled down the face of the structure made Glen Canyon Dam appear to have been "cracked."[4] Despite the efforts of the Park Service police, Coconino County sheriff's office, and the Federal Bureau of Investigation, the individuals responsible were not caught. After their dramatic action, they disappeared into the waiting crowd and joined the larger demonstration. FBI agents later dusted the plastic wedge for fingerprints, but they were unable to identify the culprits.

During the remainder of the demonstration, Edward Abbey addressed the gathering on the bridge. He recalled the glory of Glen Canyon and argued that it had been stolen from the people by state politicians, "in cahoots with the land developers, city developers, industrial developers of the Southwest . . . in order to pursue and promote their crackpot ideology of growth, profit and power."[5] He then instructed the crowd: "Oppose. Oppose the destruction of our homeland by these alien forces from Houston, Tokyo, Manhattan, Washington, D.C., and the Pentagon. And if opposition is not enough, we must resist. And if resistance is not enough, then subvert."[6] He closed his remarks by launching a nationwide petition that demanded the immediate razing of the dam,[7] and Johnny Sagebrush concluded the protest by leading the group in the singing of "Were You There When They Built Glen Canyon Damn?" and "This Land is Your Land."[8]

By all of Earth First!'s measures, the event was a success: the group made a political statement, no one was arrested, and the authorities were made to look foolish. It also yielded significant media coverage. Articles concerning the Glen Canyon Dam protest appeared in the *Rocky Mountain News,* the *Denver Post,* and the *Arizona Republic.*[9] From the movement's founding, Dave Foreman had emphasized the importance of ridicule as a political tactic, because "[l]aughter is the only way to maintain personal sanity in a world gone mad."[10] The plastic crack reflected that principle, but its allusion to *The Monkey Wrench Gang* did not inspire laughter in the government or in executives who believed their corporations were possible targets. The FBI interpreted the event as a harbinger of domestic terrorism,[11] and business interests began to express concern to the bureau's Washington office soon afterwards.[12]

These fears were not unfounded, but they were somewhat premature. Earth First! clearly intended to use almost any means at its disposal to protect the wilderness (one individual went so far as to say that he supported "any method short of machine-gunning people down in the street"[13]), but for the first half of 1981, the movement was preoccupied with ideological concerns and proselytism.

Although Earth First!'s early membership was primarily drawn from the Southwestern conservation movement, the visibility of its successful actions soon began attracting individuals from a variety of backgrounds and geographical locations. In a 1981 newsletter editorial, Foreman addressed the movement's growing diversity and in so doing clarified its doctrine. He argued that "[i]n diversity there is strength. That's an old ecological maxim, but it holds true for organizations as well as for ecosystems . . . there will be few of us who are in complete agreement . . . this pluralism is healthy—and inducive [*sic*] to greater creativity and energy. The people united in EARTH FIRST! are linked by our common love for the Earth."[14] Foreman therefore welcomed the differences among Earth First! members, but he also made it clear that the movement's ideology was to retain a broadly defined single focus: "[T]he Earth must come first."[15] In so doing, he created a tension between ideological unity and freedom of interpretation that was destined to cause problems for the movement's leadership. He had diversified Earth First!'s approach to the environmental crisis but opened its simple doctrine to a variety of interpretations. As Earth First!'s membership spread across demographic and geographic boundaries, this tension fostered a conflict that eventually split the movement.

However, the solidarity of the group was not, however, in question during 1981. During that year, the newsletter was clearly the product of an ideologically unified movement, intent on publicizing its cause and proselytizing across the United States. There were no major conflicts among Earth First!'s members, and in the late spring, the movement began a serious campaign to attract new adherents.[16]

In May, the newsletter published an article on the Glen Canyon Dam petitions, encouraging individuals to continue to gather signatures. However, that issue was most notable for two other features. First, its cover, which usually provided direct coverage of Earth First! actions, instead reprinted an editorial from another publication, the *Daily Sentinel* of Grand Junction, Colorado.[17] The article, a commentary on the

Glen Canyon Dam protest, was generally uncomplimentary. It was, however, indicative of the growing coverage that the movement and its tactics were receiving. The authors criticized the radical nature of Earth First!'s demand that Glen Canyon Dam be dismantled and noted that the movement was unlikely to gain popular support. Earth First!ers were well aware of the difficulty of their mission, however, and hostile press coverage served only to reaffirm their convictions. It also spread their message. Second, the May newsletter contained the first list of the movement's regional contacts. The editors had compiled a list of nine individuals, in locations as geographically widespread as Maine and Colorado, who were prepared to formally represent Earth First! and to "coordinate the formation of local groups and projects."[18] This charge reflected the movement's early emphasis on centralization and showed its rapid growth.[19]

The May newsletter concluded with an impassioned plea for funds,[20] but the June issue was printed on schedule, and there was no further mention of the problem. Earth First!ers were not, on average, a wealthy group, but their fervent belief in the importance of their mission insured that whenever such financial disasters threatened, funds would be found.

Early in June 1981, the group's leadership began planning the Earth First! Road Show, a three month tour of the United States that was intended to "spread public awareness of Earth First!, help organize EF! affiliates throughout the country, recruit more EF! members, and, especially, pull EF! members together and get their ideas."[21] The program was to include speeches by Foreman and songs by Johnny Sagebrush, as well as a film of "The Cracking of Glen Canyon Damn," and would be performed "for any group that would listen."[22] The Road Show depended upon the movement's grassroots infrastructure, for it required Earth First! members to arrange local performances, set up meetings with the press, provide accommodation for the performers, and provide sufficient funds for the tour. The leadership's appeal was successful. By August, a nationwide tour had been organized, with local volunteer coordinators found for the majority of cities where performances were planned.[23]

As will be seen, the Road Show effectively achieved all of its goals. This success was in part a function of its composition. The Earth First! Road Show was one of the movement's most important vehicles to display and revel in its "folklore," the creative traditions that the group used to define itself and distinguish it from other environmental groups and from society at large.[24] From poetry to songs and stories about monkeywrenching, such traditions held the promise of a meaningful life for new members. They were also a way for longstanding members to relive and redefine their experiences. It is useful to briefly examine a number of Earth First!'s creative traditions.

For Earth First!'s founders, the imminence of biological disaster necessitated a new human order and made clear the limits of an acceptable human community. Industrialized society and its attendant authority structures were antithetical to the survival of biodiversity. Earth First! therefore adopted an informal structure that was (in their view, at least) roughly modeled on tribal societies,[25] and the movement prided itself on its minimal structure and the few formal constraints it placed on its adherents. This freedom was, however, illusory. Earth First!'s membership and ideology were at all times constrained by a well-articulated panorama of symbols, songs, and stories. The movement relied on the development of a shared culture to bind its members together and to limit their interpretation of Foreman's declaration that "the Earth must come first." A formal hierarchy and organizational structure were therefore unnecessary.

Much of the movement's symbolism was deliberately chosen (for example, Glen Canyon Dam and the Round River Rendezvous), but other expressions of a shared sense of community developed organically. From the first printing of the newsletter, poetry was a common feature; early on, it highlighted authors such as Stephen Crane and D. H. Lawrence,[26] but soon their work was outnumbered by the contributions of aspiring Earth First! poets. Likewise, art became an integral part of the bond among the group's adherents.[27]

However, the most important expression of Earth First!'s shared belief system was its music. Over the course of its history, Earth First! musicians developed a body of musical compositions that fully expressed the movement's ideology. Song and dance became an important part of Earth First! gatherings, and the journal's merchandise office conducted a booming business in cassette tape sales.[28] Darryl Cherney (one of Earth First!'s best known and most controversial musicians) argued that the reason for this development was rooted in the character of the movement's goals. Because "Earth First! is essentially a warrior tribe, and we're dealing with . . . insurmountable, or seemingly insurmountable obstacles, we have a special need for the release of tension and sorrow, as well as a need to express our joy in the good fight."[29] Earth First!'s peculiar brand of folk music was a rebellion against the "technological perversion of modern music,"[30] and its "wildness and fun" were crucial to achieving the appropriate atmosphere at the group's gatherings.[31] At the same time, Earth First!'s music functioned to consolidate the group and to maintain ideological unity; it "dr[ew] everyone together."[32] Earth First! musicians wrote music that reflected their personal struggle to save the wilderness, and all Earth First!ers could empathize with their experiences. The most popular musicians (among them Dana Lyons, Cecelia Ostrow, Walkin' Jim Stoltz and Darryl Cherney) developed significant followings, and were often regarded as heroes for their ability to translate their experiences into music.[33]

While Earth First! gatherings always provided opportunities for songs, stories, and rituals, it was at the Earth First! Road Shows and the Round River Rendezvous where these creative traditions played their most important role. While Road Shows were a means to revitalize the movement's disparate local groups, the Round River Rendezvous was the movement's "annual tribal gathering"[34] held every July 4. Before Foreman and Bart Koehler embarked upon the first Earth First! Road Show, the annual Round River Rendezvous took place. That sequence is important, for it allowed a further definition of the movement's ideology prior to its first concerted attempt to proselytize.

As noted above, the first Round River Rendezvous in 1980 attracted approximately sixty interested individuals. In 1981, that number more than tripled: over two hundred people attended the meeting.[35] Only a year after its founding, Earth First! was becoming a diverse movement, and its local affiliates were scattered across the United States. Under such circumstances, the Round River Rendezvous, as the only annual meeting of all Earth First!ers, took on great importance. As the movement continued to develop, the Rendezvous' size and significance also grew. The early Rendezvous of 1980 and 1981 were loosely organized gatherings, but later meetings scheduled workshops, speeches, and concerts in order to feature as many events as possible.[36]

Earth First!ers' fundamental belief in the imminence of an apocalyptic environmental crisis made the Rendezvous uniquely important in giving adherents the opportunity to express their concerns with other like-minded individuals. Their beliefs and their way of life distinguished them from middle class America, but at the Rendezvous, they could discuss their ideas and their experiences openly with others who shared their understanding of the world. While the Rendezvous was technically just an annual meeting, the function it performed within the movement went far beyond the usual parameters of such occasions:

> [What binds us] is a very deep love of the earth . . . The biodiversity of the planet, the air, the water, everything needs to live. It's like a tribe. It's so strong, it's almost like a religion. . . . It's that sort of feeling, "you feel that way too? I felt so isolated! I thought I was the only wacko out there who wanted to throw myself in front of a bulldozer to protect a tree, and there's others like you!" It's a homecoming; it's really neat to meet your own tribe.[37]

Earth First!ers understood themselves to form a community outside the American mainstream, and the Rendezvous was an opportunity to experience that perceived reality in its most complete form. Its most important function was, therefore, to bring Earth First!ers together, "to show solidarity and camaraderie";[38] as a member of the 1986 Rendezvous committee stated, "The RRR is spiritually uplifting. You realize that there are other people who feel the way you do, and you feel free to speak your mind. For me the RRR is the only chance I get to meet people I can stand being with."[39] For these reasons, the Rendezvous was an opportunity for celebration; it was also a forum to conduct the movement's business.

The 1981 Rendezvous was held on the Fourth of July weekend at Moab, Utah, in Arches National Park. It therefore began with a celebration of Independence Day, "in traditional American fashion with waving flags; fancy oratory; stirring songs; red, white, and blue bunting; and lots of beer."[40] Not only did the nation-state and its people require the continued biodiversity of the wilderness, but the American political identity itself was based upon the existence of wilderness. Foreman declared that Earth First!ers were the real Sagebrush Patriots and that the Sagebrush Tories who supported Ronald Reagan were comparable to the Tories who supported King George during the American Revolution. "Wilderness is America. What can be more patriotic than the love of the land?"[41] Foreman clearly identified Earth First! with the American founders, linking what he interpreted as the political and commercial oppression of the twentieth century with that of the eighteenth century American colonies.[42] Indeed, he later remarked of the FBI agents who were tracking the movement, "If the people who are trying to frame me were around in 1770, they would have been calling Sam Adams, Patrick Henry and Thomas Jefferson terrorists."[43]

The spirit of the 1981 Rendezvous was celebratory; after Foreman's speech, the occasion's most notable events were poetry readings, a performance by Johnny Sagebrush, a speech by Ken Sleight (a Utah river runner who was generally acknowledged to be the model for *The Monkey Wrench Gang*'s Seldom Seen Smith), and the mock appearances of Senator Sam Hayakawa and Secretary of the Interior James Watt. "James Watt" accepted the position of "Honorary Membership Chairman of Earth First!" and declared, "I will work diligently to balloon the membership of EARTH FIRST! to three million by the end of the Ray-Gun Administration or the end of the world, whichever comes first."[44] In the movement's early years, the relaxed atmosphere of such gatherings was in part the result of the great volume of beer that was imbibed: at the 1981 Rendezvous, approximately 2500 cans of beer were consumed.[45] The drinking that took place at these events was accepted as a form of release from the stressful intensity of Earth First!'s struggle to save the wilderness.[46]

The newsletter published directly following the 1981 Round River Rendezvous provides the first direct discussions of "ecotage," or ecological sabotage, in Earth First! literature. In his editorial "The Reichstag Fire—1981," Foreman described the night of February 27, 1933. On that evening, ten Nazi agents, on orders from Joseph Goebbels, set fire to the Berlin Reichstag and blamed the communists, an event that provided Hitler with sufficient justification to establish a dictatorship.[47] Foreman compared that night with the evening of July 3, 1981, during which a Utah Power and Light transmission tower carrying a 345,000-volt power line was toppled seven miles south of Moab, the location of the Round River Rendezvous. Foreman noted that "environmentalists in general, and Earth First! in particular"[48] had been blamed for the damage. His commentary was indicative of a well-defined but as yet publicly unarticulated philosophy of ecotage. Foreman argued that it could not have been the work of Earth First!ers, because the event "had no meaning or purpose."[49] Instead, the damage had more likely been caused by corporate interests themselves, "the San Juan County Commission, Utah Power and Light, or Free-lance anti-environmental yahoos."[50] Foreman wrote that while Earth First! was not allied with "the accused reds" of the Reichstag fire, there were marked similarities "between the Nazis and the dominant political establishment of southeastern Utah."[51] He did not, however, disown the tactics of ecotage. Indeed, Foreman's condemnation of the Utah utilities corporations was juxtaposed with an open invitation to all Earth First!ers to suggest new and effective techniques of monkeywrenching.

The August 1981 issue of the newsletter concluded with the announcement of an "Ecotricks" contest, a competition intended to inspire the newsletter's readers in their defense of the earth. An "ecotrick" was defined as "any nonconventional means employed to protect the Earth Mother. It implies the use of superior wit and cunning in a form of psycho/political judo to render our/her opponents impotent . . . hopefully in the bedroom as well as in the arena of contest."[52] The newsletter provided only one guideline. The ecotrick "should not be too fellonious [*sic*] because we need you out there being active."[53] Although Earth First!ers had several times publicly declared that monkeywrenching was among their repertoire of tactics, no explicit discussion of its specifics had yet appeared in the *Newsletter*. Its appearance at this time reflects not only the growing confidence of the movement and its leadership but also the recognition that open discussion of monkeywrenching might itself be a valuable tactic. The "Reichstag" incident made clear that whether or not they were involved, Earth First!ers were likely to bear the blame for such occurrences.

Most Earth First!ers agreed that the severity of the environmental crisis necessitated the use of innovative and sometimes desperate tactics. Ecotage, or monkeywrenching, as it came to be known, was undoubtedly their most controversial weapon; its goal was to "block environmentally destructive projects, to increase the costs of such projects and thereby make them economically unattractive, and to raise public awareness of the taxpayer-subsidized devastation of biological diversity occurring in the world." Monkeywrenching would help to insure that "[w]hen the floundering beast finally, mercifully chokes in its own dung pile, there'll at least be *some* wilderness remaining as a seed bed for planet-wide recovery."[54]

Examples of monkeywrenching were plentiful in Abbey's *The Mon-*

key Wrench Gang (and they no doubt served as inspiration for many Earth First!ers' actions). Foreman suggested that such activities might include "pulling up survey stakes, putting sand in the crankcases of bulldozers, rendering dirt roads in wild areas impassable . . . cutting down billboards, and removing and destroying trap lines."[55] It was "using the tools of the devil against the devil."[56]

Monkeywrenching was never condoned or actively undertaken by all Earth First!ers; indeed, its moral justification and relative efficacy were debated throughout the movement's history. Nevertheless, monkeywrenching's occasionally spectacular consequences and its controversial nature insured that it would be this aspect of Earth First! that would attract the most media coverage and draw public attention.

In his 1985 article "Strategic Monkeywrenching," Foreman discussed the American environmental crisis and the need to protect biodiversity, suggesting a number of guidelines for safe and effective monkeywrenching.[57] He argued that the most accessible and therefore the most cost efficient areas of American wilderness had already been destroyed. The few remaining wilderness areas were difficult to access, and they would likely provide only a marginal profit. Foreman wrote:

> It is expensive to maintain the necessary infrastructure . . . for the exploitation of wild lands. The cost of repairs, the hassle, the delay, the down time may just be too much for the bureaucrats and exploiters . . . if there is a widely-dispersed, unorganized, *strategic* movement of resistance across the land. It is time for women and men, individually and in small groups, to act heroically and admittedly illegally in defense of the wild.[58]

The guidelines Foreman provided for successful monkeywrenching stressed its strategic nature; it was purposeful, not vandalism for the sake of vandalism. Monkeywrenching activities, properly performed, would be nonviolent, targeted, dispersed, and elegantly simple. In Abbey's *Hayduke Lives!*, George Washington Hayduke and Doc Sarvis outlined the "Code of the Eco-Warrior": "Rule Number One is nobody gets hurt, Rule Number Two is nobody gets caught, and Rule Number Three is if you do get caught, you're on your own."[59] Monkeywrenching could not be centrally organized or performed by groups, because such direction would invite discovery and/or infiltration.[60]

The solitary and relatively anonymous character of monkeywrenching gave that activity a peculiar role within the movement. To openly discuss specific actions was to invite arrest; in theory, Earth First!ers could not, therefore, discuss monkeywrenching activities in detail at their gatherings. Indeed, even informing local newsletter contacts of such actions was discouraged.[61] The practice of monkeywrenching was, however, an acknowledged undercurrent at Earth First! gatherings. In the words of one Earth First!er, "I don't know of anybody that's done it, I'm sure they have, but I don't know of it, or who they are. I'm sure that if you look at thirty people in a room, there are people who will have done something, but I don't know who they are . . . we realize that we're all in this together, we're working with each other."[62]

Among those who did practice monkeywrenching, there was a sense of shared accomplishment; monkeywrenchers felt their actions distinguished them among Earth First!ers. It was "definitely a kind of secret society."[63] Again, such activities were not supported by all Earth First!ers, but most understood their motivation. One such individual, asked about his attitude towards monkeywrenching, replied, "I deplore the necessity of the tactic."[64]

The solitary character of monkeywrenching, coupled with its inherent risks and dangers, served in many cases to transform monkeywrenchers into heroes and to grant the activity itself a glorified symbolic status. Monkeywrenching was celebrated both in story and in song. The lyrics of Roselle and Cherney's "Ballad of the Lonesome Tree Spiker" illustrate this point: "Well I've spiked me some redwoods and I've spiked me some pines / And they've tried to stop me with rewards and fines / The cops and the Freddies are hot on my trail / But I'm a tree spiker and I'll never get nailed."[65] In his 1990 article "Dave Foreman!," Charles Bowden characterized monkeywrenching as "The Fantasy of Direct Action against The Beast. Babylon. The Military-Industrial Complex."[66] His religious terminology was well-chosen. While monkeywrenchers believed their activity was of practical value,[67] the activity also symbolized their apocalyptic battle against the military industrial state. In this respect, monkeywrenching reveals much about Earth First!'s millenarian belief structure.

For most Earth First!ers, the American state and its institutional structures had ceased to provide a meaningful political existence. In its place, both groups looked to the environment to provide both meaning and structure for their political life. In the words of Dave Foreman, "[it is] religious in a non-supernatural sense . . . we have an ethical, reciprocal relationship with the land. We are, for lack of a better term, talking about our souls."[68] In this respect, both groups sacralized the earth. Monkeywrenching was therefore not just a political tactic but also a religious act. Indeed, in many interviews Foreman identified monkeywrenching as "a form of worshipping the earth."[69] He once commented that "[a] bulldozer is just iron ore. . . . It doesn't want to be up here destroying the earth. All we're doing is liberating its soul, allowing it to find its true self, its Buddha-hood, and go back into the earth."[70]

Monkeywrenching is thus "very much a sacrament,"[71] an outward and visible sign of inward and spiritual growth. In the context of Earth First!'s millenarian ideology, that sacrament played an important role. As one Earth First!er commented, "I don't use violence but there's a war being waged upon us and upon the planet. Every thread of fabric in the planet is currently the victim of an onslaught. . . . We are in a war. . . . I am a warrior, and I will continue to defend myself and the planet as best I can."[72] The biological crisis was so severe, the time remaining to save the planet so minimal, and the forces of ecological destruction so powerful that those who truly loved the wild had few other options.[73] To choose monkeywrenching was to choose life.[74]

The momentum created by events such as the "cracking" of Glen Canyon Dam and the second Round River Rendezvous continued into the autumn of 1981. On September 11, three hundred Earth First!ers demonstrated against Secretary of the Interior James Watt at a Western Governors Meeting in Jackson, Wyoming,[75] and in October, Foreman published an article concerning Earth First! in The Progressive.[76] Although Foreman had many times expounded his message to his fellow Earth First!ers, this article was his first opportunity to bring the message to a larger and potentially sympathetic audience, and he took full advantage of the occasion. Foreman's article provides a detailed recounting of the movement's history and doctrine, and his arguments made compelling reading. After the magazine's publication, the Earth First! newsletter was swamped by over three hundred letters of interest and inquiry.[77]

The Progressive article represented a major clarification of Earth First!'s doctrine as of mid-1981. Foreman discussed the decline of traditional Washington environmental lobbying and outlined the need for a new, radical group "[t]o fight with uncompromising passion, for Mother Earth."[78] Presaging the movement's later problems, Foreman emphasized the primacy of the earth, stating that "for a group more committed to Gila monsters and mountain lions than to people, there will not be a total alliance with other social movements."[79] At the same time, however, he left open the possibility that Earth First! would perhaps cooperate with groups such as feminists and civil rights activists, and again he stressed the importance of developing a diverse movement. All that was required was a belief that the Earth should come first.[80] Foreman also declared what was to become one of Earth First!'s standard rallying cries when he wrote, "Action is key. Action is more important than philosophical hair-splitting or endless refining of dogma. . . . Let our actions set the finer points of our philosophy."[81] This statement revealed two important facets of Foreman's conceptualization of the movement's doctrine. First, and most obviously, the group was to be one of action, not words. Second, it indicated a shared sense of precisely why that action was necessary. Earth First!ers did not need to read deep ecology; they had an intuitive understanding of why their actions were necessary.[82]

On September 9, 1981, the Earth First! Road Show began its trek across the United States. Over the course of the next three months, Foreman and Koehler (Johnny Sagebrush) brought Earth First!'s message to over forty cities, performing for audiences that ranged from twenty to two thousand people.[83] They told stories, sang, and sold memberships and merchandise.[84] When it was over, local groups had been encouraged to fight on their own issues and "come together nationally to confront the beast of industrial civilization,"[85] and the group of five had grown to become a national movement.

4

The Battle Begins

The challenge has been made, and our time is at hand. The
meek and silent will be steamrolled by the device of their
apathy. . . . Lift up your hearts and raise your voices my
friends and brethren, the last battle is about to be fought.[1]

—Letter to the *Earth First! Newsletter*

The final months of 1981 saw the end of an era in Earth First! history:
the newsletter's first editor, Susan Morgan, resigned her position and
moved to Seattle. She did not officially leave the Circle, but thereafter,
her public affiliation with the movement gradually decreased.[2] Morgan's departure left the group's leadership without a female presence
and allowed radical changes to the movement's newsletter.

During the first two years, a typewritten, photocopied newsletter had
been an adequate vehicle to disseminate news and information amongst
Earth First!'s members. By late 1981, however, the limits of that format
were obvious. Its brevity prevented lengthy issue analysis, and it could not
accommodate photographs, artwork, or the large number of "Letters to
Earth First!" that the paper received each month. It also gave the movement an amateurish appearance that did not reflect its growing size and
influence. In December, Pete Dustrud became editor and began his tenure
by publishing the newsletter in a large tabloid format, on newsprint. This
transformation overcame the difficulties of limited issue coverage and perhaps unintentionally altered the publication's content and function.

The photocopied newsletter had featured the opinions and articles
of the movement's leadership; there was space for little else. The new
format was significantly larger, and it therefore required more articles
and contributors. It also provided ample space for the publication of

"Letters to Earth First!." Between December 1981 and February 1982, the number of letters published in the paper increased from four to thirty-one per issue.[3] In its new format, the paper disseminated not only the leadership's beliefs but also the often divergent beliefs of the membership. Unintentionally, the newsletter became the public location of the movement's many internal debates. In the early 1980s this was not a problem, for there were no major ideological cleavages among Earth First!ers. In his first editorial, Dustrud declared, "The heart and soul of EARTH FIRST! philosophy is that the human race resembles a cancer, which is rapidly devastating the Earth and Her community of life, and leading toward a massive ecological breakdown."[4] Those who wrote to the newsletter expressed only agreement.

By early 1982, membership had increased to approximately fifteen hundred individuals. Drawn to the movement by Foreman's article in the *Progressive* and by the Earth First! Roadshow, these new members were geographically dispersed, and they solidified the group's status as a national political actor.[5] At the same time, however, they exerted a centrifugal force upon the group's structure.

As we have seen, Earth First!ers understood themselves to have recognized a fundamental truth, the imminence of a "biological meltdown," and believed that that recognition distinguished them from mainstream environmental groups and the public at large. In that respect, they constituted a distinct and identifiable millenarian group. Their beliefs, however, prevented them from adopting the formal organizational hierarchy that usually characterizes such groups. Organizational hierarchy was the hallmark of the industrial monolith; it stifled wildness and diversity. This subtle discordance caused a tension that was most clearly expressed in Earth First!'s governing body, the Circle of Darkness. Dave Foreman remarked of this tension, "The Circle was the ruling body of Earth First!, and at first we decided that it was going to have really solid control. We didn't want anybody selling out on us . . . and at another level, we wanted to encourage local groups to take off on their own, and avoid bureaucracy."[6]

Foreman identified this incongruity as an inconsistency,[7] but it is perhaps better understood as the logical result of the group's ideology. This tension had existed from Earth First!'s origins, but the group's ideological development, coupled with the sudden influx of new members, encouraged its resolution during the winter of 1982.

The first stage of the necessitated transformation became evident early in 1982. On the cover of the February 2, 1982 newsletter, Pete Dustrud featured an article concerning Earth First!'s national contact list.[8] He began with the statement that "Earth First! could be likened more to a movement rather than an organization," and he emphasized that the movement's strength had to come from its grassroots chapters.[9] Dustrud's article did not detail any specific responsibilities for Earth First! contacts. Individuals were asked to volunteer as contacts in order that "other folks in each area can approach their contacts and begin getting things moving,"[10] an arrangement that implied spontaneity and emphasized informality. By contrast, the first contact list, printed nine months earlier, had been notable for its emphasis on centralized authority. In that formulation, contacts were identified as central to the planning and coordination of meetings and actions. This move away from centralization reconciled Earth First!ers' unity of purpose with their doctrinal emphasis on diversity and "wildness."

These changes, among others, were formalized at a meeting of the Earth First! leadership held on February 6 and 7, in Eugene, Oregon.[11] The meeting was not advertised in the newsletters; participation appears to have been by invitation only. A number of those who attended were members of the Circle, and all were clearly "leaders" in some respect.[12] All those who attended the meeting had a strong commitment to defending the earth. They also exemplified the strong loyalty to the movement that was developing amongst its adherents. That affection was well-expressed in a story from the February meeting:

> [O]ur most unusual arrival wandered in shortly before 2 A.M. The few who were still up and staggering around witnessed a U-Haul negotiating its way around the cars out front. In a second, the front door flew open to reveal Louisa Willcox, just in from Wyoming. Seems she was barreling along when her Capri gave out near Burns, Oregon. Being in a hurry, she came upon a solution. Louisa rented the U-Haul, pushed her car into the back, and resumed her beeline for Eugene.[13]

The February meeting clarified the group/movement distinction and the issue of "membership." Bill Devall, who later coauthored the book *Deep Ecology*, stated that he felt Earth First! was more an "organism" than an "organization." Another Earth First!er, "Marcy," stated that she felt Earth First!ers were first and foremost bound by their ideals.[14] The others agreed. It was decided that given Earth First!'s status as a movement, the term "member" was inappropriate; the appellation "Earth First!er" better expressed the meaning of Earth First!'s role in history.

In his report on the meeting, published in the March newsletter, Dustrud expanded this argument. He argued that "just paying money to Earth First! doesn't necessarily make anyone an 'Earth First!er' and there are Earth First!ers who have yet to hear about EF!, let alone pay any money into the newsletter and the general fund."[15] The idea that there existed individuals who were Earth First!ers in spirit, but not yet aware of their affiliation, was based upon the knowledge that Earth First!ers shared a set of beliefs that set them apart from the rest of humanity. This notion also implied that there were individuals who by nature understood that the wilderness was intrinsically valuable, as well as those who would never understand its significance: "There are those who can live without wild things, and those who cannot."[16] In later years, Foreman speculated that the source of this difference was the "wilderness gene." Those who possessed it became human beings who were "Antibodies against the Humanpox"[17] and whose job it was "to fight and destroy that which would destroy the greater body of which they are a part, for which they form the warrior society."[18] At no point during Earth First!'s history did the majority of its adherents believe that their capacity to fight for the earth was an inherited faculty; nevertheless, this topic was at the center of one of the movement's longstanding debates.

All millenarians understand themselves to live at a pivotal point in the history of the world and to have a critical role in the consummation of that history. Every millenarian group therefore believes it is in some way a "chosen people." In response, most such movements carefully distinguish between members and nonmembers, and carefully attend to issues of human reproduction. Children have an important historical role, for they are potential inheritors of the millennium.

For Earth First!ers, the issue of human reproduction is problematic. Their belief system identifies the phenomenal growth of the species *homo sapien* as a fundamental cause of the impending environmental apocalypse. Further, many do not see Earth First!ers as a necessary part of the future millennium. They are misanthropic and pessimistic to the extent that they hope only for the preservation of sufficient biodiversity as will allow for the continuation of other plant and animal species. At the same time, however, Earth First!ers understand themselves to be elites whose awareness of the biological meltdown imparts to them a special role in saving the planet's biodiversity. Insofar as this tension became linked to the larger issue of human nature, it was to play a role in the eventual factionalization of the group. Those who believed human beings were perfectable became true millenarians, while those who believed human nature to be unchangeable became more apocalyptic than millenarian. Their primary concern was with the apocalypse and the events leading up to it, and they expressed little concern with the composition and character of the postapocalyptic world. Presaging this later conflict, the question of whether or not Earth First!ers should have children was fiercely contested early on.

Most Earth First!ers identified human overpopulation as one of the primary causes of the environmental crisis, and in response, many undertook to be sterilized. In the words of one Earth First!er, "My strongest belief is that the human population needs to allow people who want to die to have the right to die, and we need to really cut down on having kids. . . . I personally have had my tubes tied. I practice what I preach. I can't go out and tell somebody else not to have children if I have any . . . there are so many people in this world, we have to make a stand and say no."[19]

Many Earth First!ers also publicly advocated a reduction in the total human population. They believed that it was too late to reduce the population through education; the remedy therefore lay in other, quicker means. Foreman, using the pseudonym Chim Blea, suggested that the government should offer free contraceptives and free abortion, without restrictions.[20] Indicative of the movement's conservative political leanings, Chim Blea also suggested that no welfare payments or food stamps be provided to parents with more than two children, that capital punishment be the penalty for murder, rape, kidnapping, and other violent crimes, and that further immigration to the United States be prohibited.[21] Blea concluded "her" article by noting that while these measures appeared heavyhanded, they would probably still be insufficient: "What is really needed is to 1) Give every woman the right to one child. 2) Offer a $20,000 payment to anyone willing to be sterilized without producing *any* children. 3) Make sterilization mandatory for all women and men after they have parented *one* child."[22] Some Earth First!ers were even more pessimistic and draconian: "I don't think there's a solution to the population crisis—it's beyond the point of birth control. . . . I personally think we all ought to be sterilized. . . . Education's too slow."[23]

Despite this insistence on an immediate reduction in the human population, some Earth First!ers were ambivalent concerning the successful achievement of this goal. Quite simply, the sooner the inevitable "crash" came, the better; greater areas of wilderness would be left untouched. If it occurred sooner because of unsustainable population growth, then so be it.[24] Because of the imminence of this crash, and despite its desirability in some Earth First!ers' eyes, Foreman identified the current generation as the "most important generation to have lived on the planet Earth."[25]

Not all Earth First!ers, however, agreed that their own sterilization was the most acceptable way to achieve their political goals. Indeed, a number of Earth First!ers, some of whom had parented children before joining the movement, put forth an alternative argument. This segment of the movement came to believe that human beings would live through the biological meltdown and the subsequent collapse of industrialism and civilization. It was therefore necessary that some thought be given to the kind of human community that would emerge after that event. For those who already had children, that question was of particular importance. Earth First!ers did not emphasize their special place in the post-meltdown world, but they clearly believed that only those with an "ecological consciousness" would survive and have a place in that world. Moderates declared that Earth First!ers would simply be better equipped than the average person for the rigours of that world. They were "used to sleeping on the ground in the rain,"[26] and they probably already possessed the basic skills that would be necessary to live in such an environment, "the old skills every other generation has had, except the last two or three."[27]

From ideas such as these, it was not difficult for Earth First! parents to create a rationale for their families. If this generation of ecologically conscientious individuals was the most important in the history of the species, and if some of these people were likely to survive to build the new human community, it was the responsibility of Earth First!ers to reproduce. Their children would be more ecologically responsible and aware than other children. This argument emerged publicly in 1984, perhaps due in part to the barrage of "anti-reproduction" articles printed that year in the movement's paper. In his response to these articles, Reed Noss argued that there was nothing more natural than human reproduction, identifying it as the "overriding concern of our animality."[28] Noss claimed that all Earth First!ers were well aware of the need for a decline in population growth and therefore already limited their family size. He chastised Earth First! authors who felt compelled to remind readers to do so: "Compare our baby production to that of the average Catholic, the uneducated black or Appalachian, the poor Latin American, the African, the Indian."[29] At the same time, Earth First!ers had a duty to reproduce, because "all people are *not* equal in comprehending or defending the earth."[30] Noss argued that it was "time to recognize a 'deep ecology elite,' an ideological population of people who understand their kinship with the earth, their interdependence with other ecological entities, and their duty to fight for what they love and *are*. This is a true and ethical elitism, and has nothing to do with material wealth or political power."[31] Because there is a correlation between intelligence and environmental awareness, there is a genetic element to this elite. By their nature and their nurturing, Earth First!ers' children will be more environmentally aware than their peers, and they will be able to "keep up the fight, which will probably continue until the extinction of our species, when the present generation of activists is gone."[32]

Among those with children, home birthing and home schooling were typical.[33] In a 1986 letter, "Klairice" wrote that she intended to home school her son using Foreman's *Ecodefense*, in the hope that he would become a full-time monkeywrencher.[34] Those who agreed with Noss, however, remained in the minority, and many were bitter. An Earth First!er in Arizona stated that he felt the majority of young, childless Earth First!ers were closeminded concerning this issue, to the extent that they had censored his articles in the movement's journal.[35]

While this debate continued, another, equally important conflict was brewing. In the May 1982 issue of the newsletter, the column "Dear Ned Ludd" replaced "Eco-tactics." With that change in name, a highly visible institutionalized format was created for the publication of monkeywrenching tactics.

Ned Lud (or Ludd) was a British craftsman who, in the late eighteenth century, deliberately broke two stockingframes in a Leicestershire stocking mill. Later, in the early nineteenth century, British craftsmen rioting against the mechanization of their factories adopted the name "Luddites" in his memory. The workers destroyed their own machinery in an effort to slow mechanization and thus to keep their jobs. In the words of one such individual, "[P]lunder is not our object, the necessaries of life is [*sic*] what we at present aim for."[36]

As has been noted, Edward Abbey's novel *The Monkey Wrench Gang* served as a prototype for the development of Earth First!. For Abbey himself, Ned Ludd was an inspiration; the novel is dedicated in memoriam to "Ned *Ludd* or *Lud*."[37] That influence is also evidenced in the text of the book. It is Ned Ludd who inspires the Monkey Wrench Gang to embark upon their campaign to save the wilderness: "Dr. Sarvis told his comrades about a great Englishman named Ned. Ned Lud. They called him a lunatic but he saw the enemy clearly. Saw what was coming and acted directly. And about the wooden shoes, *les sabots*. The spanner in the works. Monkey business."[38] The new name implied that the column would provide advice on tactics that were possibly violent, probably illegal, and usually targeted against corporate property, specifically the implements of environmental destruction.[39]

Preparing the way for this change, Foreman's March editorial was entitled "Violence and Earth First!." In that article, he recounted his remarks to a representative from the conservative Mountain States Legal Foundation: "If you come home and find a bunch of Hell's Angels raping your wife, old mother, and eleven year old daughter, you don't sit down and talk balance with them or suggest compromise. You get your twelve gauge shotgun and blow them to hell."[40] While Earth First! did not advocate violence or monkeywrenching (the decision to use those tactics was identified as a personal choice), those kinds of actions were understandable and acceptable. The earth was in grave danger, and those responsible were proceeding unchecked. Foreman asked that Earth First! be large enough to allow a wide diversity of tactics, but he closed his article by revealing his personal assessment of appropriate tactics: "If we report on the activities of monkeywrenchers it is not because we want *you* to do it, too. But there are people out there trying to save their Mother from rape and their story must be told too."[41]

This declaration was supported later in the March newsletter in Foreman's draft plan for a publishing venture, Ned Ludd Books. Foreman outlined several upcoming books to be published under that name, but he identified a book entitled *Ecodefense: A Handbook on the Militant Defense of the Earth* as the most requested and the most controversial.[42] Foreman proposed that *Ecodefense* include technical information on such topics as making explosives, wrecking a bulldozer, and destroying an oil rig, as well as suggestions on effectively harrassing "villains," and subsequently, going underground, creating a new identity, and minimizing legal charges.[43] Foreman's editorial on violence, and his proposal to publish a "how to" guide for monkeywrenchers, represented a renewed emphasis on monkeywrenching. The newly named "Dear Ned Ludd" page featured tactics that were more than just "ecotricks"; the first column included instructions on such actions as sabotaging dirt bike paths with roofing nails, and disabling seismic crews.[44]

The publication of monkeywrenching tactics and the movement's implicit support of such activities became a controversial issue amongst Earth First!ers in the late spring of 1982. The newsletter's new editor, Pete Dustrud, became concerned that coverage of such material had over time "progressed from relatively harmless and humorous pranks to ones which I feel border on outright violence. In addition, most of the few reader responses on this subject seemed to reinforce my concerns."[45] One letter, which offered instructions on spiking roads with a metal punji stake, proved to be Dustrud's breaking point. He told Foreman of his worries but was informed that he had to publish the material. In response to this disagreement, the Circle fired Dustrud. He then resigned from the Circle and declared he had resigned from the newsletter.[46]

Foreman's August editorial was an attempt to explain these events to the Earth First! constituency; it was also an opportunity for him to reassert his authority. Although Earth First! had no legitimized leadership hierarchy, Foreman's role in the movement's founding, coupled with his magnetic personality, allowed him to continue to play a dominant role in its development. His editorial reinforced the "non-hierarchical" and "anarchistic" character of Earth First!,[47] but it also clarified the limits of the movement's ideology. Foreman declared that Earth First!ers were not terrorists, but in the context of the mainstream environmental movement, they were radicals, and he reminded his readers that the symbol of the movement was a clenched fist. That radical character required adherents to actively champion their cause: "We will engage in peaceful civil disobedience. . . . We will go to jail if necessary. We will not officially spike trees or roads but we will report on the activities of those who do. They are heros."[48] In reasserting Earth First!'s philosophy, Foreman stated that this radical stance did not "encompass the entire left-wing of the environmental movement."[49] As he wrote the following month, "We've been nice for too long. I don't plan to fight with one hand tied behind my back. I might even have a shiv or some brass knucks in my boot."[50] Wilderness was intrinsically, not instrumentally valuable,[51] and Earth First! would not compromise.

As editor, Dustrud had left his mark on the movement's newsletter by changing its format and increasing the range of contributors. On assuming the editorship, Foreman also initiated important changes.

By the early spring of 1982, Earth First!ers had come to understand themselves as a movement. Their journal, however, had remained an eponymous "newsletter." With the August 1982 issue, the publication became simply *Earth First!*. The new name was intended to reflect the character of the movement and a more philosophically appropriate relationship between the movement and the journal. In Foreman's words, "Let EARTH FIRST! be a movement, a non-organization. But within that movement is the publication *EARTH FIRST!*, an independent entity serving the movement as a communication medium."[52] Subscribing to the paper did not necessarily make one a "member" of Earth First!, conversely, one did not have to subscribe to the paper in order to be an Earth First!er.[53]

In reflecting on this period in Earth First!'s history, Foreman identified Dustrud's departure as an important milestone[54]—and not only because the change in editorial direction reinforced Earth First!'s acceptance of monkeywrenching tactics. At its origins, Earth First! was a group of friends who shared the same beliefs about the environment, and their ideals and folklore were conducive to maintaining a relaxed and friendly atmosphere amongst adherents. However, with its growth in size and its ever more public identity, it became necessary to impose some ideological boundaries. Despite their insistence on diversity, some principles were sacrosanct, and Foreman and the other members of the Circle could no longer assume that all Earth First!ers shared those principles and interpreted them in the same way. The imperatives of managing a movement dictated that important ideological issues sometimes drove "friends" apart. Within Earth First!, Dustrud was the first individual to pay the price for that tension. Foreman's interpretation of the movement as a "group of friends" did not, however, completely disappear. Earth First!'s eventual factionalization was due in part to his unhappiness with the group's ideological clashes and infighting.

In taking over the journal's editorship, Foreman reasserted Earth First!'s "no compromise" position in terms of both its philosophy and its demands. The most startling of his autumn 1982 articles, written under the Chim Blea pseudonym, concerned the prospect of nuclear war. It reflects Foreman's ambivalence about the future of humankind in a postapocalyptic world. In "The Terror of Nuclear War," Chim Blea downplayed the destructive nature of nuclear war and encouraged all activists to believe they could survive. Blea noted that most popular accounts of the devastation caused by nuclear war described a blackened, barren earth, with few survivors. Blea asserted this description was "buncombe";[55] while millions would die in the attack, and millions more from radiation sickness, all was not lost. It was possible to survive nuclear war and perhaps even to benefit from it. The earth was resilient, and nuclear war offered the possibility that civilization would collapse: "I don't think nuclear war is the worst ecological disaster imaginable. I think the continuation of industrial civilization is the worst ecological scenario, that that will destroy more species, ravage more land, and poison the planet more thoroughly than a major but brief exchange of nuclear warheads."[56]

In November 1982, this increasingly radical perspective was put into practice. The movement went "past the point of just talk and capers to real confrontation"[57] by undertaking its first civil disobedience protest, at New Mexico's Salt Creek Wilderness Area.[58] The region was threatened by Yates Petroleum, whose lease on it expired November 1. In an effort to avoid that deadline, the company cut through a wildlife refuge, "bulldozed an illegal road, and started drilling."[59] Although the U. S. Fish and Wildlife Service cited the company for trespassing, it did not have the means to stop the drilling activities. In response, a Sierra Club group from Texas blockaded the company's illegal road. Foreman and Wolke then started a separate blockade.[60] This protest was initially successful: the Earth First!ers prevented further drilling until a judge issued a restraining order against Yates Petroleum. The protest also served the movement well by drawing the attention of the national media, including a sympathetic CBS news team.[61]

The "Bisti Mass Trespass," Earth First!'s second major direct action, was undertaken to preserve the Bisti Badlands area, a wilderness region located in the northwest corner of New Mexico. The area was a proposed Bureau of Land Management wilderness area, but was also the proposed site of a stripmining operation.[62] To help prevent its development, fifty Earth First!ers entered private lands, burned effigies, flew the American flag, and sang "America the Beautiful."[63] The protest was peaceful; no one was arrested, and the action suggested to Earth First!ers that such activities were potentially powerful weapons against large corporations and the government. They understood themselves to be on the side of "right," and the authorities, in the form of security guards and the state police, had not dared to touch them. Ever conscious of their use of symbols, Johnny Sagebrush (Bart Koehler) and Nagasaki Johnson (Mike Roselle) remarked, "We'll be arrested soon enough. We just have to make sure we pick *our* time and place."[64] The protest was at least marginally successful in achieving its aims: although James Watt had dropped the Bisti Badlands as a BLM study area in early November, he reinstated it almost immediately.[65]

Although Earth First! had obtained some favorable coverage in the mainstream press, its political agenda and rhetoric remained uncompromising. A December letter in *Earth First!* applauded the leadership's decision to continue to print "Dear Ned Ludd" and reminded fellow Earth First!ers that they were "in a state of war with industrial capitalism."[66] It was this certainty of their role in "the war," coupled with these initial successes in the Bisti Badlands and Salt Creek, that prompted the movement's leadership to create an Earth First! SWAAT team (Save Wilderness at Any Time). The team was to be modeled after the individuals at Salt Creek who (in Foreman's words) "did not worry about . . . mundane questions. We did not care if we were alone in standing against Yates, did not care if our cars broke down on the way, did not care if we had money for food. We had a duty."[67]

The two actions in New Mexico had illustrated that "the enemy" could effectively launch surprise attacks. The movement therefore required an organizational response plan and a dependable group of individuals who were willing to implement it. In his December editorial, Foreman requested that interested individuals complete a sign-up form and also emphasized that such an enterprise required funds. Thus, Earth First!ers had to be "ready with bail money for those who are arrested. . . . We must have an emergency fund to pay for gas, food, phone, etc. for future actions of this kind (often it is those who are unemployed who are free to go at a moment's notice)."[68] Eco-warriors fought for a higher cause, but they were not entirely free of pragmatic constraints.

The Earth First! SWAAT Team emerged from what had become a large and influential movement. By December 1982, the monthly list of contacts had grown to include over fifty local Earth First! groups; it had even become international in scope, with a group in New South Wales, Australia, and the journal began to report on environmental protests that country.[69] Earth First! had supported two successful direct action protests, and those events had given the movement momentum. Indeed, the leadership was so busy that the final 1982 issue of *Earth First!* was printed as a double Yule/Brigid (December/February) edition. The momentum continued in early 1983, supported by an article in *Outside* (a national periodical), another Earth First! Road Show, and numerous direct actions.

An article by Stewart McBride in the December issue of *Outside* emphasizing the movement's "cowboy image"[70] attracted many new Earth First!ers from across the United States and Canada. Half of the letters to the editor in the March issue of *Earth First!* mentioned that article as having brought the movement to their attention. One writer compared Earth First!'s activities to the "Ghost Shirt Dance," implying that its efforts were noble but doomed to failure[71]; he or she declared a willingness to join the movement anyhow.[72] The movement's growing success was also reflected in the publicity surrounding the Earth First! Foundation, in theory an entity separate from the Earth First! movement: "[T]he Earth First! Foundation is an independent entity, [but] it hopes to act as a major fundraiser for other aspects of the Earth First! movement. The Foundation believes in the necessity for a fundamental restructuring of our ideas and behavior in regard to civilization and nature."[73] The Internal Revenue Service granted the foundation tax exempt status, and it became a vehicle for funding many Earth First! projects and publications, among them the Earth First! Wilderness Preserve System. The foundation also offered the opportunity for "academics, people in government agencies, [and] professional people" to contribute to Earth First! projects.[74]

In January, Foreman, Roselle, Johnny Sagebrush, and Cecelia Ostrow conducted the second Road Show, in Oregon and California. In the space of twenty-one days, they gave seventeen performances and drove about fifteen hundred miles.[75] Their effort and dedication were not wasted, for like the first such venture, this Road Show was a particularly effective proselytizing tool. Of the approximately twenty-five hundred people who heard their message, almost three hundred were sufficiently moved to volunteer for the Earth First! SWAAT team.[76] This enthusiasm arose in part from the fact that the Road Show coincided with two major Earth First! direct action campaigns: the Gasquet-Orleans Road protest in California, and the Kalmiopsis and Bald Mountain Road action in Oregon.[77]

The Gasquet-Orleans Road protest was aimed at preventing the Forest Service from constructing a road between the two northern California towns.[78] Earth First!'s involvement in the cause began in January and continued throughout the spring of 1983, resulting in at least one arrest.[79] Although the "No G-O Road" protest was successful,[80] it did not leave a lasting mark upon Earth First! folklore,[81] simply because it was overshadowed by the Bald Mountain/Kalmiopsis direct action. For Earth First!ers, the battle over Bald Mountain was a fight to save what little remained of the Pacific Northwest's old growth forest ecosystem.[82]

Oregon's Kalmiopsis Wilderness was a protected wilderness whose northern boundary cut across the crest of Bald Mountain. The mountain's north face, and over 160,000 acres of wilderness that spanned outwards from it—at the time, the largest unprotected wilderness in the Northwest—were in danger of being destroyed.[83] The United States Forest Service had finalized several timber sales in the North Kalmiopsis in the 1982–85 period,[84] and to facilitate logging, was building a road that would carve up Bald Mountain.

A central tenet of Earth First!'s creed was the belief that "humans have no divine right to subdue the Earth, that we are merely one of several million forms of life on this planet. [Thus we] reject even the notion of benevolent stewardship as that implies dominance."[85] As a result of this fundamental certainty, the movement advocated that "significant" areas of the earth be declared "off limits to industrial human civilization."[86] This demand could not be satisfied simply by the creation of more national parks; as Foreman wrote, "It is not enough to preserve the roadless, undeveloped country remaining. We must re-create wilderness in large regions: move out the cars and civilized people, dismantle the roads and dams, reclaim the plowed land and clearcuts, reintroduce extirpated species."[87] The Earth First! Wilderness Preserve System therefore encompassed over 716 million acres of the United States, an area that included both existing wilderness and areas that were to be turned back into wilderness. The California and Oregon north coast—including the Kalmiopsis—was, at approximately 15 million acres, one of the largest and most important of the identified preserves.[88] Thus, Earth First!'s battle to save Bald Mountain and the Kalmiopsis Wilderness was not just an attempt to save a particular wilderness area, but a campaign to save an entire ecosystem. It was a goal intrinsic to the movement's vision.

Earth First!'s attempts to stop the building of the Bald Mountain Road were well organized: the journal offered a list of suggested activities, which included participation in blockades, providing logistical support to those involved in blockades, and attending the 1983 Round River Rendezvous, which was to be held in the Kalmiopsis Wilderness.[89] *Earth First!* also published a Kalmiopsis Hotline phone number and a "No G-O" Hotline number for further information, and offered to provide a "Blockade Handbook" for both actions to anyone who requested it.[90]

Earth First!'s blockade of the Bald Mountain Road began on the morning of April 25, 1983, when four Earth First!ers blocked the path of a caterpillar tractor involved in the construction project.[91] The "war" continued for over three months, during which time the blockades continued in waves. In the end, forty-four Earth First!ers were arrested. The movement was proud of those who stood between civilization and the wilderness; the journal published an "honor roll" and featured the personal accounts of some of those arrested. The warriors believed that their action had made them even more committed to their cause, and they modestly refused accolades:

I no longer have doubts about my commitment to action NOW for wilderness. It must be done. If we wait and go through the "proper channels" one more time, there will be no forests left.[92]

I don't believe any of us are particularly brave, but we were given strength at that moment by something outside ourselves . . . there's something on our side that's bigger than any bulldozer. If we can act out of love for Mother Earth, rather than hatred for the enemy, and with the humility that comes from knowing that we're a small part of something greater than ourselves, our power is unlimited. We can stop this road.[93]

By far the most notable story to come out of the Kalmiopsis blockades, however, concerned Dave Foreman. Although many of those involved in the blockades had directly confronted "the enemy," most had escaped without serious injury; Foreman was the exception, and (once again) his story became part of the movement's folklore. On the morning of May 12, Foreman and another Earth First!er, wheelchair-bound Dave Willis, created a log roadblock ten miles from the construction area, a tactic intended to stop company workers from reaching the site. A sheriff's deputy who arrived at 6:00 A.M. removed the log, leaving only Foreman and Willis blocking the road. Fifteen minutes later, the construction workers arrived in a large pickup truck. Although they first tried to drive around the men, Foreman continually blocked them. Eventually, the driver of the truck, Les Moore, lost his patience. The truck struck Foreman several times, but he continued to stand his ground until he was inevitably forced to move backwards. The driver then accelerated, and Foreman could neither move out of the way nor maintain his balance. He fell under the truck and was dragged over one hundred yards before the driver stopped. In an encounter that was to be repeated on hundreds of subsequent occasions, Foreman then bested the driver in a verbal exchange. *Earth First!* recounted the story as follows: "The five construction workers piled out of the truck and surrounded Foreman. . . . 'You dirty communist bastard,' yelled Les Moore, 'Why don't you go back to Russia where you came from?' 'But, Les,' Foreman replied, 'I'm a registered Republican.' "[94] Foreman was arrested and charged with disorderly conduct but was released on bail that afternoon.

The events on Bald Mountain ended abruptly on July 1. Earth First!, along with the Oregon Natural Resources Council, had previously filed suit against the Forest Service; on that day a temporary restraining order was issued against the Forest Service to immediately halt the construction of the Bald Mountain Road.[95]

Although the success of the lawsuit was not assured,[96] Earth First!ers felt they had won a great victory. The 1983 Round River Rendezvous, which had been planned as a giant protest against the Bald Mountain Road, became instead a giant celebration, with over three hundred Earth First!ers in attendance.[97] In a speech at the gathering, Marcy Willow recounted why she had become an Earth First!er, even though her commitment had caused her friends to question her sanity and her family to disown her.[98] Willow described Earth First!ers' connection to the wilderness as giving meaning to their lives and as the necessary foundation of their existence: "[N]o matter how alone you get, as long as there is the Wilderness, there is wild Nature, who is your mother, your child, your lover, ancient, new-born, and the same age as you. From your lips comes a certain knowledge. You will fight for Wilderness, 'tree by tree' if you have to. You're a hero and the whole world is in awe. You stopped the road."[99]

As had become traditional, Foreman gave his annual speech on the last night of the Rendezvous. Ever conscious of the need for symbolism, he combined myth wth a plan for practical action in his address. In a fictional story that was to become a standard element in all his speeches, Foreman told of a camping trip he and Mike Roselle had taken with President Reagan, James Watt, John Crowell, and Anne Gorsuch.[100] Among Earth First!ers, its themes and phrases were already familiar,[101] but even so—and indeed because of this familiarity—it remained an effective inspirational tool. Foreman was a charismatic leader, and his speaking style has been compared to that of a Southern evangelist.[102] In his mythical confrontation with James Watt, Foreman alluded to Earth First!ers' link to the environment, their wildness, their power, and one of their most important symbols, Glen Canyon Dam. He also made clear their hatred of those who participated in the destruction of wilderness:

> Look at me! Sired by a hurricane, dam'd by an earthquake, half-brother to the cholera, *nearly* related to the smallpox on my mother's side! Why, I could eat 19 oil executives and a barrel of whiskey for breakfast when I'm in robust health, and a dead bulldozer and a bushel of dirt-bikers when I'm ailin'. . . . I crack Glen Canyon Dam with a glance. The blood of timber executives is my natural drink, and the wail of dying forest supervisors is music to my ears.[103]

The final months of 1983 were a time for reflection on the movement's history and its future development. Earth First! had enjoyed much success during the year, both financially and in terms of its political goals.

These successes had drawn even more adherents, and while the movement was strengthened by their participation, it once again experienced potentially divisive problems.

During the last quarter of 1983, *Earth First!* exhibited a peculiar duality. The journal emphasized unity: this was perhaps best expressed in a retrospective photo essay of the movement's first three years.[104] Under his own name, Foreman asserted that all tactics that aimed at preserving wilderness were appropriate and useful; they were "tools in a tool box."[105] Through Chim Blea, he argued that "[a]t no time in human history have so many suffered from oppression, hunger, poverty, and the threat and actuality of war. We fool ourselves, I fear, with human arrogance when we visualize human beings filling the role of cerebrum in the body of the living Earth."[106] For millennia, human beings had struggled for peace and freedom, but to no avail. A "Golden Age of Deep Ecology" was an illusion. Earth First!'s philosophy therefore required more "monkeywrenching in the dark than . . . noble Gandhian direct action,"[107] because "it is not so important to make a moral statement, to convince the general public with our courageous and ethical stance, as it is to just stop the goddamned destruction."[108]

While Foreman clearly retained his original views on tactics and goals for Earth First!, the journal became the focus of a debate between those who espoused this perspective and those who advocated civil disobedience aimed at transforming society. Foreman encouraged that debate, however, by offering space for it within *Earth First!* and by encouraging further growth in the movement at a time when many new adherents were likely to come from northern California.[109] In so doing, he set the stage for the movement's eventual fragmentation.

During the Bald Mountain Road campaign, a California environmental group had criticized Earth First!ers for their "combative" attitude and logo.[110] While the individuals concerned did not respond to Foreman's invitation to illuminate that position in *Earth First!*, another individual did: Mike Roselle. Amongst the five founding members of Earth First!, Roselle was an anomaly. He was the youngest and the only one who had not devoted his entire adult life to the preservation of American wilderness.[111] Prior to Earth First!'s creation, Roselle had been a member of many left wing groups aimed at the transformation of the social order. Those personal differences ultimately led to a different perspective on Earth First!'s tactics and goals.

Foreman and Wolke's involvement in the Kalmiopsis action reinforced their belief that the preservation of wilderness should be Earth First!'s ultimate aim. It was not proof that "civilization" was changing. Rather, it was the first step in establishing Earth First!'s Wilderness Preserve System and the first indication that it might be possible to save some wilderness to allow for recovery after the ecological apocalypse: "The battle grows. It is overwhelming. With each tussle we discover the greater venality of those who see the Earth as 'resources.' They are the Capitalist-Communist Industrial Managers—the two headed monster 'Capicom.'"[112] However, Roselle did not agree with Foreman and Wolke's interpretation of the Kalmiopsis protests. For Roselle and for a significant proportion of younger Earth First!ers, the success of protests such as the Kalmiopsis suggested that education could change human nature. These victories might eventually lead to the transformation of human consciousness, and following that, a more appropriate relationship between human beings and their environment. It might even be possible to prevent the occurrence of the "biological meltdown."

Roselle's reinterpretation of Earth First!'s millennial belief system did not happen suddenly. His earliest entry into the debate illustrates this point. In the journal's first major forum on nonviolent action, his contribution was a cartoon showing Gandhi and Hayduke (the wildest member of Abbey's Monkey Wrench Gang) holding hands and meditating.[113] Roselle's preference for nonviolent direct action over monkeywrenching, and his reinterpretation of the movement's goals and belief system, were encouraged by the role he played in the movement's first major California action, which occurred in October of 1983: the preservation of the Sinkyone coast, a wilderness area located in the northwest corner of Mendocino County, California.[114]

Prior to the autumn of 1983, Roselle received moderate to little coverage in the movement's journal. Although a founder, he was clearly not a leader. Roselle was, however, the principal Earth First! representative in the Sinkyone campaign, and with its rise, his articles and activities began to receive front page coverage.[115] While some Earth First!ers later intimated that Roselle's transformation had more to do with self-interest than principle, such charges are difficult to substantiate. What is clear is that the autumn of 1983 saw Earth First!'s youngest and most left wing founder given a position of authority. He was geographically isolated from other Earth First! leaders in an important direct action in northern California, an area with, in the words of one Earth First!er, "the highest per capita of activists of any place in the United States."[116] Roselle was surrounded by individuals who believed that civilization could be transformed and who by their way of life seemed to realize that possibility. It is difficult to imagine better conditions for the development of an ideologically-based faction.

5

The Eve of the Apocalypse

> The reshaping of our power systems is the only means to save
> Earth. . . . It would be a shame if people who share those
> values, led astray by the anarchists' wholesale rejection of our
> systems, contented themselves with outrage at the abuse of
> power, and scorned to enter the arena of power where our
> destiny will be decided.[1]
>
> —Andrew Bard Schmookler

Between 1984 and 1987, Earth First! engaged in hundreds of protests across the United States; a small number of these campaigns were successful but most were not. Earth First!ers' monkeywrenching activities and direct action events raised public awareness of environmental problems, but they saved little wilderness. Within the movement, that experience fostered two different responses. Among the "first generation" of Earth First!ers, including Dave Foreman, it gradually yielded a retreat to a belief system that was more apocalyptic than millenarian. For more recent converts to Earth First!, the experience had the opposite effect: with Mike Roselle, those individuals became more fervently millenarian, convinced that they, along with those they converted, could create a new and perfect society.

Earth First!ers numbered in the thousands by 1984, but despite the movement's size, most adherents felt bound to their colleagues by more than just a common interest. For them, Earth First! was infinitely more than a political pressure group pursuing its goals through unusual tactics. It was the community wherein meaningful political life occurred.

Earth First!'s doctrine redefined morality, the good life, and the best political society, and in so doing, it reoriented its adherents' lives. This transformation engendered a change in values that caused many individuals to grow apart from families and friends who did not make environmental concerns a priority. Earth First!ers preferred to spend time with those who shared their vision. In the words of one Earth First!er, "I started hanging around with [Earth First!ers] because they had certain attitudes . . . and my whole circle of social relationships changed . . . it was organic, something natural that happened."[2] This development was not deliberate, but it was, perhaps, inevitable. Those who were not sympathetic were gradually left behind:

> I'm transitioning some of my priorities. . . . I have very few friends who aren't involved in [actively working to protect the environment]. . . . I don't have time, and I don't have the patience. . . . It's a level of respect. . . . I have several housemates that pay lip service to [environmental activism], and I have a few who are a little bit more involved. And I have seen within myself a growing intolerance of their lack of doing anything.[3]

This separation was reinforced by the practical requirements of Earth First!'s doctrine. The movement demanded of its adherents a willingness to act, and in this commitment to action, Earth First!ers became further isolated from the American mainstream. Earth First!'s major campaigns often lasted a number of months. In order to fully participate in such actions, Earth First!ers had to be available at short notice for extended periods of time. To facilitate this, many took temporary and/or low-paying jobs that they could leave at short notice: "[U]ntil a few years ago, I'd probably had about twenty or more jobs, from pumping gas and painting, to driving forklifts . . . to working on a farm . . . it was a good way to make money in concentrated periods, so I could be active."[4] Moreover, many Earth First!ers frequently moved, oftentimes crossing state lines. This transient behaviour was the result of their desire to be where they were needed and was facilitated by the movement's network of contacts. In virtually every state, Earth First!ers could find colleagues who would willingly offer them shelter.

This transience also served another goal. It was difficult for law enforcement agencies to track monkeywrenchers at the best of times. When the monkeywrenching population changed frequently, individuals were better able to remain anonymous, and their activities were harder to predict. It also made it more difficult to arrest those responsible for illegal activities.[5]

Earth First!'s doctrine therefore effectively isolated its adherents. In that process, the movement became correspondingly more important to them, both emotionally and intellectually; for some it became a "surrogate family."[6]

By 1984, Dave Foreman was running Earth First! on a full-time basis, and the movement's journal as well as its commercial ventures were self-sustaining.[7] These changes were a result of the movement's growth and early success, and they allowed Earth First!ers a new assurance that their beliefs and their cause were well-founded. As this success continued, Earth First! expanded its purview in several ways, among them a new attention to international environmental problems.

Beginning with the March 1984 issue of *Earth First!*, the "Letters to the Editor" section of the journal included, with increasing frequency, contributions from foreign nationals.[8] These letters encouraged American Earth First!ers to believe that the movement was growing internationally, whether or not that was actually the case.[9] Coupled with this development, *Earth First!* began reporting on international environmental issues, focusing on two major international campaigns: the Rainforest Beef Campaign and the Australian Rainforest Campaign.

The Rainforest Beef Campaign was an international protest against Central American deforestation. Activists in thirty countries targeted deforestation caused by the production of new farm pastures. (Most often, the cattle raised on these lands were destined for fast-food restaurants in the United States and Europe.[10]) The American protests were led by Earth First!, and (as will be discussed below) this leadership role involved coordinating demonstrations at more than twenty locations across the United States.[11]

The second international campaign of 1984 was the Australian Rainforest Campaign. Although only a small number of Earth First!ers (among them Bill Devall) actually traveled to Australia to participate,[12] the movement offered its support in other ways. John Seed, an Australian activist, participated in the 1983 Road Show, and the journal provided wide coverage of Australian issues. Seed's "Letter from Australia" column, coupled with issue-specific articles, insured that Earth First!ers were familiar with Australia's environmental problems and with the activities of their colleagues in that country.[13] In the latter half of the year, *Earth First!* also covered issues in the Amazon basin, Japan, India, Germany, and Denmark.[14]

Earth First!'s new openness to international events did not lessen its attention to domestic environmental issues; indeed, the number and scale of the movement's activities at the individual, regional, and national levels increased dramatically. Reports of monkeywrenching incidents rose sharply. Among the most notorious of these events were major tree spiking actions in Washington's Wenatchee Forest, Virginia's George Washington National Forest, and unnamed forests in British Columbia, Canada.[15] In Oregon, the "Hardesty Mountain Avengers"[16] and the "Bonnie Abbzug Feminist Garden Club"[17] also spiked trees. Another notable incident was the destruction, through arson, of an illegal woodchipping site in Hawaii; the fire caused over $300,000 worth of damage and forced the owner out of business.[18]

Earth First!ers also increased the number of their legal protests. Each edition of *Earth First!* featured a variety of articles focusing on specific issues; in 1984, the editorial staff introduced the practice of closing these articles with a section entitled "What you can do." Usually this segment of the article included the addresses of relevant government officials and corporate executives and a request that letters of protest be sent to them. Often, it also included the names and phone numbers of the Earth First!er(s) coordinating other protest activities (such as direct action events).[19]

At the same time, regional Earth First! organizations grew in number and visibility. These groups served as informal umbrella organizations for the many cell groups that existed in certain areas, such as Florida[20] and Montana.[21] They organized and supported independent direct actions concerning "local issues," and they often sponsored regional Round River Rendezvous. When a major national campaign was held in a particular location, the relevant regional organization often formed the backbone of the protest. The national leadership supported this development. As one of its first major activities, Montana Earth First! occupied the Missoula office of Senator John Melcher, an event that was given a front page column and two full pages of coverage in *Earth First!*.[22] Older regional groups, such as Arizona Earth First!, were also active.[23]

While 1983 was dominated by two major events, the Kalmiopsis and "No G-O Road" protests, 1984 was remarkable for the large number of national campaigns that Earth First! initiated. In February, as a direct response to the Coors corporation's attempt to build an industrial complex in Shenandoah National Park, the journal began to feature a campaign to boycott the company's beer.[24] Although this effort was not labor intensive, it was significant. Earth First!'s anti-Coors stance had begun in 1982 as a reaction to the company's ties to the Reagan administration.[25] Coors's continued willingness to directly inflict "visual and chemical pollution" on a protected wilderness area, as shown in the Shenandoah affair, reinforced Earth First!'s determination to boycott its products. As has been noted, beer played an important role in Earth First! rituals and folklore; it reinforced the movement's antinomian tendencies. Coors was therefore an especially meaningful symbol. Earth First!'s boycott continues to this day.[26]

Also in the spring of 1984, as the American segment of the international Rainforest Beef Campaign, Earth First! organized a successful nationwide protest against Burger King's use of Central American beef. Between April 24 and 28, Mike Roselle coordinated more than twenty separate protests across the United States,[27] working with other environmental groups when he believed it necessary (among them the Friends of the Earth and the International Indian Treaty Council).[28] The Rainforest Beef protest was reasonably successful: it provoked Burger King into taking some action on the issue,[29] and it illustrated that Earth First! was capable of sustaining a nationwide campaign. It also furthered Roselle's career within Earth First!. His leadership of this campaign extended his efforts to carve out his own territory within the movement and presaged the path of his philosophical development. Roselle was becoming increasingly convinced of the capacity of civil disobedience to change the world, and his experience with the Rainforest Beef campaign reinforced that conviction.

During this period several other major protests were organized. In February, plans were made for a protest to prevent the Tuolumne River (in California) from being further dammed. The rally was held in April and drew over three hundred Earth First!ers to a site in the Sierra Nevada;[30] it received considerable media attention, including a feature on the *MacNeil/Lehrer Report*.[31]

If one protest stands out among the many Earth First! actions of

1984, it is the movement's role in the effort to save the Middle Santiam forest in Oregon, a campaign undertaken in the second half of the year.[32] Oregon environmentalists had long struggled to prevent the Middle Santiam from being logged. When Earth First! joined the protest, its efforts were part of what many interpreted as the last chance to preserve those forests. Although the Oregonians were grateful for the participation of all sympathetic individuals, they feared that Earth First!'s reputation for illegal activities would taint their efforts: "[T]hey didn't like the attitude, they didn't like the militance [sic], they didn't like the talk of direct action to the point of violence, and they didn't like the fist logo. They were pacifists . . . but they were willing to do civil disobedience."[33]

The Earth First!ers decided that the campaign's goal was more important than Earth First!'s public affiliation with the cause. On May 5, the coalition of environmentalists working in the Santiam officially became the Cathedral Forest Action Group (CFAG),[34] but this name change did not entirely sever the perceived connection between Earth First! and the Santiam protest. George Draffan, an Earth First!er who participated in the protest, remarked, "There were known Earth First!ers involved in it, the place was spiked, we were doing civil disobedience, (which no other group did), so it was pretty obvious to everybody concerned that it was Earth First! under a new name."[35] From May 5 onward, however, CFAG was officially linked only with civil disobedience actions.[36]

Throughout 1984, Earth First!'s doctrine remained explicitly millenarian. One example of this was Reed Noss's May article "Deep Ecology, Elitism and Reproduction." All Earth First!ers emphasized the importance of the movement as a collectivity, but in this article, which represented a small but significant minority, this belief is strikingly evident. Although Noss stressed that he was not making an argument for the eugenic breeding of individuals "more receptive to environmental values,"[37] his essay focused on the special role of Earth First!ers in the process of human history. By highlighting the argument that those who completely understand deep ecology form an elite and by linking that capacity to a genetic capability, Noss evoked the notion of a "chosen people." His article was indicative of the feeling that still remained prevalent within the movement: Earth First!ers had a moral responsibility to fight for the earth; after the biological meltdown, their ecological consciousness would allow them to create a new, perfect, and ecologically sustainable world.

Dave Foreman's speech at the 1984 Round River Rendezvous stressed that Earth First!ers were a people chosen to fight the evils of corporate America and to recover the Pleistocene, the golden age when "humans knew their rightful place in the big picture . . . as natural people, we knew our proper place in the world."[38] He proclaimed that "[i]n just a few generations, we and our forebears have taken the most magnificent and diverse of all the continents on Earth—in essence, the Pleistocene, with its great flowering of large animals, those thundering herds of biomass—and we have turned it into freeways and condominiums and Pac-Man and Pop Tarts. And we call that *progress*. We call that *civilization*."[39] Foreman identified "growth-crazed tyrants" as the architects of this evil, individuals who "don't know anything about what's truly valuable in life, or about what *sacredness* is."[40] For Foreman and Earth First!, the standard by which all human activity was to be measured was Aldo Leopold's land ethic. The natural world had a right to exist for its own sake; actions that recognized that were good, actions that did not were evil. That year's Rendezvous focused on the destruction of Montana's Cabinet Mountains wilderness and the resulting loss of grizzly bear habitat.[41] Therefore, Foreman concluded his talk by demanding that the grizzly be returned to its rightful range (from New Mexico through the Canadian border) and stated, "That's how we save the grizzly bear . . . and it's how we save ourselves."[42] By acting in defense of wilderness, Earth First!ers could restore the Pleistocene, and in so doing redeem themselves.

During interviews given during 1984, Foreman was clearly optimistic about the future of the movement and the possibility that it would achieve its goals. He had good reason to adopt a positive outlook. Between July 1983 and July 1984, Earth First! had doubled in size; public estimates put the total number of American Earth First!ers at approximately ten thousand.[43]

Despite such optimism, the December issue of *Earth First!* addressed the question of whether or not progress had been made in saving designated wilderness areas. While the authors conceded that some wilderness had been preserved, much more had been opened for commercial development. Earth First!'s hard fought battles may have been successful, but little overall progress had been made.[44] In absolute terms,

Earth First! was losing the war, a fact that would soon begin to wear on Dave Foreman.

In 1985, the movement grew and prospered, but again, it achieved little absolute success. Wilderness that Earth First!ers thought they had saved was once again threatened, and the Cathedral Forest campaign also continued. After five years of existence, however, Earth First! was financially stable. The journal was still self-supporting, and Foreman and others who worked full-time for the movement received a modest salary (Foreman was given $250 per month).[45] Additionally, the Earth First! Foundation began to be more heavily publicized in the journal.[46] The Foundation's articles of incorporation declared that it was based on the principles of deep ecology, and its funds were intended "to preserve and restore environmental quality and to promote the conservation and protection of natural resources."[47] An *Earth First!* article invited any interested parties to apply for grants, providing a lengthy explanation of acceptable uses for such funds. Owing to the Foundation's tax-exempt status, its monies could be used for indirect support of civil disobedience actions but not for the support of monkeywrenching activities. Following the publication of those articles, the Foundation attracted substantial donations; by 1986, its annual income was over twenty thousand dollars.[48]

Two major events influenced Earth First! during the early months of 1985; both concerned the movement's use of tactics. In February, Dave Foreman's book *Ecodefense* was published. Subtitled *A Field Guide To Monkeywrenching,* the book gave "detailed, field-tested" instructions on many standard eco-sabotage tactics, from "decommissioning" heavy equipment and airplanes to tree spiking, destroying roads, and avoiding arrest.[49] Foreman jokingly said that he hoped it would initiate a new era in "citizen involvement in public lands management,"[50] but his purpose was a serious one: "It is time for women and men, individually and in small groups, to act heroically and admittedly illegally in defense of the wild. . . . John Muir said that it if it ever came to a war between the races, he would side with the bears. That day has arrived."[51]

While monkeywrenching tactics had for years been published in the journal's "Dear Ned Ludd" pages, the publication of those tactics in book form had several important consequences. It gave Earth First!ers and other interested environmental activists a pocket "how to" guide, an event that was bound to increase the frequency and scope of monkeywrenching. According to Roselle, it also brought ecotage "out of the closet": "[A] lot of ecotage was going on at the time . . . but it was being reported as 'mindless vandalism.' [*Ecodefense* allowed it] to be reported for what it was."[52] The book's publication drew negative attention from government officials and law enforcement agencies,[53] but it also drew more individuals to the movement.[54]

In response to this influx, Foreman was compelled to print an article in the May issue of the journal that outlined Earth First!'s founding principles. Foreman wrote that all Earth First!ers believed in biocentrism and practiced "putting the Earth first." He also emphasized the movement's tribal nature, stressing that it was not an organization and did not have officers or a hierarchy, and enthusiastically wrote of Earth First!'s acceptance of diversity. There was room for everyone, from "animal rights vegetarians to wilderness hunting guides, from monkeywrenchers to followers of Gandhi . . . from bitter misanthropes to true humanitarians."[55] He cautioned, however, that Earth First! represented a particular militant philosophy and that the movement would not change to suit those who did not like it. If people were uncomfortable with its vision, they should leave, because "everyone has their own tribe."[56] Further, Foreman sometimes revealed his own uneasiness with the movement's size: "We never envisioned Earth First! as being a huge mass movement (in fact, some of us are downright surprised that there are *that* many Earth First!ers out there.)"[57] Foreman's comments evince a continued belief that Earth First!ers were by nature separate from the rest of humanity and that they possessed "the wilderness gene." Those remarks, however, also suggest that he was reconceiving the character of the Earth First! movement and its role in history.

The second major development during the early months of 1985 was the emergence of what was later to become one of Earth First!'s standard tactics. The previous year's protests in Oregon's Middle Santiam had resulted in the arrest of thirty-four individuals,[58] but despite these efforts, old-growth timber sales had continued. In 1985, those sales were to include a stand of trees that Earth First!ers called Millennium Grove, so named because of the age of its trees (many of which had been growing since the fall of Rome).[59] Desperate to save the grove,

Mike Jakubal, a rock climber, and his friend Ron Huber recalled the tree sitting tactics of Australian environmentalists, who had climbed small trees to prevent felling. Jakubal and Huber determined to use rock climbing methods to scale the much taller Douglas firs of the Pacific Northwest.[60]

Jakubal and Huber thus introduced tree sitting, the practice of hauling a platform seventy to eighty feet up a tree and remaining there until law enforcement authorities safely removed the protester. The technique was reasonably effective in realizing its short term goal; loggers would not cut down a tree when doing so would probably kill the individual ensconced in its branches. Moreover, tree sitting events always drew media attention, a fact that limited the logging company's range of choices.[61] The tree sitters would inevitably be removed, but not before their efforts had caused the logging company concerned unwanted publicity and a considerable sum in extra security and labor costs.

At Millennium Grove, Jakubal left his tree and was arrested after only one day, but Huber remained in his tree for over a month. He was finally removed when the Forest Service, using a mobile crane brought in from Portland, forcibly removed him from his perch. The entire affair cost Williamette Industries over $100,000.[62]

Despite its success, the tree sitting at Millennium Grove indirectly caused controversy within Earth First!. In his June *Earth First!* editorial, Foreman praised the "heroics" of Jakubal and Huber. He was pleased at this militant endeavor by Oregon Earth First!, which had distanced its activities from those of the more moderate Cathedral Forest Action Group. Foreman did not, however, stop there, but went on to criticize CFAG: "As much as I admire most of the folks in CFAG, there are a few who seem to me to bog down the effort to save the big trees with their self-righteous journey to heaven."[63] His comments were aimed at those whom he felt were pursuing their own spiritual development at the expense of action. The impending crisis made such endeavors irrelevant: "[Y]our significance pales beside that of the old growth forest, the grizzly or the Grand Canyon. Protection of a place is the bottom line. Excessive emphasis on the personal growth element is *Me First!*, not *Earth First!*."[64]

Foreman later apologized for these comments, but he made no attempt to hide his feelings. In August, he wrote that he regretted any disharmony he might have caused but concluded by saying that his remarks were "sincere," even if they were "inappropriate in that context."[65] Preserving wilderness remained his top priority, and this episode illustrates that he was becoming increasingly uneasy with the influence on Earth First! of those whom he believed were "New Agers." With some justification (many Californian Earth First!ers could be characterized as New Agers), Foreman identified these individuals with the movement's social justice faction.

Foreman understood these difficulties to be the result, in part, of the increasing number of civil disobedience and direct actions in which Earth First!ers were participating. These were frequently long and painful battles, and they often did not achieve their goals. Foreman believed that in such circumstances it was inevitable that some Earth First!ers would question their beliefs because "[y]ou work your heart out to save a particular tree or piece of ground and when you 'lose,' you wonder what it was all for. . . . Was it a waste because you didn't 'succeed' in your immediate goal?"[66] Foreman cautioned Earth First!ers to relate their activities and achievements to the movement's end purpose, instead of looking for meaning in their own personal development. Every action to preserve wilderness was by its nature good, and that was the measure by which it was given meaning.

Throughout 1985, Earth First!ers faced many disappointments that required such reinterpretations. In June, Howie Wolke, one of the movement's founders, became the first individual to be arrested for monkeywrenching. Wolke was alleged to have pulled out survey stakes in Bridger-Teton National Forest in Wyoming, and he was charged with destruction of property.[67] The Chevron Oil Company, whose project had been "desurveyed" twice before, was anxious to prosecute him. He was convicted and sentenced to six months in jail.[68] Wolke's arrest and subsequent incarceration were unexpected. He later confessed that he had been afflicted with the "nothing-can-happen-to-me syndrome."[69] Because he was pursuing what he believed to be morally right, he assumed that he was infallible.

Although the movement initiated several new campaigns in 1985 (among them actions in East Texas[70] and in Meares Island, British Columbia[71]), much of its time and energy were spent continuing efforts that had begun the previous year. As has been noted, the fight for Oregon's Middle Santiam Forest continued in 1985; likewise, protests concerning the loss of Yellowstone's grizzly habitat[72] and the Kalmiopsis wilderness[73] continued.

Despite the fact that they seemed to have made little progress, Earth First!ers did not lose their enthusiasm for their cause. The 1985 Round River Rendezvous, held on the Uncompahgre Plateau in Colorado, drew over two hundred people from thirty-five states.[74] It was the first week-long meeting and the first to feature scheduled workshops and training sessions. Foreman's speech called Earth First!ers to action and reminded them of their role in history. Marcy Willow summarized his speech in the journal, recounting that Foreman had argued that "[p]eople are afraid to die . . . because they are afraid to live. Modern society insulates us from real life. He also called on us to recognize the Neanderthal in ourselves, that we have been called out of the dimness of the ice age to act as antibodies against the destruction of the earth."[75]

At the same time, however, the journal's report of the 1985 meeting also made reference to possible FBI infiltrators, the first such incident reported in Earth First!'s national publication.[76] Despite their inability to achieve substantial wilderness protection, Earth First!ers appeared to the outside world—and in particular to law enforcement agencies—as a real threat to public order.

Foreman closed 1985 with a reassertion of his apocalyptic hopes: "[R]ecord-breaking cold and snow ripping through the land, and it's only early October as I write this. . . . *The ice,* the ice may be coming soon to wipe our nasty little case of acne off the broad smile of Ma Gaia. . . . And good riddance too."[77] On the fifth anniversary of the journal's creation, he celebrated the size of the movement and the fact that it had been "taken away from its founders" to become a "tribe."[78] He wrote with enthusiasm of the movement's many regional groups[79] and of the heroics of individual Earth First!ers, but missing from his article was any reference to their pivotal role in the founding of the millennium. That element was conspicuous by its absence; it gave to his essay a sense of distance from the movement, and it suggested that he had begun to reevaluate his beliefs. Although Foreman closed the article by looking forward to the movement's next five years, it appeared that he was no longer certain of Earth First!'s future.

Despite these difficulties, 1986 began on a positive note. Earth First!'s annual budget was well over $100,000,[80] and in the first months of the year, the movement received heavy media attention.[81] Foreman gave over twenty speeches across the United States and debated Montana congressman Pat Williams on *The Today Show*.[82] These events prompted him to declare in his February editorial that "Earth First! is moving into a new and exciting phase."[83] Foreman was correct in that assertion but mistaken in his optimism. During 1986, a series of events occurred that presaged the development of intractable problems within the movement.

On January 27, Mike Roselle was named national campaign coordinator for Greenpeace USA[84] Roselle's preference for civil disobedience that was aimed at changing public opinion had long been evident, and his move to Greenpeace reflected that predilection. It also emphasized his distance from the other founders of Earth First!, individuals who were completely disillusioned with the character and tactics of large Washington lobbying groups. Foreman optimistically and tactfully wrote, "We do not view this as a situation of Earth First! losing Mike Roselle, but rather as Earth First! gaining Greenpeace."[85] His comment reflected Earth First!'s policy of accepting diversity, but it also illustrated its inherent problems. Greenpeace prescribed change through education, and its goal was to prevent the apocalypse by making industrial civilization more environmentally sensitive. Those tactics and goals were in direct opposition to Foreman's vision of Earth First!. While in his more reflective moments Foreman admitted that there was a role for such groups (in their own way, they helped preserve some limited wilderness),[86] admitting Greenpeace's goals and tactics into Earth First! would fundamentally alter the latter movement. Ultimately, it would allow Roselle and other likeminded individuals to come together as a faction, with the tacit support of Earth First!'s leadership.

In early 1986, Earth First! also began to suffer from problems caused by the rapid spread of monkeywrenching. In March, monkeywrenchers destroyed a small Montana firm's logging equipment and left a banner that declared "Earth First!." Foreman chastised them for committing an act that he felt was more vandalism than strategic environmental protection.[87] He argued that it had caused Montana Earth First! public relations difficulties, and in so doing had harmed the cause of Earth First! as a whole.

That event summarized well the problems inherent in Earth First!'s tacit support of monkeywrenching. As has been noted, the movement did not officially condone eco-sabotage, but the journal's "Dear Ned

Ludd" columns and the publication of *Ecodefense* meant that it would inevitably be linked to any monkeywrenching actions. Earth First!'s "tribal structure" further magnified this problem. Without a hierarchy of responsibility, it was difficult to control the actions of individual Earth First!ers: "The idea of a decentralized monkeywrenching movement which feeds off youthful rebellious energy is certainly releasing a lot of energy, but it's not controlling the direction in which it's released. . . . All you're getting that you can count on is that release of the wild spirit. If you believe it has to have strategic value too, then you've got problems."[88] One person, acting alone, could commit an act that might conceivably have repercussions for the entire movement.

In May 1986, one such event occurred, unnoticed by most Earth First!ers. A group of Earth First! monkeywrenchers cut the electrical power lines leading to the Palo Verde nuclear plant, a complex located twenty-five miles west of Phoenix, Arizona.[89] Their goal was unclear, but the Federal Bureau of Investigation argued that such activities could conceivably cause a nuclear meltdown.[90] The FBI had been accumulating material on Earth First! since its inception,[91] but the Palo Verde sabotage gave it cause to begin a thorough investigation. Initially, however, the movement was unaware of the increased level of FBI surveillance that began in May and Earth First!ers continued their usual activities. Many Earth First!ers did suspect that the movement had been infiltrated by the FBI, but they took no more than the usual precautions to prevent their illegal activities from being discovered.[92]

In 1986, Earth First!'s roster of campaigns again included many familiar names. In March, the Siskiyou National Forest sold more of the Kalmiopsis wilderness. Earth First! once again organized protests, thus continuing a battle it had begun in 1983.[93] The movement also continued to fight for the preservation of grizzly habitat, this time in Yellowstone National Park;[94] that protest continued for most of the year, and again little progress was made.[95]

In March, another significant loss occurred: tree fellers entered Millennium Grove and began to cut its trees. The Forest Service and law enforcement agencies had learned from their experiences the previous summer and attempted to prevent tree sitting protests through the use of heavy security, including "guarded barricades miles from the cutting site, invisible UV-sensitive dust on all signs and equipment, 24-hour guards in the Grove, and armed patrols cruising the (public's?) roads."[96]

In a final attempt to save the grove, mainstream environmental groups filed for a temporary restraining order, and Earth First!ers entered the forest during the night. While they successfully evaded security and were able to tree sit for a day, they did not succeed in stopping the felling. Millennium Grove was "murdered."[97]

The destruction of Millennium Grove was a devastating loss for Earth First!. A four-year fight to preserve some of the oldest forests in the United States had failed. Many of those who participated, however, chose to interpret those events in a different way. Representative of that faction was Mike O'Rizay, who wrote in the journal that "Millenium [*sic*] Grove now resembles other stumpfields. . . . That one vile act of destruction spurred more people into action and aroused more support for old growth than months of protest the previous summer. The old growth preservation movement appears to have reached a critical mass . . . a radical proposal—not one more tree!—has now become common opinion."[98] Earth First! had failed to preserve wilderness, but it had changed public opinion.

Such an interpretation may have appealed to Earth First!ers such as Mike Roselle; it could not, however, satisfy Earth First!ers such as Dave Foreman. For the latter, the preservation of wilderness was of absolute importance and the only true measure of success. Indeed, while 1986 saw the rise and establishment of Roselle's reinterpretation of the Earth First! doctrine, those who disagreed with him were not silent.

In November, the first of three articles by "Miss Ann Thropy" appeared in *Earth First!*. (The latter two will be discussed in chapter 6.) "Technology and Mortality" addressed the question of whether or not education could solve one of the most critical components of the environmental crisis: overpopulation.[99] While the author concluded that education had occasionally worked in industrialized economies (for example, post-war Japan), for that very reason it could not provide a solution to the problem. Any children born into industrialized countries consumed ten times the resources of those in rural societies; they therefore contributed disproportionately to the earth's overpopulation problem. Miss Ann Thropy's biocentric redefinition of overpopulation took this imbalance into account. "She" wrote that "any human population is overpopulated when it disrupts the cycles of nature so as to threaten to permanently reduce global diversity. By this definition the US and all industrial nations are vastly overpopulated. . . . Industrialization means overpopulation."[100] Miss Ann Thropy also implied that modern birth control and family planning are inherently flawed because they "are linked to the technocratic control responsible for the ecological crisis in the first place."[101] This connection was not explored further, but the author asserted that in any case, "Technological solutions to technological problems do not work."[102]

For Miss Ann Thropy, the only real solution to overpopulation was through natural population stability. From the golden age of the Pleistocene until the Middle Ages, human populations were held in check through high infant mortality rates: "People in the Pleistocene didn't drop dead at 35—if they lived past infancy they probably lived to 70 as people always have. . . . But since approximately half the population died in childhood, the average was 35."[103] The solution to overpopulation was therefore to dismantle the technology of medical science that saves the lives of sick children. To let children die was a tragedy, but the alternative was far worse. Dismantling that technology was not as difficult as it seemed because "[t]he technological complex is more fragile than its discourse lets on. We have seen in the area of wilderness preservation how monkeywrenching succeeds in undermining the plans of corporations."[104]

Miss Ann Thropy's suggestions for attaining natural population stability included: 1) preserving areas where mortality rates were still natural, 2) taking back areas controlled by technology, 3) fighting technological advances by monkeywrenching in universities, research institutes, and corporations, 4) extending monkeywrenching to all urban areas, and 5) "spiritually rejecting" technology.[105] For Miss Ann Thropy and those Earth First!ers who agreed with her, changing the beliefs and behavior of the American masses was a useless enterprise.

The publication of "Technology and Mortality" and the ensuing controversey surrounding it[106] revealed that there were many Earth First!ers who still held a strong commitment to biocentric equality as well as many who shared Roselle's faith in change through education. For most of the year, the coexistence of these factions caused few problems. The 1986 Round River Rendezvous, for example, was perhaps one of the movement's most successful annual meetings. It drew more than five hundred Earth First!ers from six countries to the Challis National Forest in Idaho.[107] Foreman was still outwardly enthusiastic about the future of the movement, and he chose his annual address to declare the imminence of the apocalypse.[108]

A complete transcript of Foreman's speech does not exist, but its content is referred to in every journal article concerning the 1986 Rendezvous. In his August editorial, Foreman wrote that in early July, he "received two signs from Earth that told me that we—Earth First! [were] doing the right thing."[109] The first of those signs occurred during the Rendezvous. Foreman had planned to speak on "the inevitable collapse of the industrial state," and a freak snowfall during the July 4 rally further inspired him: "'Mother Nature is coming, and she is pissed!' proclaimed Dave. He painted a vivid image of the returning ice sheet sweeping the continent clean of man's trashy edifices, and identified our mission to preserve natural diversity to assure that Earth remains peopled by all forms of life. Snowflakes on a cold wind added weight to Dave's vision."[110]

The second "sign" occurred after the Rendezvous had concluded. Foreman, Roselle, and seventeen other Earth First!ers were arrested during a protest over the loss of grizzly habitat in Yellowstone National Park. On their way to jail (transported in a Park Service tour bus), a grizzly bear and two cubs appeared at the side of the road. "Ranger Paul Miller passed binoculars around for all of us to look. Rationality be damned. The ecstatic pagans in that bus had just received a sign from the wild—*Keep on!*"[111] Foreman's prediction that the apocalypse was imminent and his assertion (through "signs") that Earth First! was taking the right type of action undoubtedly served as his symbolic response to the movement's lack of absolute success during 1986. In that respect, it provided sufficient motivation for Earth First!ers to continue their protests throughout the second half of the year.[112]

Foreman's impassioned Rendezvous speech might also have been the result of intimations that Earth First!'s unity was dissipating. If he had hoped that his speech would restore that friendship and unity, however, he was mistaken. The camaraderie that had marked the movement's early years was becoming increasingly difficult to maintain. Simple measures that worked in the past were no longer effective. In an open letter to the 1987 Rendezvous Committee, for example, Nancy Morton and Roger Featherstone wrote of one example that illustrated this problem well. The evening campfire at the Rendezvous could no longer accomodate all of those who wished to attend it, because "300 people don't fit around one fire, no matter how big it is."[113]

In a large and diverse movement without an established hierarchy, disputes could not be easily resolved, a situation that led to some bitterness and acrimony between the rapidly emerging factions. Foreman's December editorial admitted this growing problem: "We need to chew over many questions and there are going to be strong feelings on opposite sides of them. You can . . . state your position in strong terms, even passionate terms, and still maintain a degree of respect for someone with whom you disagree. . . . Before you write a letter . . . remember that you are writing to friends. Be strong, but be civil."[114] Underlying these difficulties, however, was the fact that by the close of 1986 the movement had clearly developed two factions. The conflict between these two groups was nowhere better expressed than in the movement's continuing debate over the best society and in two articles by Miss Ann Thropy that would appear in 1987.

6

Misanthropy and Social Justice

In everything we do, the primary consideration should be for the long-term health and native diversity of Earth. After that, we can consider the welfare of humans. We should be kind, compassionate and caring with other people, but Earth comes first.[1]

—Dave Foreman

I have a song called "Dave Foreman's Nightmare." The refrain is "Gay Ethiopians Coming Across the Border." . . . I am not a big fan of the human species [but because we didn't endorse their misanthropic beliefs] . . . they have decided we are some kind of "human lover" faction.[2]

—Darryl Cherney

During 1986, the conflict within Earth First! had steadily escalated; in a few short months, friendly debates became bitter arguments. In 1987, this dissension crystallized into two factions. The first group upheld the principles of biocentrism and the preservation of biodiversity as its primary goals. For its adherents, wilderness, not the human species, was the measure by which all actions should be judged. The second group, whose adherents might be described as "career activists," maintained that issues of biocentrism and social justice were interrelated and of equal importance. No human community could be fully biocentric without also attending to issues of social justice.

Over the course of the year, individuals in the first group, best represented by Dave Foreman, became increasingly apocalyptic. They cared only for preserving wilderness and biodiversity, and they had come to believe that it did not matter who survived the imminent environmental crisis and its biological meltdown. Individuals in the second group, which included Mike Roselle, became increasingly millenarian. By widening the scope of Earth First!'s doctrine to include issues of social justice, they hoped to create the foundation of an environmentally responsible and just society. After the collapse of industrial civilization, their community would be the human nucleus of a reborn, perfect world.

One of the first public indications of this dispute could be found in the movement's journal. Between September 1985 and September 1987, Andrew Schmookler (an author who had an interest in the movement) and a number of Earth First!ers (including Edward Abbey) engaged in a printed debate concerning the character of human nature and the virtues of civilization. Although their discussion was known amongst Earth First!ers as "the anarchy debate," it actually focused on determining the best postapocalyptic human community. The dialogue was friendly,[3] but it evidenced the growing division within the movement. Notably, Foreman did not participate.

The exchange began with the journal's review of Andrew Schmookler's book *The Parable of the Tribes.*[4] Schmookler's argument was that primal peoples lived in harmony with the ecosystem but that once civilization began, individuals and tribes were free to "invent their own way of life," a situation that ultimately resulted in anarchy. *Earth First!*'s reviewer "Australopithecus" summarized the consequences of this argument: violence between people and against the earth was then inevitable[5] because "as soon as any one tribe becomes aggressive, all tribes must adopt the ways of violence. . . . The peaceful tribe can surrender, flee or fight; any of which amounts to a victory for the ways of violence."[6] In order to gain and maintain power, societies then exploited each other and nature, and just as natural evolution selects for the fittest species, social evolution selected for the most powerful societies. As a result, Schmookler wrote, the world had become "a dismal mess."[7] Australopithecus praised Schmookler for his celebration of primal life but strongly criticized him for not providing a solution to "the world's desperate plight."[8]

Schmookler responded to Australopithecus primarily because he found this last criticism so distressing. In his own *Earth First!* article, he argued that competition in natural systems created a "synergistic and harmonious order that protect[ed] the viability of all components of the system."[9] Anarchy, defined as the capability of a creature to invent its own way of life, was not, therefore, the natural condition of the world. It was an unnatural state,[10] and it was not life-serving. The establishment of a new "life-serving order" would restore the balance of the ecosystem. In a later article, Schmookler further clarified his vision of the future. As long as human beings lived in civilization, he argued, they would inevitably suffer from the evils of anarchy and competition. It was therefore necessary that, even after an apocalyptic event caused the decentralization of the world's power structures, some form of government should be restored. Those who survived the event would require some form of protection. He also recommended that a world government be established in order to "protect communities from the unjust intrusion of others in the form of war and environmental degradation . . . the solution to our problems requires structures to govern the play of power."[11] Schmookler closed his article by praising the American Constitution, particularly with respect to its management of factions. This last remark was guaranteed to provoke Earth First!ers.

The first individuals to respond to Schmookler's article were Christopher Manes and Edward Abbey. Both of them argued against Schmookler's belief that any form of centralized government was necessary and/or useful. Indeed, both authors identified centralized government itself as an evil.[12] Manes focused his argument on the evils of centralized power, claiming that it was centralized authority, not anarchy, that yielded violence; Abbey took this argument further in directing his attention to the postapocalyptic future. Arguing against Schmookler's definition of anarchy, Abbey asserted that rather than violent chaos, anarchy was "democracy taken seriously,"[13] propounding a vision of an anarchistic community with Jeffersonian overtones. True anarchy would be "a voluntary association of free and independent families, self-reliant and self-supporting, but bound by friendship, kinship, and a tradition of mutual aid."[14] Abbey stated that although the founders of the United States had attempted to create such a nation, their attempt had failed. Rather than Jefferson's vision of a land of freeholders or Lincoln's vision of a land governed by the people, the country had followed "the scheme devised by Madison and Hamilton." As a result, it had become "a nation of helots ruled by an oligarchy of techno-military-industrial administrators."[15]

Abbey confidently predicted the end of the military-industrial state within fifty years. He wrote that it would be replaced by a "higher civilization" comprised of "scattered human populations modest in number that live by fishing, hunting, food-gathering, small scale farming and ranching, that [would assemble] once a year in the ruins of abandoned cities for great festivals of moral, spiritual, artistic and intellectual renewal."[16] Abbey's argument was clearly apocalyptic, but not necessarily millenarian. Although he stated that those who would live in the postapocalyptic world would be "a people for whom the wilderness is not a playground but their natural and native home,"[17] he made no reference to Earth First! or Earth First!ers. A sense of community was missing from his vision; those who survived the meltdown would do so by luck or by wit, not by their ideological or spiritual affiliation. Foreman introduced Abbey's article in his editorial but made no comment on its content.

In Schmookler's next article, he reiterated his argument but effectively distanced himself from both Earth First! factions by praising American government and arguing that reform would be the most effective means to achieve change in the system.[18] Schmookler accused Manes and Abbey of criticizing "our representative democracy as if it were essentially equivalent to an oligarchical tyranny" and warned of "the dangers of revolutionary utopianism."[19]

The first response to Schmookler's criticisms came from Jamie Sayen, an Earth First!er from New Hampshire.[20] Sayen wrote that the present situation was intolerable and stated that his own vision of the future resembled Abbey's prophecy. His principle concern, however, was with the transition "from here to there." He was deeply troubled by the possibility that the apocalyptic fall of "the Machine" would cause severe and unnecessary damage to the earth: "[T]here isn't much time because the mighty do not 'go gently into that good night'—they crash and take as many with them as they can."[21]

For Sayen, however, this problem had a solution. He did not sympathize with Schmookler's hope for a world government, but he did admit that such an institution might "buy time." Unlike Schmookler, Manes, and Abbey (and Foreman), he believed that human nature could be changed—indeed, improved. In that faith, Sayen, perhaps unwittingly, gave voice to the movement's growing social justice faction. Although he wrote disapprovingly of Schmookler's humanism, Sayen believed that human beings had learned from civilization: "I feel it is essential to point out a critical difference about a second-coming of primalism: we will not be embarking with a tabula rasa. We would reenter the natural world with our memories of the failed experiment of the past 10,000 years profoundly imprinted in our minds and souls."[22] Because of this, it was possible that a significant number of individuals could be made aware of the evils of civilization prior to the apocalypse. This would not prevent its occurrence, but it might lessen its violence: "I hope that as the Bhopals, Chernobyls, Love Canals and Space Shuttles accelerate our understanding that modern centralized civilization is a death trip, more and more people will reawaken to the simple joys and wisdom of deep ecological living. . . . And hopefully as the ability of the Machine to tyrannize our lives weakens, the biocentric, decentralized tribes will be able to throw off the yoke."[23] For Sayen, the ideal community of the future included not just Earth First!ers but all those who could be convinced of the necessity of biocentric living.

The conclusion to the anarchy debate added little to these basic arguments. In the four final articles, Schmookler reasserted that there was need for a political order to control violence, Robert Goodrich argued that with the removal of centralized government, anarchy would also disappear (and natural life would remain), and Manes repeated his criticisms of centralized power.[24] Foreman did not comment on the debate, but within the journal, Manes's article appeared last. The final words in the anarchy debate thus belonged to a biocentrist. Responding to Schmookler's earlier critique, Manes declared that he was proud to be a "utopian." To have earned such a title meant that he and other biocentrists had freed themselves from the limits of technological culture and its discourse.[25]

Schmookler's attempt to fully explain his conception of anarchy thus developed into a debate that provoked clear and divergent statements on the postapocalyptic future. Its tone was generally friendly, but over the course of 1987, the relationship between the two factions changed. Animosity between them grew rapidly, and by November Foreman (writing as Chim Blea) was lamenting the venomous nature of their arguments and pleading for tolerance.[26]

During the first months of the year, the content of the movement's journal changed noticeably. Although *Earth First!* was in the hands of individuals who were for the most part aligned with the biocentrist faction, the editors were under increasing pressure to include a larger number of civil disobedience and social justice articles than they had in the past.[27] This change was not made easily, and problems developed at the journal office.[28] For a short period, the editorial board was reasonably accommodating to those demanding a new focus. Many civil disobedience actions received front page coverage,[29] and a few articles that were concerned only with "social justice" also appeared.[30]

At the same time, in the larger public arena, Earth First! was again drawing extensive media coverage. *The Utne Reader, The Nation,* and *The Whole Earth Review* featured articles on the movement. By this point, however, it was clear to many Earth First!ers that such attention was a mixed blessing. Although it was an effective way to publicize their cause (and continued to draw more adherents to the movement), it also had drawbacks. In his June editorial, Foreman remarked that "some folks are getting involved with Earth First! because it's the 'in' group right now, because it's easy to gain a high media profile . . . and because it's fun."[31] One such individual was Darryl Cherney, one of Earth First!'s well-known social justice campaigners, who (according to Foreman) had once declared that he was an Earth First!er "because it gave him instant media access."[32] Such statements were far removed from the pronouncements of first-generation Earth First!ers, whose concern for preserving wilderness meant that all other issues were secondary.

Although Earth First!'s social justice faction successfully dominated the journal for the first few months of the year, the biocentrists were quick to respond. In the March and May issues, two articles by the pseudonymous "Miss Ann Thropy" were published. Many people assumed that Foreman had written the essays, but in fact the author was Christopher Manes. As with Miss Ann Thropy's earlier "Technology and Mortality" (discussed in chapter 5), the arguments made in "Overpopulation and Industrialism" and "Population and AIDS" were extremely controversial.[33] They moved the social justice/biocentrism debate into the public realm and forced many Earth First!ers to take sides.

"Overpopulation and Industrialism" furthered the arguments made by biocentrists in the anarchy debate.[34] Discussing the relationship of overpopulation to industrialization, Manes argued that the developed nations were largely responsible for overpopulation and emigration in the Third World. Western technological and humanitarian aid (including medical assistance) supported overpopulation in underdeveloped nations by sustaining people who would have otherwise died. However, industrialism was incapable of sustaining this false security forever; inevitably, it would end. Thus, for Manes, the issues of overpopulation and technology were inextricably linked, and in such a technological context, justice did not exist: "Justice and freedom and all higher values are at home only in a decentralized, anarchistic setting, which presupposes Earth as wilderness."[35] To pursue justice in a technological society, he argued, was to permit technology to continue to "propagate its power relations."[36] Manes closed the article by challenging other biocentrists to take the overpopulation debate beyond its traditional boundaries. There was no one else, he believed, who was prepared to do it.

In the following issue of *Earth First!*, Manes, still using the "Miss Ann Thropy" pseudonym, did indeed take the overpopulation debate far beyond its traditional boundaries. In an article guaranteed to create controversy, he suggested that AIDS might be a welcome and effective means to reduce the earth's population. Although its author and the journal's editor knew that "Population and AIDS" would cause controversy, they were also confident that many other Earth First!ers shared their views. When Manes informed editor John Davis of his intentions, he simply stated: "Somebody's obviously going to do this article. It might as well be me."[37]

Conceding that conservation, social justice, and appropriate technology were nice to discuss, Manes asserted that these issues did not address the real cause of the earth's problems. "The only real hope for the continuation of diverse ecosystems on this planet," he argued, was "an enormous decline in the human population."[38] Such a decline was inevitable, either through nuclear war or environmental cataclysm, but in such a situation "we would inherit a barren, ravaged world, devoid of otters and redwoods, Blue Whales and butterflies, tigers and orchids."[39] Although education might be effective, the imminence and severity of the environmental crisis rendered it irrelevant. A disease such as AIDS, however, had the potential to reduce the human population significantly and quickly. Manes pointed to three reasons for the potential environmental benefits of AIDS. First, the disease affected only human beings, which would permit a reduction in the human population without harming other species. Second, it had a long incubation period, which would allow one infected individual to infect many others before his or her death. (This feature would also insure the continued survival of the virus.) Third, AIDS is spread through sexual activity, which Manes argued is "*the* most difficult human behavior to control."[40]

Manes suggested that these characteristics of the AIDS virus could have phenomenal success in preserving the environment. If, like the Black Death in Europe, AIDS could eliminate one-third of the human population, it would benefit endangered wildlife on every continent. More importantly, just as the Black Death contributed to the end of feudalism, AIDS had the potential to hasten the end of industrialism. If enough human beings died—Manes estimated that the population of the United States, for example, would have to decline to fifty million—then industrialism would cease to function: "Capital dries up, governments lose authority, power fragments and devolves onto local communities which can't affect natural cycles on a large scale."[41] Manes recognized that long before this happened, governments would likely implement "draconian" measures to prevent the spread of the disease. However, he suggested that these measures, in and of themselves, would probably cause a breakdown in the development and export of technology, an event that could also cause a decrease in the human population.

Manes did not, strictly speaking, advocate the spread of AIDS, and he closed his article by stating that it was not his intention to discount the suffering of AIDS victims. He explained that there would inevitably be victims of overpopulation, either through war, famine, and/or poverty. In this respect, AIDS could therefore be seen as a solution: "To paraphrase Voltaire: if the AIDS epidemic didn't exist, radical environmentalists would have to invent [it]."[42]

The next *Earth First!* contained letters responding to certain articles from the May issue, but none of them concerned "Population and AIDS." Foreman left the controversial essay to be discussed at the 1987 Round River Rendezvous; instead, he used his June editorial to remind Earth First!ers of the movement's founding principles, which he identified as strictly biocentrist. This reminder was necessary because he had recently seen "some definite attempts to change, 'sanitize' or 'mellow-out' the Earth First! image and style."[43] This decision to reassert Earth First!'s original principles was the first of three such attempts that Foreman made during 1987.

Foreman began his editorial by stating that Earth First!ers put the Earth first in all of their decisions, "even ahead of human welfare if necessary."[44] Although that principle had been a part of Earth First!'s doctrine from the movement's inception, it had become strangely controversial in light of Miss Ann Thropy's recent article (and in the context of a sharply-divided movement). He went on to add that Earth First!ers were pleased that they lacked legitimacy among the "gang of thugs running human civilization," questioned and even demonstrated antipathy toward progress and technology, refused rationality, and recognized that there were "far too many human beings on Earth."[45] In an indirect attack upon those who advocated social justice, he also stated that the doctrine of Earth First! superseded those of traditional right/left politics and that real Earth First!ers did not set any "ethnic, class or political group of humans on a pedestal and make them immune from questioning."[46] Earth First!ers did not use human beings or human welfare as the measure of the good; wilderness was the "real world" and stood as the measure of all actions.

Following those principles, Earth First!ers had a commitment to action and a responsibility for living their lives in a way that would support natural diversity. Foreman added that while all Earth First!ers did not necessarily participate in monkeywrenching actions, they had to accept that tactic as a legitimate tool for the preservation of biodiversity and wilderness. In any case, they had to be "unwilling" to condemn it.[47] Foreman acknowledged that the movement had evolved in a way he would not have chosen but stated that he had accepted that fact. However, although his was only one voice ("albeit a rather loud one"), he strongly believed that if any individual or local group could not agree to the principles that he listed, they were better off in another environmental group.

Foreman's attempt to remind Earth First!ers of the movement's original principles was not welcomed by those who also advocated social justice. Many of them began to question the legitimacy of Foreman's leadership; his personal popularity, long a crucial factor in the movement's unity, was waning.

In the same editorial, Foreman also reported a bizarre incident involving a letter he had received from an individual who did not want Earth First!ers to bring dogs to the annual Round River Rendezvous. The anonymous note, which lacked a return address, threatened the poisoning of any dog that was brought to the gathering.[48] Foreman had given it to the Rendezvous committee, and in order to warn dog owners, the letter had been published in the May issue of the journal. In a remarkable turn of events, the journal then received an outpouring of letters accusing Foreman of wanting to kill dogs.[49] While Foreman had in the past made clear that he did not support the ownership of domestic pets, the assumption that he could be guilty of such an act was surprising. Exasperated and insulted, Foreman could not understand why many Earth First!ers blamed him for the letter and/or wondered why he had not dealt with the problem himself. He questioned, "Would you have preferred not to know about this character's plans so you couldn't prepare for it? Or do you want some Big Daddy to take care of everything and not trouble everyone else with the problem? We're a grassroots group . . . it's all of you who need to deal with the problem."[50]

Since Earth First!'s inception, Dave Foreman had served as its prophet and leader. Indeed, many Earth First!ers looked upon the tightly-knit movement as a surrogate family, and "Uncle Digger" as their surrogate parent. Although Foreman had to battle daily with a social justice faction that wished for more freedom and independence, many of those same individuals still understood him to be their prophet and leader. Even if they disagreed with his beliefs, many still had great affection for him: "Dave Foreman has said some stupid things, but he's also spoken to my heart on many important things."[51] This paradox later added to the bitterness of the movement's ideological conflict. Darryl Cherney illustrated this peculiar contradiction well. Reflecting upon the factionalization of the movement, he remarked, "The problem with Foreman is that he set up everything that we believe, and now that we believe it, he's saying that we're a bunch of commies."[52] Foreman's adoption of a purely apocalyptic belief system and his eventual departure from the movement were for many a personal betrayal.

Despite these difficulties, the 1987 Rendezvous went ahead as scheduled; it was held July 6–10 at the north rim of the Grand Canyon. Although it began well with a speech by Abbey,[53] the Rendezvous was marked by namecalling and factional conflict. The most notorious incident concerned a group from Washington state that called itself "Alien Nation."[54] The individuals in Alien Nation were self-described "anarchist communists," and they advocated "eco-mutualism."[55] Alien Nation was particularly concerned with "anti-authoritarianism and non-hierarchical relationships":[56] "We must learn to live in an harmonious relationship with each other and the natural world without dominance of any sort as part of our lifestyles."[57] Not surprisingly, its members took issue not only with Miss Ann Thropy's article on AIDS but also with a letter written by Abbey to the *Bloomsbury Review* that argued for the closing of American borders to all immigrants. Their philosophy was, for the most part, in agreement with the beliefs of Earth First!'s social justice faction.

In accordance with Earth First!'s policy of accepting diversity, it was common practice at the annual Rendezvous to allow special interest groups such as Alien Nation to set up information booths to publicize their causes and sell merchandise. At the 1987 Rendezvous, members of Alien Nation operated such a table. Abbey approached them, and he, the individuals at the table, and approximately twenty bystanders became involved in a debate concerning his letter to the *Bloomsbury Review*. Subsequently, the Rendezvous organizing committee requested that Alien Nation abandon its table.[58] That evening, a small group of Earth First!ers disrupted the members of Alien Nation: "[A] group paraded up and down the campsite under the guise of darkness, cracking a bullwhip and chanting 'No more Earth First! wimps.' 'Down with humans.' . . . Many of us considered this behavior nothing short of KKK type tactics."[59]

Upon their return to Washington state, members of Alien Nation published a newsletter that featured an article entitled "Dangerous Tendencies in Earth First!." They criticized elements of the Rendezvous (specifically, the flying of the American flag and the "Sagebrush Patriots Rally"), argued that the movement had a centralized power structure (as evidenced in the dominance of the Tucson Earth First! office), and asserted that their group had been censored by the Rendezvous committee. Alien Nation's newsletter concluded with a final condemnation of the "fascist tendencies within Earth First!."[60]

These criticisms echoed charges made that summer by environmentalists outside of Earth First!. Murray Bookchin, for example, called Foreman a fascist and a racist and referred to him as an "eco-brutalist."[61] In his annual Rendezvous speech, Foreman addressed such critiques; his talk was an expanded version of his June editorial and was reprinted as a feature article in the November issue of *Earth First!*.

Foreman began by praising the movement's diversity, but he quickly moved on to state that he thought that Earth First! was becoming too diverse: "[D]isagreements over matters of philosophy and style

. . . threaten to compromise the basic tenets of Earth First!, or make [it] impotent."[62] He stated that Earth First! was not born of the anarchist movement or the political left and was never a part of the reform environmental movement. To this he added, "I simply do not want to go to my tribe's annual gathering and hear debates in workshops on whether there is or isn't a problem with overpopulation, or hear Ed Abbey intemperately denounced as 'racist' and 'fascist.'"[63] Foreman then went on to list again the basic principles that he felt were the foundation of the Earth First! movement. In this reassertion, he changed the arrangement of the list to emphasize biocentrism and took direct aim at those in Earth First! who advocated social justice: "An individual human life has no more intrinsic value than an individual Grizzly Bear life (indeed, some of us would argue that an individual Grizzly Bear life is more important . . . because there are far fewer Grizzly Bears). Human suffering resulting from drought and famine in Ethiopia is unfortunate, yes, but the destruction of other creatures and habitat . . . is even more unfortunate."[64] Foreman went further by adding two components to his list. The first was a reminder that Earth First!ers should have a sense of humor ("Most radical activists are a dour, holier-than-thou, humorless lot"), and the second was "an awareness that we are animals."[65] Declaring that Earth First!ers knew that they were, first and foremost, "Animal," he wrote that "we are not devotees of some Teilhardian New Age eco-la-la that says we must transcend our base animal nature and take charge of our evolution in order to become higher moral beings."[66] For Foreman, the state of the human soul was of little relevance, and he firmly believed that human nature would not, indeed could not, change.

To drive his point home, Foreman ended the speech by offering to leave the movement if the majority of Earth First!ers felt that his statements were outside the mainstream of their beliefs. He stated that to continually debate the principles of biocentrism and social justice distracted Earth First!ers from the real work at hand, and it was tiring. He then declared that he had "no energy to continually debate the above points within my tribe and [would] seek my campfire elsewhere" if the problems continued.[67]

While the 1987 Rendezvous featured some enjoyable events,[68] it was for many, including Dave Foreman, an unhappy milestone in the movement's history. The Round River Rendezvous, the movement's only real opportunity for tribal renewal and camaraderie, had been marked by bitter infighting. In reflecting on Earth First!'s development, Foreman identified that meeting as the point "where the very obvious splits in Earth First! became not healable."[69]

That experience was not redressed by the direct action that was held in conjunction with the Rendezvous: a protest at a uranium mine on the north rim of the Grand Canyon. The action was exceptionally chaotic, and Earth First!'s confrontations with the police were violent.[70] Foreman's wife, Nancy Morton, as well as Peg Millett and several other protesters were hurt by a police officer; Foreman was angered and yelled at the officer. The experience caused him to question whether or not he was "Gandhian" enough to take part in such events. In a transformation bound to further alienate him from the social justice faction of the movement, Foreman decided he did not have the right "emotional make-up" to participate in direct action events; he then began to question the very utility of direct action in preserving wilderness.[71]

In the September issue of *Earth First!*, Mike Roselle wrote a guest editorial. In it, he indirectly responded to Foreman's attempt to define the movement, and requested donations for a special Earth First! Direct Action Fund.[72] Roselle's editorial was not obviously hostile (making no mention of the social justice/biocentrism conflict), but in it he argued that "Earth First! means direct action."[73] Most of his article was taken up with a call for financial support for the Direct Action Fund and the Nomadic Action Group (NAG), a select number of Earth First!ers who specialized in organizing and running direct action campaigns. Roselle promised that all money that was raised would go toward funding "uncompromising activism and providing support for those activists on the front lines."[74]

Roselle's editorial, coupled with a letter mailed by the journal to all subscribers, succeeded in drawing over $18,000 to the Direct Action Fund in less than three months.[75] Although Roselle had clearly created his own definition of Earth First! and had likewise created his own agenda for the movement, Foreman praised him as "probably the best direct action catalyst for natural diversity in the world."[76] With the Direct Action Fund, Roselle had a budget with which to further implement his social justice agenda and to increase his authority within the movement.

The November issue printed an extended version of Foreman's 1987 Round River Rendezvous speech, entitled "Whither Earth

First!?"—the third time Foreman offered that material to Earth First!ers during 1987. Foreman further challenged the movement by publishing with it the article "Is Sanctuary the Answer?," an essay which continued the argument that Abbey had made in his controversial letter to the *Bloomsbury Review*. Foreman wrote that the individuals who came to the United States from the nations of Latin America were of two types: political refugees escaping tyrants and economic refugees seeking a better life.[77] He maintained that the United States's continued openness to refugees postponed inevitable revolutions by removing the politically active and economically dispossessed from their homelands. Furthermore, allowing vast numbers of refugees into the United States had a significant environmental impact. In seeking a better life, those individuals would further pollute southern California, consume vast resources, and create the need for more environmentally destructive development. "In the long run, the most humane solution is the one advanced by Edward Abbey: send every illegal alien home with a rifle and a thousand rounds."[78] Foreman also explained that his sole purpose in writing the article was to clarify his position on immigration; he had been accused of being a racist and a fascist, and he wanted Earth First!ers to know his real position. Perhaps anticipating another round of vitriolic letters from the social justice faction, Foreman then declared that his statement closed the debate over this issue in the journal.

In December, Foreman reported to readers that the journal had received a great deal of mail concerning both his own article "Whither Earth First!?" and Alien Nation's critical essay on the movement. He wrote with much pleasure that the vast majority of letters had supported his position.[79] He celebrated this victory with the publication of Miss Ann Thropy's response to Alien Nation along with a second article on AIDS, which he introduced as one of the most important articles ever presented in the journal.[80]

Miss Ann Thropy's response to Alien Nation briefly reasserted the points that had been made in "Population and AIDS." The majority of the article, however, was spent addressing Alien Nation's charges that Miss Ann Thropy (Christopher Manes) was an "eco-fascist."[81] Manes's defense was simple, and consistent with the principles of biocentrism and biocentric equality. He suggested that the term "eco-fascism" was usually used in such a way as to imply that radical environmentalists wished harm upon humanity and were therefore "a morally repugnant lot."[82] Manes found such moral criticism boring, and he doubted that the universe cared at all about the purity of his soul. Human rectitude was, in the context of the environmental crisis, virtually meaningless: "What matters is . . . *wilderness.* Old growth forests and Black-footed Ferrets are what's important, not the prestige of spiritual beautification."[83] Manes argued that the "academic environmentalists" who criticized his argument were merely supporters of the corporate industrial monolith, who wanted the benefits of technology but did not recognize its destructive consequences. In concluding his article, Manes made it clear that given a choice between a cure for AIDS and the loss of technology, he would choose the latter and happily "goose-step to the nearest wilderness."[84]

Daniel Conner's "Is AIDS the Answer to an Environmentalist's Prayer?" furthered the arguments originally made by Manes.[85] Conner's essay, however, was more substantial (almost three full pages in length) and somewhat less inflammatory than Manes's effort. He spent much of the article explaining the potential size and effect of the AIDS epidemic and the role of overpopulation in fostering the environmental crisis. Although the publication of such a lengthy article might have seemed like an overbearing attempt by Foreman and editor John Davis to reassert the authority of biocentrism in *Earth First!,* that impression was somewhat mitigated by the style of Conner's article. Unlike Manes, he cited scientific evidence and even provided a reading list for anyone interested in pursuing the issue further. However, Conner went even further than Manes in one of his assertions. Manes had argued that the appearance of the human immunodeficiency virus at this point in history was simply a happy coincidence. In response, Conner briefly summarized James Lovelock's Gaia hypothesis, which argued that the earth (or Gaia, after the Greek earth goddess) might itself be considered a single living organism, capable of regulating its own chemical and physical environment. Conner then strongly suggested that HIV and AIDS were Gaia's response to the pressures of overpopulation, pollution, and species extinction. He closed his article with three predictions: 1) AIDS would spread rapidly amongst the heterosexual population; 2) AIDS would likely mutate into a variety of related strains; and 3) even if a vaccine and/or cure was found, Gaia would create a new and even more virulent disease.[86]

The final 1987 issue of the movement's journal included within it a pull-out "introductory brochure" for Earth First!ers to distribute amongst potential adherents, the first such effort since Foreman's 1980 "Membership Brochure." The insert included information on Earth First!'s lack of formal organization, its program for the creation of international wilderness preserves, its Road Shows and Round River Rendezvous, and direct action and monkeywrenching tactics. The four-page insert thus contained most of the information a new Earth First!er would need to know, but it was also strangely bland. It addressed Earth First!'s apocalyptic doctrine, but it did not refer to Earth First!'s millenarian hopes: "Today is the most critical moment in the three-and-a-half billion year history of life on Earth. Never before . . . has there been such an intense period of extinction as we are now witnessing . . . [our battle] is a battle for life itself."[87] Neither did it refer to the movement's inner turmoil. The flyer proclaimed that Earth First!ers "tolerate each others' varying beliefs, but are united in our concern for Earth above all else. Quite simply . . . EARTH FIRST! believes in wilderness for its own sake."[88]

In its avoidance of Earth First!'s major schism, the insert presented what was by the close of 1987 a misleading picture of the movement. Foreman and others in the "biocentric faction" had come to believe in a doctrine that was wholly apocalyptic. Although they acknowledged that Earth First!ers might have a critical role to play in preserving wilderness prior to the apocalypse, they had no hope for a postapocalyptic Earth First! community. Roselle and the social justice faction had modified some of the movement's original tenets, but they remained truly millenarian. They believed that the Earth First! community not only had to save wilderness but also educate the American public; further, they still maintained that the Earth First! community itself was intrinsically valuable. Earth First! had evolved into two separate groups, each of which possessed a distinct belief system.

As noted in chapter 2, the movement had in its early years envisioned a salvation for itself and for the earth that clearly fit the model developed by scholars of millenarianism. It was imminent, ultimate, this-worldly, and total. The original Earth First!ers had anticipated an apocalyptic event that was comprised of the collapse of the industrial infrastructure and a biological meltdown. After its occurrence, the earth could begin anew. This salvation was also understood to be collective. Earth First! began as a small, tightly-knit group of individuals who were convinced not only that they were living at the most important moment in human history but also that they had a crucial role to play in that history. In a world reborn, their community and its relationship with all other species would stand as the model and foundation for a new human civilization.

For Dave Foreman and the movement's original core of adherents, that shared hope and understanding were supported by the similarity of their education, upbringing, and political experience. Most of those who were originally drawn to the movement were lifelong conservationists who were in their early thirties and from the American Southwest. While many held dear the traditional symbols of the American polity (for example, the flag) and had participated in the traditional political process (often as conservation lobbyists), they believed that their government had been taken over by business interests. Most described themselves as conservatives, and they identified their political and intellectual forebear as Thomas Jefferson.

The political beliefs of these individuals provide a context for their ecological principles. Although their belief system became more sophisticated over time, its emphasis on biocentrism and the preservation of wilderness never wavered. Most importantly, its very foundation—the assertion that a true biocentrism was comprised of a belief in both biodiversity and biocentric equality—never changed. Foreman declared in the movement's first "Statement of Principles" that "[a]ll life forms . . . have an inherent and equal right to existence" and that "[w]ilderness has a right to exist for its own sake."[89] Those themes continued in his writings and his speeches throughout the 1980s. Their logical conclusion—"All human decisions should consider Earth First, humankind second"[90]—also remained as a central theme. As a result, these Earth First!ers engaged in activities that were specifically aimed at preserving species and wilderness. They preferred monkeywrenching and direct actions such as blockades to civil disobedience activities that were aimed at raising public awareness of environmental issues: "Reality is out there. In the Big Outside. And my action in defense of it—raw, rank, brawling, and boorish as it may be—is vastly more important than all the enlightenment with which I can swell my head in the several score years in which my consciousness exists."[91] Only the fittest of each species could survive in that reality.

Foreman and those around him believed that human nature was

unchanging; education could effect only limited and temporary changes over an extended period of time. They understood themselves to comprise an exceptional group and to be in possession of what Foreman later referred to as "the wilderness gene."[92] For the first years of the movement's existence, that assumption included all Earth First!ers.

During the mid-1980s, Earth First!'s growing diversity, coupled with its lack of real accomplishment as a collective, fostered an ideological split within the movement. Foreman and those around him came to emphasize the immediate preservation of biodiversity and wilderness, and they ceased to look beyond the imminent meltdown. They anticipated and hoped for that event, but nothing more. They became apocalyptic rather than millenarian.

The movement's second faction was comprised of younger individuals, most of whom had joined the movement in the mid-1980s and whose geographic roots, education, and political backgrounds differed substantially from those of the original Earth First!ers. Mike Roselle had been exceptional amongst the movement's founders, and he symbolizes well the individuals in this faction. Roselle was in his early twenties, and therefore younger than the other founders; he had participated in many left wing political groups and had a practiced disdain for many of the more "red neck" endeavors of his colleagues.[93] Those individuals who came to support his vision of Earth First! were also young and lived predominantly on the West Coast, particularly Oregon and California. They joined the movement after it was well-established, as Road Show proselytes and civil disobedience devotees. Their political experience was not obtained in traditional conservation groups nor in the offices of Washington lobbyists. Rather, they came to Earth First! with an assortment of activist backgrounds, from unions to the peace movement, and they brought with them the conviction that social change was both desirable and possible. Although they often participated in monkeywrenching activities, they emphasized direct action and civil disobedience that would both save wilderness and raise public awareness. Unlike Foreman and the biocentrists, they did not distinguish between Jeffersonian and Hamiltonian America. To them, the state and all its symbols were simply oppressive.

Most individuals in the social justice faction had little trouble believing in Earth First!'s basic millenarian doctrine. They too anticipated an imminent apocalyptic event that would combine the crumbling of the industrial infrastructure with a biological meltdown. In anticipation of that event, however, they advocated social change through education, an emphasis that transformed Earth First!'s original doctrine into a new type of millenarian belief system. In preparation for the apocalypse, those in the social justice faction advocated an emphasis on biodiversity and social justice at the expense of biocentric equality. If all citizens could be convinced of the severity of the impending crisis, they might change their way of life and thus lessen its effects. Likewise, they might be convinced to become Earth First!ers. In this way, the social justice faction expanded the original "collectivity" that would be saved. All individuals could now be included, not just those with "the wilderness gene." The elite character and conservatism of Foreman's original vision were abandoned in favor of a more typical revolutionary ideology. All those who were converted could participate and become a member of their community. Proselytism and public awareness were therefore extremely important. This perspective also altered the nature of Earth First!'s millennial vision, as the original movement's anticipation of a future world characterized by biological and social Darwinism was discarded. The new millennium would embody social justice, equality, peace, and biocentrism.

Without a shared millennial vision, Earth First!ers had little to hold them together. Dave Foreman's apocalyptic views were not intrinsically unifying, and despite his optimistic declaration that most Earth First!ers supported him, individuals in the social justice faction had not abandoned their principles. As 1987 drew to a close, Earth First! was weakened from its lengthy spate of infighting, and its adherents no longer shared a common vision of the future. These weaknesses could not have occurred at a worse time: in 1988 and 1989, Earth First! was the subject of intense FBI surveillance and infiltration, and the ensuing pressures soon threatened the movement's very existence.

7

A Parting of the Ways

It used to be when we had disagreements, we'd get together at the national gatherings, and the two people would get drunk and [argue]. That was fine. But when they started having followers, it became factions. . . . They'd always called each other names, but then they started believing them.[1]

—George Draffan

The uneasy coexistence of Earth First!'s two factions continued into 1988, but the tension between them soon ripened into a full-fledged ideological conflict. Between 1988 and 1989, the movement's problems were exacerbated by internal bickering and external pressures. Disagreements concerning the character and content of *Earth First!*, coupled with the culmination of the Arizona FBI investigation, pushed the movement to the breaking point.

In 1988, Dave Foreman expressed his apocalyptic views by continuing to assert that biodiversity issues should dominate Earth First!'s agenda. In an attempt to achieve that goal, he restructured the movement's journal in the first months of that year. In the February issue, he stated that *Earth First!* was simply not large enough to include topical essays, wilderness proposals, and Ned Ludd columns as well as cover all of the movement's direct action activities.[2] In order to have space for lengthy articles on biodiversity, he created three new columns that condensed coverage of Earth First!'s direct actions in the journal's back pages.[3] He also intimated that Earth First!'s regional newsletters should be responsible for publishing full direct action coverage.[4] This reorganization of the journal was not well received by those in the movement's millenarian social justice faction. For them, direct action and civil disobedience were inextricably linked to biodiversity, and they interpreted Foreman's editorial decision as a heavyhanded attempt to control the ideological direction of the movement.[5]

Foreman's February editorial also drew attention to the movement's growing financial success. By 1988, *Earth First!* was making a profit. Its budget was over $200,000,[6] and its Ned Ludd Books and "Trinkets and Snake Oil" offerings had grown tremendously.[7] Further, the Earth First! Foundation had a yearly budget of over fifty thousand dollars.[8] As noted above, however, this success also became a source of conflict[9]: Foreman and the journal's other staff members never issued a public statement that indicated where those profits were channeled. According to Zakin, Roselle deduced that Foreman was using the money to selectively fund monkeywrenchers whose illegal activities could not be supported by the Earth First! Foundation.[10] He reasoned that while Foreman's financial beneficence might have been motivated by altruism, it also served a less lofty purpose. Because the journal's profits were not a matter of public record, Foreman was free to provide financial support to whomever he chose. Roselle assumed that Foreman could therefore fund those of whom he approved (usually biocentrists) and neglect those with whom he disagreed (usually individuals from the social justice faction). In this way, Foreman was capable of financially reinforcing his power base within the movement. According to Zakin, it was this possibility that most angered Roselle.[11] (Foreman insisted that all of these funds went directly to support the Journal.[12])

In early 1988, Roselle had the time and occasion to nurse his anger. In late January, he participated in a Greenpeace protest at Mount Rushmore, South Dakota[13]; as a result, he was arrested and spent four months in jail.[14] During that time, he publicly accused Foreman of using the journal to pursue his own agenda. He also implied that Foreman was behaving like a dictator, angrily referring to his supporters as "Foremanistas."[15] Zakin argues that Roselle was angry simply because Foreman had unfettered access to *Earth First!*'s profits. It is more likely, however, that Roselle's main concern was that civil disobedience and direct action tactics (such as the one that resulted in his imprisonment) were not fully recognized or appreciated by the Earth First! hierarchy. Foreman's failure to fund more of those activities was merely a symptom of that more fundamental complaint.

Initially, neither Foreman nor the other members of the journal's

Tucson staff acknowledged Roselle's accusations. As a result, the tension between the two men continued to grow. This animosity only exacerbated the tensions that existed between the apocalyptic and millenarian factions.[16]

During February and March, Foreman went on a speaking tour in New England, New York, and Alaska. He drew large crowds and a great deal of media attention, and as a result many new adherents were drawn to Earth First!.[17] Foreman implored his listeners to actively halt environmental destruction by any means necessary, but he focused on biocentrism, and he did not mention social justice.[18]

Foreman's tour was followed on April 21, 1988, by the largest protest in Earth First!'s eight-year history. The "National Day of Outrage Against the Forest Service" was a nationwide coordinated protest against the "outrageous policies and ruinous methods of the Forest Service."[19] It was organized by Karen Pickett (a California Earth First!er who later married Mike Roselle) and included direct action events in seventy-five locations across the United States.[20] Foreman publicly supported that event; he congratulated Pickett on its success, and he allowed *Earth First!* to feature coverage of the protest in its June issue.[21] At the close of that article, Pickett thanked Roselle's Direct Action Fund for financially subsidizing the event.[22]

With the success of his speaking tour and of the "National Day of Outrage," Foreman was once again faced with the possibility that Earth First! might become a mass movement. From the beginning, he had hoped that Earth First! would remain a small, ideologically united tribe. The movement's growth had seen him transformed from a millenarian into an apocalyptic prophet. Now, Earth First! was on the verge of another growth spurt, and Foreman was unhappy. He felt that if the movement continued to grow, it would be forced to completely abandon its radical political stance. His apocalyptic message would be lost, and the character of the movement itself would change. As a result, he once again broached the subject of Earth First!'s growth and diversity in the movement's journal. In May, Foreman announced that the Arizona staff would produce a special issue of *Earth First!* later in the year that would focus on issues related to the movement's growth.[23]

In the end, however, Foreman did not wait for that issue to express his views. Later that month, he began the lengthy process of withdrawing from Earth First!. He formally retired as editor of the journal, naming John Davis (who had been the paper's managing editor for three years) as his replacement. His decision to appoint Davis was well reasoned: the latter had significant practical experience and was also a confirmed biocentrist. Indeed, on many issues, Davis's beliefs were more extreme than his own.[24] Foreman would continue to run Ned Ludd Books, write his "Dear Ned Ludd" column, and occasionally write "Around the Campfire" commentaries, but he was tired of being the "most visible spokesperson for Earth First!." He yearned to represent "only Dave Foreman."[25]

In his next "Around the Campfire" column, printed in the final pages of the June issue of *Earth First!,* Foreman explained why the movement's continued growth would eventually effect changes in its character: "There is a cumulative effect from growth which requires more bureaucracy just to communicate, coordinate, and 'manage,' and which thereby fundamentally alters the nature of the group."[26] He envisioned a small, avant-garde movement for the hardcore, misanthropic Earth First!ers, whose principal goal was to save a significant portion of the American wilderness before the apocalypse occurred. He implied that a large, unwieldy, and ideologically diluted mass movement could only be appropriate for those who compromised their biocentrism with a hope for social justice and who believed that education could produce social change.[27]

The Earth First!ers who believed in social justice and dreamt of a perfect millenarian community, however, refused to leave the movement. Instead, they became even more insistent in their demands that the journal publish direct action news and social justice articles. According to John Davis, their demands were felt at the journal's Tucson office: "We were under a fair amount of pressure from some of the direct action activists. . . . They wanted us to cover direct actions, and very little else. . . . Dave and I wanted to have a very strong focus on conservation history and conservation biology, and that caused tension between the journal staff and the people out doing the actions."[28] As a result, Foreman's editorial changes had little permanent effect. Direct action reports still found their way to *Earth First!*'s front pages, and the debate between the two factions continued to dominate the paper.[29]

The individuals responsible for exerting that pressure were predominantly northern California Earth First!ers. During the time that their *de facto* leader, Mike Roselle, had spent in prison, another leader had emerged: Judi Bari. As was typical of many West Coast Earth First!ers, Bari's political and educational background were not rooted in the American conservation movement, and environmental issues were not her only concern. She had grown up in the eastern United States and had enjoyed an upper middle class family life that was made exceptional by the fact that her parents were socialists.[30] Before she moved to California in 1979, she was a shop steward at a Maryland mail sorting center; after her move to the West Coast, she worked as a carpenter. She soon became involved both in antinuclear protests and in demonstrations against U.S. involvement in Central America.[31] Eventually, she added environmentalism to her list of causes and searched for a group in which to participate. Earth First!'s radical doctrine appealed to her, but as a radical feminist, she was "appalled" by the movement's macho image.[32] One of her activist colleagues, however, convinced her to become an Earth First!er. Darryl Cherney accomplished this feat by stressing the movement's radical reputation, which would "make the timber companies quake in their boots," and by claiming that Earth First!'s lack of organizational structure would allow them to "make our [local] group any way we wanted."[33]

Bari quickly became well-known in California Earth First! circles. She was assertive and outspoken—and vehement in her belief that environmental problems were inextricably linked to social justice issues. Not only did she insist on bringing Earth First!'s message to other activist groups, she also brought their messages to Earth First!. Bari was particularly determined that Earth First! and Earth First!ers should embrace feminism. In late 1988, she wrote an account of the annual California regional Round River Rendezvous that illustrated that point. She declared, "[A] significant facet of this rendezvous was the absence . . . of the male machismo with which EF! has become associated. This was partly because California has such a strong feminist contingent, and partly because some of the worst offenders didn't show up . . . in the women's caucus we had to reluctantly admit that, hey, these EF! men may be assholes, but at least they're trying."[34]

For many Earth First! women outside of California or the movement's social justice faction (and even for some within them),[35] the very idea of women's caucuses was puzzling. Helen Wilson (from Tucson) remarked, "I was very disgruntled at the Council of Women. We went, and the first thing some women did was pull off their shirts . . . then they just started ragging about the men."[36] For many of those in the biodiversity faction, feminist concerns were irrelevant to wilderness preservation, and it was frustrating to spend valuable Rendezvous time discussing women's issues and/or complaining about men: "I was very upset because I was thinking 'we're here to talk about environmental issues. This is not just a "women's issue"!' I found out from my husband who was with the men, that they didn't talk about women. . . . They didn't pull down their pants. They talked about wilderness."[37]

Taken alone, Bari's feminist challenge had little noticeable effect on Earth First!. Those in the social justice faction were predisposed to accept it, and those in the biodiversity faction simply lumped it in with the wide variety of social issues that they felt had no role in the movement. Bari, however, brought more than feminism to Earth First!: she also brought her experience as a labor organizer, and it was in this area that she was to have her greatest impact. As early as May 1988, she began to forge an alliance between the Industrial Workers of the World (IWW, or "Wobblies") and Earth First!.[38] In so doing, she was unwittingly following the lead of Dave Foreman.

The IWW has had a long history in the United States. It began in June 1905 as a labor organization that included three major departments: Mining, Metals and Machinery, and Transportation.[39] Most successful between 1915 and 1919, it was in a state of decline by the early 1920s.[40] Despite its difficulties, a small remnant of the original Wobblies continued to keep the organization alive into the 1990s. Melvyn Dubofsky suggests that the Wobblies's principal rallying cries, which included a distrust of establishment politics, a derision toward bureaucracies, the favoring of community action, and an emphasis on participatory democracy, are the reasons for the group's endurance. Those themes remain appealing, he says, to "all who prefer a society based upon community to one founded on coercion."[41]

Foreman had long admired the IWW, and he had originally modeled some of Earth First!'s protest methods on those of the old labor organization.[42] He believed that the Wobblies—who also advocated both small scale industry and population reduction—were, as their literature proclaimed, "the only group in the history of North American labour to have been consistently on the side of the Earth against its commercial and industrial despoilers."[43] Foreman also appreciated their tactics, and he adopted their use of stickers (known as "silent agitators") as a staple of Earth First!'s "Trinkets and Snake Oil" merchandise selection. Foreman and the anonymous coeditor of *Ecodefense* acknowledged these links in the selection of the latter's pseudonym: "Bill Haywood" took his name from one of the IWW's most notorious early leaders. The real Haywood and 164 other members of the IWW were arrested in 1917 for such crimes as conspiring to hinder the draft. Haywood jumped bail and fled to Russia, where he later died.[44]

As might have been expected, Bari attempted to form a different kind of link between Earth First! and the Wobblies than the one that Foreman and his associates had created. From her point of view, the IWW could be more than just an Earth First! folk myth. By the late 1980s, the IWW was a very small organization, but she hoped to use it to forge a practical political alliance between California loggers and Earth First!ers. The Wobblies could serve as the vehicle through which loggers and environmentalists realized they had a shared interest in seeing the fall of the corporate industrial monolith that was destroying the environment. If workers and environmentalists realized they were on the same side, Bari reasoned, they could create a mass movement that would destabilize that monolith and bring about real social change.[45] Bari began working on that alliance almost immediately, and it soon made her the target of numerous death threats.

The 1988 Round River Rendezvous was held from June 29 through July 4 in the Kettle River mountain range of Washington state. The size of the gathering reflected the movement's continued growth; between four and five hundred Earth First!ers were in attendance.[46] Although the meeting appeared similar to those that had preceded it, the 1988 Rendezvous was distinguished by two features. First, the annual meeting evinced a remarkable degree of openness regarding the movement's most controversial tactic, monkeywrenching.[47] Although *Earth First!* was always careful to publish disclaimers regarding such tactics, the 1988 Rendezvous publicly featured instructional workshops on various monkeywrenching tactics (including disabling large machinery and tree spiking).[48] The movement had perhaps grown more confident and careless as it grew in size. This open advocacy of illegal tactics was somewhat ironic given a related circumstance of the meeting: a notice posted at the meeting jokingly declared "F.B.I. Welcome,"[49] but there in fact was at least one such undercover officer at the gathering.[50] Second, dissatisfaction over the journal's style and content became the substance of public disagreement at this meeting. In his speech to the Rendezvous, Howie Wolke argued that the journal should focus on wilderness issues and eliminate all of what he referred to as "excess baggage." On his view, "articles on matters most relevant to social reform, animal liberation, paganism, the peace movement [and/]or feminism . . . do not belong in the Journal."[51] In his August editorial, John Davis stated that he agreed with Wolke's arguments but that he would not "summarily reject" such articles if they were "clearly linked to saving wilderness and wildlife"[52]—in effect reiterating Wolke's priorities.

Although Davis attempted in the editorial to present an evenhanded perspective on the other events that occurred at the 1988 Rendezvous, he was bitter. At the meeting, he had been accused of making the journal into a drab and tedious publication. In print, he responded coldly that if "[h]umor has been lacking in recent issues . . . it is the writers' responsibility to restore it."[53] Although criticism of *Earth First!* had been common during Foreman's editorship, he had been capable of limiting public discussions of its content and function. With Davis's written report of the Rendezvous debate, a new era in the journal's history began. Without Foreman to commandingly declare that discussion of the issue was finished, open and unending criticism of *Earth First!* became not only acceptable but also respectable among individuals in both factions. The apocalyptic faction wanted a return to strict coverage of biodiversity issues, while the millenarian faction wanted greater coverage of social justice issues. As a result, no one was satisfied with the paper's content, and the power struggle between the movement's two factions continued through the autumn. The September issue, for example, featured California tree sitters on the cover but was dominated by biodiversity articles (among them, a three page article on snakes.[54])

In the November journal, Wolke returned to writing his "Grizzly Den" column simply in order to further the remarks he had made at the Rendezvous concerning the movement's "excess baggage." To this, however, he added a further request that was sure to anger many Earth First!ers from the social justice faction (many of whom had declared themselves to be pagans, and who regularly took part in pagan rituals).[55] He asked that the journal stop using pagan dates in its masthead (a practice that had been initiated by Foreman—who had no interest in paganism—only in order to further distinguish Earth First! from the environmental mainstream). Wolke wrote, "I speak English . . . and long for the day when I'll be able to pronounce the names of Journal issues . . . many of us do not consider ourselves 'Pagans.' Many potential supporters are put off by the Journal's *apparent* subscription to Paganism."[56]

Further evidence of dissatisfaction with *Earth First!* was that a new journal, entitled *Live Wild or Die*, began publication during this time. As described in an *Earth First!* advertisement, it promised to serve as an outlet for the most radical anarchists in the movement. Published in northern Washington state, it was primarily the vehicle of Mike Jakubal, an Earth First!er who had earlier promoted a nonexistent faction he called "Stumps Suck." Both Stumps Suck and *Live Wild or Die* created a minor stir amongst the Tucson staff (who no doubt anticipated that they were about to be attacked on yet another front). Although they were a response to the journal's editorial direction, neither *Live Wild or Die* nor Stumps Suck became the official voice of the social justice faction. Mitch Friedman, one of the individuals involved in their creation, noted that "*Live Wild or Die* was a reaction to the so-called censorship at the Journal. It was intended to cover more of the revelry and the nihilistic [spirit] . . . wilderness protection wasn't the ultimate goal, but release of the wild human spirit, which might lead to wilderness protection, but not necessarily."[57] *Live Wild or Die* enjoyed only a brief existence; after just a few issues, it disappeared.[58]

As squabbling continued over the control and content of *Earth First!*, a series of events occurred in northern Arizona that eventually helped to cause the movement's final fragmentation. A small, tightly-knit cell group unwittingly allowed an FBI infiltrator into their midst. Although usually careful to monkeywrench only with individuals they knew well,[59] they admitted a man known as "Mike Tait" into their circle.[60] Tait, whose real name was Mike Fain, accomplished this feat by emotionally manipulating one Earth First!er, Peg Millett, and ingratiating himself with her friends.[61]

The previous year, in October 1987, the group had sabotaged the Fairfield Snow Bowl ski area by cutting the support bolts on twelve towers at the bottom of the Snow Bowl chairlift on Agassiz Peak.[62] Calling themselves EMETIC (a play on words, as well as an acronym for Evan Meecham Eco-Terrorist International Conspiracy), the group declared by way of press releases that it was protesting the commercial development of Navajo and Hopi sacred lands. EMETIC threatened to chain the Fairfield CEO to a tree at the 10,000 foot level and feed him shrubs and roots until he understands the suicidal folly of treating the planet primarily as a tool for making money. . . . [Fairfield] should consult with appropriate spiritual authorities on the Navajo and Hopi reservations and agree not to operate at all on the days of greatest religious significance . . . if our compromise is accepted Fairfield should place a small ad in the classified personals [saying] "Uncle!" Otherwise, better hire more security.[63]

On September 26, 1988, this small group chose another politically meaningful target: under cover of darkness, EMETIC cut twenty-nine electrical power poles that served the Grand Canyon Uranium Mine. Their action cut power to the mine for four days, and cost the company over $200,000.[64] Almost one month later, on October 25, EMETIC struck the Fairfield Snow Bowl resort a second time. On this occasion, its members severed the chairlift's main support pylon.[65]

Although other Earth First! cell groups were committing similar actions with perhaps more dangerous and costly results, the FBI deliberately chose the Prescott, Arizona circle as a focus for its investigation. Its agents wanted to arrest Foreman and deduced that they could best achieve that goal by implicating him in that group's plans.

The FBI investigation continued through the winter of 1988 and into the first few months of 1989. It was by no means inconsequential in its cost or its scope; in its investigation of EMETIC, the Bureau employed fifty agents for over two years. By the operation's conclusion, it had amassed over thirteen hundred hours of secret recordings.[66] Estimates concerning that evidence suggested that over fourteen thousand work hours of transcription would be required and that such a process would yield over twenty-four thousand pages of documents. The entire process would cost an estimated one million dollars.[67]

While the undercover investigation was underway, ideological conflicts continued to rage within the movement. In February 1989, Davis announced Foreman's official retirement from "his role as publisher of the Journal and as spokesperson for the Earth First! movement."[68] Davis then pleaded with Earth First!ers to stop their constant bickering and focus on environmental issues: "We receive numerous articles and letters lambasting some rival person or faction. Frequently, writers complain to us because their critiques of rivals are not printed. Hence, the following suggestion: given that the present quarreling seems to be fulfilling some social need, why don't we begin instead to debate more pressing questions?"[69]

Davis's intentions were good, and he was clearly concerned about the movement's loss of community and direction, but as might have been expected, his definition of "more pressing questions" were those that concerned conservation and biodiversity issues.[70] The examples he cited were such questions as "When is it best to replant damaged lands, and when is it best to leave natural succession to begin anew? When if ever, are captive breeding programs justified?" As a result, his plea was interpreted by those in the millennial faction as yet another attempt to silence the discussion of social justice issues: "'How to replant damaged lands' is certainly not the only valuable debate. Wilderness and human freedom are simultaneously murdered by *organizational* systems. Oppression is the nature of stratification. Avoiding analysis of organization versus tribal anarchy legitimizes the structural systems we are fighting against."[71] The letters to the editor continued. Davis had again failed to stem the journal's coverage of the ideological conflict between the two factions.

Against this backdrop of infiltration and conflict, however, Earth First! did achieve some remarkable successes. The February issue of the journal reported on the initiation of a Mid-West Road Show that had scheduled over thirty performances. Plans for an "Ancient Forest Expedition" were also announced: a group of Earth First!ers from Washington state planned to take a ten-foot diameter Douglas fir across the United States and schedule protests to coincide with their arrival. The expedition was a success. By its conclusion, the group had visited over twenty-five cities, from Kansas City to New York and Nashville.[72]

Earth First!'s major financial endeavors were also doing well. The Direct Action Fund year-end report recorded that over thirty thousand dollars had been distributed to various campaigns,[73] while the Earth First! Foundation treasurer reported that during the previous year almost fifty thousand dollars had been used to fund legal activities and protests.[74] The movement had also attracted corporate sponsors: Earth First!'s Redwood Action Team had received a five hundred dollar donation from Patagonia Clothing.[75] On the surface, it appeared that the movement was capable of functioning, even while it was riven by factions. In the early spring of 1989, however, two events initiated the final stage of its fragmentation.

On March 20, 1989, at the age of sixty-one, Edward Abbey died. Dave Foreman learned of his death upon returning from a vacation in Belize, and the occasion gave Foreman the opportunity to reflect on Earth First!'s origins and development. In the end, this reflection reinforced his conviction that Earth First! was no longer his spiritual or political home.[76]

Most Earth First!ers realized that Abbey, through his life and work, had inspired the founding of the movement. In celebration of his contribution, the journal featured a four page tribute to him. It began with an article by Foreman, who took the opportunity to praise Abbey, and perhaps inadvertently, provoke Earth First!'s social justice faction:

> In his death Abbey joined a small company. Perhaps only Henry David Thoreau, John Muir, Aldo Leopold and Rachel Carson have touched so many souls so profoundly. Edward Abbey was a great man because he articulated the passion and wisdom of those of us who love the wild. He was a spokesperson for our generation and for generations to come of those of us who understand where the real world is.[77]

Foreman's words reflected his belief that Abbey's understanding of the environmental crisis was, in fact, correct: "Whether we live or die is a matter of absolutely no concern whatsoever to the desert."[78] The preservation of wilderness was vastly more important than social justice issues. Finally, Foreman praised Abbey's ability to "prick the inflated egos of those who take themselves too seriously. The self-righteous humanists who hated Abbey never understood what he was saying. It is their loss."[79]

Ironically, Edward Abbey's last attempt to deliver his message was at a Tucson Earth First! gathering in February 1989, where he was introduced by Cat Clarke, a woman who was later identified as an FBI informant.[80] His death also occurred as the FBI's investigation of Tucson Earth First! approached its conclusion.[81]

On the evening of May 31, 1989, Mike "Tait"/Fain, Mark Davis, Marc Baker (a biologist), and Peg Millett headed out into the desert near Wenden, Arizona. Their goal was to cut the power lines that served the Central Arizona water lift project. It was intended as a dry run for far more ambitious undertakings; eventually, the group planned to cut the power lines that led to the Palo Verde nuclear power plant in

Arizona, the Diablo Canyon nuclear plant in California, and the Rocky Flats atomic weapons facility in Colorado.[82] The small group did not, however, achieve their goal. As they cut the first leg of the tower,[83] a flare went up into the sky and fifty FBI agents encircled them. Davis and Baker were arrested on the spot. Millett successfully evaded the trap, hiked through the desert, and hitchhiked back to her home in Prescott (a journey of over sixty miles). She gamely went to work the next day, but FBI agents soon arrived at her office and arrested her.[84] That same morning, the Bureau's officers burst into Dave Foreman's Tucson home and arrested him, thus completing the roundup of the "Arizona Four." Foreman had not been present at the monkeywrenching site, but he was accused of financing the project and of distributing two copies of his book *Ecodefense* to the conspirators.[85]

Thus, by mid-1989, Earth First!'s apocalyptic faction had not only lost its mentor Edward Abbey, but the FBI had successfully targeted Dave Foreman. Ironically, though the Earth First! leader had distanced himself from the tension-fraught movement, the FBI investigation drew him back to it. By this point, however, the movement's balance of power had shifted. The publicity Earth First! had received had expanded its numbers, and the new adherents were predominantly from the West Coast. By sheer force of numbers, the millenarian social justice faction had come to dominate Earth First!'s committees and campfires.

8

The Resurgence of Millenarianism

Dave Foreman wants Earth First! to remain small, pure and
radical. I want it to be big, impure and radical.[1]

—Judi Bari

We don't want Foreman in Earth First! if he's going to be an
unrepentant right-wing thug.[2]

—Mike Roselle

Between 1989 and 1990, the Earth First! movement underwent the
final stages of its metamorphosis. During that time, it evolved into two
completely separate groups, linked by their apprehension of an imminent biological meltdown but divided by their understanding of its
implications.

The Earth First! movement threw its support behind the individuals
who were arrested in Arizona, but for the sake of presenting a united
front, it also attempted to function as if nothing unusual had happened.
In mid-June, the journal published a special edition documenting the
arrests,[3] but the story was not given any special emphasis in the regular
June issue.[4] Similarly, Earth First! continued with its plans for the 1989
Round River Rendezvous with little change.

The millenarian social justice faction had by sheer numbers come to
dominate many of the movement's committees, including the Round
River Rendezvous organizing committee. In 1989, for the first time in
Earth First!'s ten-year history, the organizing committee did not plan
the annual meeting for the July 4 weekend. In a decision unrelated to
the arrests, its members determined that the Rendezvous would occur

June 19–25, in the Jemez Mountains of New Mexico. As noted above, at Earth First!'s founding, Foreman had deliberately chosen July 4 for the Rendezvous because in his view, Earth First! represented a true celebration of the American founding. The new dates were a deliberate rejection of Foreman and that vision. They also recognized the social justice faction's version of paganism by encompassing both a full moon and the summer solstice.[5] The new dates were an attempt to create a community that located its origins and meaning outside the ideological foundation of the American republic.

The Rendezvous committee's published meeting plan also included a special invitation to a new workshop entitled "Beyond Debate—Shared Actions!: Ecofeminism, Anarchy and Deep Ecology." The workshop's goal was to encourage the movement's diversity: "These various forms of rethinking and changing the world share the passionate desire for both expanded wilderness and a wilder expression of our beings."[6] The workshop was highlighted in the 1989 Rendezvous advertisement in the journal, and it was yet another example of the growing influence of the millenarian faction.

Although most Earth First!ers were angered by the FBI infiltration, the arrests did not provide a sufficient impetus to heal the movement's internal conflicts. The possibility of further arrests, coupled with the likelihood of continued internecine bickering, kept many Earth First!ers away from the Rendezvous. The 1989 gathering was one of the smallest in the movement's history, attended by only one hundred Earth First!ers.[7]

As expected, the 1989 Rendezvous saw the movement's biodiversity/social justice conflict discussed yet again. On this occasion, however, a number of individuals from the apocalyptic biodiversity faction suggested that the movement should undergo a "no-fault-divorce."[8] In their view, there was simply not enough time left before the apocalypse to continue to debate (let alone pursue) social justice issues and "woo-woo" rituals.[9]

This sudden escalation in the conflict was prompted by an event that had provoked the more conservative first generation Earth First!ers. During the first day of the Rendezvous, one such individual, Helen Wilson, was sitting at a booth that displayed an American flag when she was verbally attacked: "I was called a Nazi. . . . They [members of the social justice faction] were upset because of the flag. I told them 'I'm an American, not a Native American, but I was born here, and I love the country. Just because some politicians have made the flag distasteful to you, doesn't mean it's distasteful to me.'"[10] Later that evening (the summer solstice), the social justice Earth First!ers went further: they burned the flag.[11] For many of the first generation Earth First!ers, that event was the final straw.

Despite these difficulties, and perhaps because of them, a new Earth First! institution emerged at the 1989 meeting. In a number of *Earth First!* articles, Foreman had written about the Zuni Indians's "Mudhead Kachinas," individuals who served as the tribe's official clowns.[12] On the morning after the flag burning, Earth First! created its own Mudhead Kachinas, and individuals from both factions participated. Mitch Friedman stated that the Kachinas served as a kind of release from the tension that had built up within the movement: "[After] all those intense proceedings, the screaming, the yelling . . . somebody sang a Bob Marley song, 'Pressure gonna come down on you you you.' And it just kind of gave me an idea. When it came around to me, all I said was 'there's going to be a Mudhead Kachina meeting right after this.' And everybody said ya; they just seemed to know what I meant."[13] The Earth First! Mudhead Kachinas attempted to recapture the movement's unity through lighthearted ridicule of its most important institutions. Friedman recounted, "We got naked, we rubbed mud all over, and we just started making fun of everyone and everybody. I did Dave Foreman. I got up, I wore his hat, his cigar, (his 'ceegar') . . . and I tried to create the idol myth about Karen Pickett."[14]

The Kachinas were evidence that Earth First!ers could still recover some joy out of their shared history and their commitment to preserving wilderness. In reporting on the Rendezvous, Loose Hip Circles wrote that "it was the Mudhead Kachinas who really made this rally special. This mysterious band of mischievous beings had no mercy and no reverence. EF! icons and luminaries were ridiculed. . . . Let's have more Mudhead Earth First! actions. Our irreverence may be our salvation."[15] In his annual Rendezvous speech, Foreman (the only one of the Arizona Four to be released on bail) focused on the recent arrests, and with typical Earth First! bravado warned the FBI that he did not intimidate easily.[16]

In his June editorial, John Davis took up where the Rendezvous had left off. He suggested that the movement's diversity might indeed be sufficient to cause an eventual split, but he implied that it was the millenarian faction that should leave. He also intimated that such a break might be constructive,[17] arguing that the benefit of such a fragmentation would be the spread of Earth First! ideas into other environmental groups.[18] He also remarked that the recent tendency among West Coast Earth First!ers to found new groups (for example, the fictional Stumps Suck) could also be beneficial, for it "might humble us."[19] Davis closed his editorial with a warning to those who would found new groups: he cautioned Earth First!ers that the decision to take such an action should be based on "the ramifications for the health of the planet."[20]

Thus, despite the Tucson arrests, Earth First! did not close ranks. The journal published photographs of FBI informants and featured a "Dear Ned Ludd" column entitled "A Monkeywrencher's Guide to Lawyers and the Law,"[21] but the June "Letters to the Editor" page was still dominated by conflicts over the movement's ideology.[22]

During the summer, *Earth First!*'s main office was relocated to Canton, New York. The move was prompted by events completely extraneous to the movement's politics,[23] but Davis stated that in relocating to New York, the journal hoped to strengthen the alliance between "EF!ers from the East, Midwest, and West" and that the movement's further decentralization would also serve to "confuse the federal goons."[24] If Davis had also thought that *Earth First!*'s move to New York would help defuse the social justice faction's antipathy towards the editorial staff (often referred to as "the Tucson junta"), he was mistaken. Letters complaining about the journal's editorial policies continued to pour in. He recounted in September that "EF!ers have been grumbling that the articles are too long. Anarchists have been heard to apply toward the Journal such opprobrious adjectives as insipid, prolix, and turgid."[25] In response, he attempted a Mudhead Kachina of his own: the September issue was brief, but it included in its pages a parody entitled *Mirth First!*. Among its articles were such titles as "The Strato-Ecology of Person/Planet/Tenure Bio-Ethics"[26] and "The Misanthrope Quiz (or, Are You an Eco-Brute?)."[27]

Davis's humor may have dissipated some of the tension that surrounded the publication, but it did not put an end to its problems. Discussions over *Earth First!*'s content and character continued through the end of the year, and Davis was clearly losing patience. In his December editorial, he responded to charges that the journal was difficult to read by making a deliberate point of writing in words that did not exceed eight characters in length.[28] He reminded Earth First!ers to keep their own articles short and stated that if the journal had been too dry of late, it was because "[a]ctivists ain't sending us funny stories no more."[29]

In late December, another individual was arrested for her involvement in the EMETIC monkeywrenching schemes: Ilse Asplund was charged with conspiracy to sabotage the Canyon Mine power poles, the sabotage of chairlifts at the Fairfield Snow Bowl, and planned attacks on nuclear power plants in Arizona, California, and Colorado. The Arizona Four thus became the Arizona Five.[30]

The first months of 1990 brought some relief to the beleaguered movement. While transcribing the FBI's recorded evidence, Dan Conner (of the Arizona Five's Legal Defense Fund) found a conversation among some of the FBI agents involved that indicated that Foreman was the real target of the investigation. Inadvertently, Mike Fain had recorded the following statement on his FBI body tap: "[Foreman] isn't really the guy we need to pop . . . in terms of the actual perpetrator. . . . This is the guy we need to pop to send a message, and that's all we're really doing. . . . If we don't nail this guy . . . we're not sending a message."[31] That discovery was later used by Foreman's defense team to argue that the whole investigation was "one of the most 'blatant, unlawful' entrapment schemes in U. S. history."[32] It reinforced Foreman's belief that he had been targeted in an effort to "intimidate the entire environmental and social-action movement in this country."[33]

In the February issue of the journal, however, Roselle continued the apocalyptic/millenarian battle by responding to Davis's flippant December editorial. Roselle argued that the FBI's persecution of Earth First!, and environmental problems as a whole, should not be regarded as a crisis; they were an "opportunity."[34] The individuals who had been arrested should not be pitied, because they had been doing something that they believed in. The events of the past year, he suggested, were yet another result of the fact that Americans had no control over "an elite, aggressive, and authoritarian government backed by a corrupt legal system."[35] What had happened to the Arizona Five was clear evidence that the millenarian social justice agenda was the most appropriate plan of action for the Earth First! movement. Roselle called for a renewed Earth First! to be founded by individuals who would "address some of the root causes of the environmental crisis, and see how they are linked to the present distribution of wealth and power."[36]

Roselle directly addressed Foreman's apocalyptic beliefs by arguing that the movement's erstwhile leader, both in his approach to preserving the environment and in the movement he had created, was simply "man[ning] the barricades." He and his followers were content with preserving wilderness and had isolated themselves from other protest movements. Roselle argued that it was more appropriate to build a movement of active people who could "relate to the words Earth First! on a deep and personal level."[37] Those individuals would not see monkeywrenching as a kind of "chivalry" but instead act to challenge the entire system, "or at least the parts of it that threaten us with extinction by holding both us and nature captive."[38] Roselle ended his article with a criticism of Davis's editorship of *Earth First!*, stating that he felt that Davis had responded to criticism in a purely defensive manner and had not made any significant changes in the journal's content. Roselle's conclusion was straightforward: "Talking down to people you see as hippies and pondering whether or not AIDS has any positive benefits might be speaking your mind, but it sure the hell isn't going to make it any easier to organize a movement."[39]

Roselle's article was a direct challenge to the biodiversity faction. Davis, its new standard bearer, did not respond to those charges; instead, his March editorial outlined issues that he felt had not been adequately addressed in the pages of the journal. He solicited articles on those topics, none of which concerned social justice issues.[40] In so doing, he made clear that he did not intend to compromise or make peace with Roselle. Moreover, he published no letters that supported Roselle's arguments. Later, when questioned as to why this was so, assistant editor Dale Turner stated that the journal staff had received several telephone calls supporting Roselle's views, but no letters.[41]

As the movement tore itself apart from within, it gained further public exposure on a massive scale. In March 1990, it was featured on the CBS television show *Sixty Minutes*. For the segment, host Ed Bradley interviewed several prominent Earth First!ers, among them Dave Foreman and Darryl Cherney. The program, aided by Earth First!ers themselves, sensationalized the movement's activities; in a quote that was soon to come back to haunt him, Cherney declared, "If I knew I had a fatal disease, I would definitely do something like strap dynamite on myself and take out Grand Canyon Dam. Or maybe the Maxxam Building in Los Angeles after it's closed up for the night."[42]

The *Sixty Minutes* feature resulted in yet another growth spurt for Earth First!: during the next month, the journal received over five hundred new subscriptions.[43]

Despite this boon, the battle between the movement's two factions continued into the late spring of 1990, fueled by Judi Bari and other California Earth First!ers. In April, Bari publicly defied Dave Foreman and Earth First!'s own history by renouncing tree spiking, the movement's trademark tactic. In so doing, she hoped to forge an alliance between timber workers and environmentalists, a link she perceived as a necessary step towards the overthrow of the industrial system. Bari was also anxious to stem the escalating threats of violence against Earth First!ers. Her statement was followed by a press release signed by seven northern California Earth First!ers (including Roselle) that formally renounced tree spiking.[44] This renunciation was not a complete rejection of monkeywrenching, nor was it permanent; the group's press release tacitly encouraged mill workers to sabotage their equipment, and later many individuals (again including Roselle) once again advocated tree spiking.[45]

Foreman was displeased by these activities, but he was preoccupied with the Arizona court case. In that context, he was anxious that Earth First! present a united public front. He therefore wrote a private letter to Bari but took no public action against her.[46]

By May, it was clear that *Earth First!*'s staff had grown tired of the constant bickering between the two factions. That month's issue reflected their weariness. Davis's main editorial was deliberately brief, and then he, Nancy Zierenberg, and Dale Turner each wrote lengthy articles explaining "How the *Journal* Works." Their efforts were, for the most part, a repetition of previous statements that they had made concerning the nature of Earth First!, such as "Earth First! is a movement not an organization."[47] In this issue, however, Davis went one step further. He declared that the movement was now so large and diverse that the journal could "no longer even pretend to be a voice for the whole movement."[48] Instead, it would "stress wilderness and biodiversity almost to the exclusion of the debates over style, emphasis, and politics that have arisen lately. We will not facilitate internecine squabbling."[49] Additionally, the editorial staff changed the paper's masthead: it was now titled the *Earth First! Journal,* and its subheading read "In Defense of Wilderness and Biodiversity."[50] Davis argued that the change was made in order to highlight the journal's role in the movement. It had always been, said Dale Turner, "an independent voice within the movement . . . and not the 'official newsletter.'"[51] The new name was intended to emphasize that partisanship. It was also another attempt to purge social justice issues from the journal's pages.

The staff also made another significant change to the journal, removing the pagan dates from the masthead and offering as an explanation only the fact that "almost nobody could pronounce them."[52] The journal had used those dates since the publication of its first issue, chiefly in order to distinguish Earth First! from mainstream environmental groups.[53] In the minds of many in the biodiversity faction, however, they were linked to the social justice faction's "woo-woo" beliefs; quite correctly, their elimination was interpreted by the latter faction as yet another rejection of their millenarian convictions. Davis concluded by stating that the editorial staff was not trying to direct the movement, but simply refocusing the journal in order that it could "best speak for Gray Wolf, Grizzly Bear, Cahaba Shiner, Socorro Isopod, Kretchmarr Cave Mold Beetle, and the myriad other imperiled creatures, and the wilderness that sustains us all."[54] Davis's attempt at diplomacy would perhaps have been better received if his commentary in the new *Earth First! Journal* had been consistently tactful. On the second page of the May issue, however, he added insult to injury by including an "Index to Gratuitously Offensive Remarks," a feature that poked fun at "politically correct" members of the social justice faction.[55]

Those individuals did not immediately respond to Davis's slants; at the end of May, their attention was taken up with other problems. In the early months of 1990, Judi Bari was busy planning "Redwood Summer," an event that she hoped would mobilize mass civil disobedience protests in the redwoods of northern California. Bari modeled the protest after the civil rights protests of the 1960s, and specifically 1964's Mississippi Summer. Redwood Summer's goal was to delay the cutting of redwood trees until the autumn, when Californians were scheduled to vote on two initiatives concerning the protection of the trees.[56] In order for Redwood Summer to succeed, Bari depended upon a number of factors: the support of Earth First!'s leadership, the capabilities of those immediately around her, and the notoriety she had acquired as a political organizer. Before the protest even began, however, the first two elements failed her, and the third element turned against her in a way she had not anticipated.

Despite his withdrawal from many Earth First! activities, Dave

Foreman remained the *de facto* leader of the movement. Many individuals still believed him to be their prophet, and his ideas and actions therefore still held influence. Moreover, the editor and employees of the *Journal* were his friends and political allies. Foreman had long had misgivings about civil disobedience as a form of political protest. He disapproved of Bari's renunciation of tree spiking and her attempts to form an alliance with those in the logging industry. He also did not care for Redwood Summer's specific goal, believing that Earth First!'s attention should be focused on publicly-owned lands, not privately-held forests. While he provided her with advice regarding death threats she had received and supported her efforts with limited funding,[57] neither he nor the *Journal* staff threw their full weight behind her. Similarly, other prominent northern California leaders, including Mike Roselle, shared some of Foreman's misgivings about Redwood Summer's goals. Roselle remarked of the campaign, "I would have liked to see us [Northern California Earth First!] focus on public lands a long time ago, but most of the activists have wanted to really concentrate on redwoods."[58]

Adding to these problems was Bari's association with Earth First! musician Darryl Cherney. Cherney was one of Bari's closest associates; indeed, for a short period of time, she was romantically involved with him. Cherney was a willing follower, but he was also overly fond of media attention. That tendency saw him claim responsibility for a poster that advertised "Earth Night," which encouraged monkeywrenching actions on the eve of Earth Day. More than one person followed the poster's recommendation, with the result that several California towns suffered downed power lines for much of the next day.[59] For his efforts, Cherney got more attention than he had bargained for; he was rewarded with both media interviews and death threats.[60]

Bari's close association with Cherney, coupled with her efforts to bring loggers and environmentalists together, had long made her the subject of public attack. Her activities in aid of other social justice causes further increased that tendency. As might be expected, given her background, Bari's organizing efforts extended beyond the realm of traditional Earth First! activities. She had gained notoriety in Ukiah, California, for her efforts on behalf of the town's prochoice lobby. At the 1987 opening of a Planned Parenthood clinic, Bari and Cherney had enraged local prolife groups with their outspoken and unusual protest methods.[61]

Bari and Cherney thus began organizing Redwood Summer while they were very much in the public spotlight. That notoriety helped them publicize the redwoods protest, but on the morning of May 24, 1990, it backfired. On that day, the two were driving through Oakland on their way to Santa Cruz, where they hoped to marshall support for the protest.[62] Just before noon, a pipe bomb exploded underneath Bari's seat. Cherney's left eye was damaged by exploding debris, but Bari, who was driving, suffered the worst of the damage. The bomb shattered her pelvis, and she spent the next six weeks in traction; as a result, she was crippled for life.[63] The Oakland police concluded that Bari and Cherney were transporting the bomb, naming them as the only suspects in the blast.[64] Those charges were later dropped, but no one was ever arrested for placing the bomb.[65] (The two activists later filed a civil rights lawsuit against both the Oakland police and the FBI for the failure to investigate the crime.[66])

In the end, Redwood Summer went on as planned, with the organizational help of other Earth First!ers as well as activists from other concerned groups, among them Greenpeace, the Earth Island Institute, and the International Indian Treaty Council.[67] Over three thousand people participated in the event, and by Labor Day 1990 over 150 of them had been arrested.[68] The protest itself, however, generated much less mainstream media coverage than the Bari/Cherney bombing. Indeed, the popular press concluded that Redwood Summer had failed to achieve its goals; during the summer, the logging of northern California's redwoods continued, virtually uninterrupted.[69]

Against the backdrop of Davis's changes to the journal, the impending trial of the Arizona Five, and Redwood Summer and the Bari/Cherney bombing, the 1990 Round River Rendezvous took place in the Gravelly Mountain range of southern Montana. The date and character of the event were the subject of controversy as early as March. In their advertisement of the meeting, the Rendezvous committee was forced to renounce an earlier, unauthorized announcement by one of its members. Jake Krelick, a member of the biodiversity faction, mailed a letter to Earth First!ers that stated that the Rendezvous would be held at the traditional time (July 2–8) and that "anything that prevents EF! from defending wilderness, biodiversity and those brave folks engaged in this struggle *does not* belong and *will not* be tolerated at the 1990 RRR."[70] The official committee advertisement politely corrected the dates (July

9–15) and stated that the theme of that year's meeting was to be "NO CONTROL."[71] Social justice concerns were again set to dominate the Earth First! Rendezvous, and for the first time, Dave Foreman chose not to attend the annual meeting.

While the 1990 Rendezvous featured many of the same workshops as its predecessors (meetings concerned such topics as deep ecology, wolves, and grizzlies), it agenda was determined by the movement's millenarian faction. The Friday night gathering around the campfire, for example, featured a war dance that "commenced to the beat of drums, starting with the weaving of the web of life, which was torn apart by the Machine, only to arise again and destroy the evil Machine."[72] Those who participated clearly believed that their movement could overthrow the system, and they celebrated in a truly antinomian fashion: "General chaos then erupted: naked, painted bodies writhing in muddy heaps, heathens twisting and shouting to the incessant beat, infiltrators watching in awe and consternation."[73]

Amidst those celebrations was a workshop that Earth First!ers later identified as the most important meeting of the event.[74] The workshop concerned the role and ownership of the *Earth First! Journal,* and it was inspired by the refusal of the journal's editorial staff to publish two letters written by Mike Roselle. In a letter read aloud by another Earth First!er, Roselle claimed that the purpose of the *Journal* was to build the Earth First! movement, that the staff was "in a phase of denial" if it thought otherwise, and that in his opinion, the *Journal* had been "hijacked" by a small, unrepresentative group of Earth First!ers.[75] Roselle wanted the *Journal* to represent the social justice faction and to be a vehicle for it to achieve its goals. The *Journal's* four staff members attended the meeting, along with approximately forty other Earth First!ers, all of whom wished to have some say in the evolution of the paper. With the acquiesence of the staff, it was decided that an advisory committee would be created to monitor the paper's content.[76]

Despite the apparent progress that was made in solving the conflict over the *Journal,* and despite the many celebrations that took place, the 1990 Rendezvous was not a particularly happy time for most Earth First!ers. The major issues that separated them were not dealt with, and the compromise solution concerning the *Journal* did not heal the personal animosity that had developed amongst Earth First!ers over the course of the year. At that Rendezvous, not even the Mudhead Kachinas could draw everyone together. Mitch Friedman remarked that "Friday of every Rendezvous was always kind of like the inspiring time, but [then] it was just a humor time. Making fun of every tradition. And nothing mattered any more."[77]

Earth First!ers of both factions were still united by their love of wilderness, but the deep divisions that existed among them meant that they could no longer appreciate even that shared loyalty. The apocalyptics believed only in preserving wilderness, while the millenarians of the social justice faction wanted to create a movement that could build a perfect, environmentally-sustainable society. They believed that after the apocalypse, humans would realize the necessity of living in harmony with the natural world. In the words of Darryl Cherney, "As we heal the earth, we will heal ourselves."[78] These differences led to a general unhappiness and a lack of focus: "What was gone seemed to be a sense of knowing where Earth First! was going. Not a belief in its value, or a commonality among the Earth First!ers, but the struggle to get back the feeling that we used to have, that we knew where it was going."[79] Finally, and absolutely, Earth First!ers had realized that with two such different visions of the postapocalyptic world, they could no longer work together. They did, however, make one further attempt to remain united; as a result of a Rendezvous meeting, the *Journal* staff allowed themselves to be governed by an "oversight committee."

The minutes of that meeting were reprinted in the August issue, accompanied by a note from John Davis that stated: "To accommodate the wishes of EF! direct activists, we'll make some changes in future issues. The letters section will be longer, "Ramblings" [Davis's editorial column] will be eliminated, and action articles will be more prominent."[80] The tone of Davis's note indicated that he was less than pleased at the turn of events.[81] That month, the paper contained four pages of letters to the editor and was dominated by articles concerning direct action events.

In mid-August, Foreman finally broke his official silence on Earth First!. For the purpose of presenting Earth First! as a united front during his trial, he had not publicly commented on the movement's activities in almost a year.[82] On August 12, however, he publicly denounced the changes that had occurred in Earth First!, stating that "West Coast yippies and hippies ha[d] taken over" and that they were "more interested in pursuing the wildness within than the wildness out in the forests."[83] Foreman declared that he was therefore demanding "a no-fault divorce" from the movement.[84]

His departure was followed almost immediately by the mass resignation of the *Journal*'s editorial staff: in September, Davis, Zierenberg, Sommerville, and Turner announced that they were quitting, effective the end of 1990.[85] They had received the first report of the newly-formed "voluntary oversight committee," and they were unhappy. Sommerville wrote, "The basic philosophical disagreement within the Earth First! movement (biocentrism, i.e., wilderness vs. anthropocentrism, i.e., social issues) and the latest incendiary brawl over content and staff of the journal have pushed me over the edge."[86] The committee had done little to convince them that their work was valued by the majority of Earth First!ers. (Emphasizing that point was the fact that its first report was accompanied by a poem that could only be interpreted as both insulting and inflammatory.[87])

The remainder of the September *Earth First! Journal* included a formal "good-bye" letter from Foreman and Nancy Morton, as well as several columns concerning possible directions for the *Journal* and the movement. The apocalyptic biodiversity faction had given up its struggle to retain control, and they would return to their independent fight to save American wilderness. The millenarian social justice faction was left to determine Earth First!'s future.

Thus, by September 22, 1990, the Earth First! movement, as Dave Foreman had created it, had ceased to exist. In the space of ten years, it had grown from a small millenarian movement into a large and diverse community that had both apocalyptic and millenarian factions. Those tensions eventually destroyed it. The protection of wilderness for its own sake is a fundamentally different goal than the transformation of the human political community and its relationship to the environment.

9

Conclusion

Like winds and sunsets, wild things were taken for granted until progress began to do away with them. Now we face the question whether a still higher "standard of living" is worth its cost in things natural, wild, and free. For us of the minority, the opportunity to see geese is more important than television, and the chance to find a pasque-flower is a right as inalienable as free speech.[1]

—Aldo Leopold

At the close of the twentieth century, the United States is one of the world's most technologically advanced nations, and its massive governmental apparatus oversees one of the world's largest democracies. For most American citizens, these facts constitute reason for celebration. A small minority, however, believe that the coincidence of these triumphs, and their mode of expression, are problematic.

The founders of Earth First! are indicative of one fragment of that minority population. The creation of that movement was their response to the diminishing of the American wilderness and to their perception of the American government as unresponsive to that decline. They believed that an imminent biological meltdown threatened the continued existence of many species (among them *homo sapiens*). Recognition of this situation and the adoption of a new morality emphasizing biodiversity and biocentric equality would yield a rejuvenated and ecologically sensitive political community comprised of those who possessed "the wilderness gene." At Earth First!'s origins, all of the movement's adherents shared this specific belief, and their tactics and goals reflected that conviction.

Earth First! thus began as a small, tightly-knit millenarian movement. As it grew in size, however, it also grew in diversity. This initial belief system was challenged by many new adherents and, as a result, the movement became unstable, eventually splitting into two factions. The first faction remained focused on biodiversity but became apocalyptic in nature; its adherents were not interested in the postapocalyptic future, but were primarily concerned with preserving wilderness prior to the biological meltdown. The second faction emphasized both social justice and environmental issues, and it developed a doctrine that was millenarian in character. In returning to a millenarian belief structure, this faction resembled the original Earth First! doctrine. Individuals in this faction hoped to convert as many adherents as possible to their cause, in order to create a just and ecologically sensitive community.

Earth First!'s emergence, character, and development can therefore be explained through an analysis of its millenarian doctrine. A review of the final stages of Earth First!'s factionalization will set the stage for a more complete analysis of the movement's evolution.

The Final Stages of Earth First!'s Factionalization

In the immediate aftermath of Dave Foreman's departure from the movement, there was little disruption in the publication of the journal. In the November 1990 issue, the main editorial was written by Karen Pickett. She commented that the split had been "long in coming" and "in part inevitable,"[2] but that the movement had not become a "new" Earth First!. The original movement had simply evolved: "A truly subversive approach compels people to re-examine assumptions. How else do we get rid of the dominant paradigm?"[3] Pickett spent the majority of her column attempting to explain the social justice faction's criticisms of the journal, but her article did contain an attempt at reconciliation. She concluded by reminding Earth First!ers to attack the movement's real enemies: "It's been a drag to deal with the level of bitterness and hostility I'm encountering in people whom I think have the same basic goals as me. . . . It's also a waste—hurl your hostility toward Charlie Hurwitz or . . . Mike Fain where it's better spent."[4]

John Davis, who was still officially the journal's editor, also included a brief note in its November issue. In it, he announced that he and Foreman intended to begin work on a new "biocentric biodiversity journal."[5] Later that month, all *Earth First! Journal* subscribers received a memo from the journal office offering them the choice of continuing their subscription to *Earth First! Journal* (under the social justice faction's editorship) or moving their subscription to the new *Wild Earth Journal,* which would focus "strictly on wilderness, wildlife, habitat and biodiversity."[6]

It is impossible to determine the exact number of subscriptions that went to each periodical and thus gauge the size of each faction.[7] It appears, however, that *Earth First!* received the larger proportion of subscribers. Aside from the subscribers' philosophical inclinations, there were other pragmatic reasons for that development. First, that journal was the "default" periodical: if subscribers neglected to respond to the memo, their subscriptions to *Earth First!* continued. Second, a good number of the original Earth First!ers, many of whom comprised the apocalyptic faction, had acquired lifetime subscriptions to the original journal by giving a one-time donation of several hundred dollars.[8] Rather than transfer a non-income-generating subscription to *Wild Earth,* they retained their original subscription to *Earth First!* and acquired a new subscription to the biodiversity journal in order to give it funds.[9] The transfer of *Earth First!* to the social justice faction marked the movement's formal separation.

The apocalyptic biocentrists subscribed to *Wild Earth,* the first issue of which was published in the spring of 1991; its masthead listed Dave Foreman as the executive editor and John Davis as the editor. Echoing the statement of principles that Foreman had written over ten years earlier for the fledgling Earth First!,[10] the new journal proclaimed its purpose to be "the restoration and protection of much—preferably at least half—of this continent as true Wilderness, with its full complement of native species and ecological processes."[11] Foreman and the other biocentrists, however, had changed one important element of their belief system during the preceding decade: they no longer believed that human nature was perfectible, and as a result, they no longer hoped for or desired a postapocalyptic community. They would now work independently towards their goal of "damage control until the machine plows into that brick wall and industrial civilization self-destructs as it must."[12]

As the first issue of *Wild Earth* was distributed, the trial of the Arizona Five began; it lasted throughout the summer of 1991. In the end, the individuals concerned negotiated a plea bargain.[13] Ilse Asplund, Marc Baker, Mark Davis, and Peg Millett each received jail sentences.[14] Foreman's defense team, which included Gerry Spence, successfully separated the Earth First! founder from the rest of the defendants. Foreman had not been a direct participant in any of the monkeywrenching activities under investigation, and his lawyers believed that the FBI had undertaken to entrap him.[15] In the end, Foreman plead guilty to a felony conspiracy charge (for distributing copies of *Ecodefense*), and he was placed on probation for five years.[16] That sentence allowed him the freedom to work on *Wild Earth* and to travel on the lecture circuit, attempting to gain support for his apocalyptic cause.

In February of 1991, the social justice faction published the first edition of the newly renamed *Earth First!* (complete with pagan dates on the masthead). During the next two years, that publication suffered. It lost many of the subscriptions it had retained after the split;[17] further, its new editorial system caused a number of problems. In an attempt to prevent any one individual or group from controlling the journal, the new *Earth First!* advisory board devised a system wherein there were seven paid editorial positions. Four of these positions were semipermanent (applicants had to agree to work on the paper for a minimum of six issues) and three were more temporary (they ranged in duration from one to three issues). In addition, the board did not allow anyone to work on any more than six out of eight issues per year.[18]

Although the new system effectively disallowed the formation of another editorial "junta," it resulted in near chaos. It proved difficult to attract an editorial staff on such a temporary basis,[19] and as a result, the journal's editorial continuity and quality declined. In the November 1991 issue, for example, the then-editorial board published an article entitled "A Hunting We Will Go," which appeared to encourage the shooting of hunters.[20] As a result of that article, several northern California Earth First!ers, among them Judi Bari and Darryl Cherney, cancelled their subscription to *Earth First!*. An earlier article that advocated the shooting of cattle had provoked similar outrage among some Earth First!ers.[21] The then-editor of the paper, Allison Slater, responded that she was tired of reading letters from people who were "quitting Earth First! because they don't like something they read in the journal. Some animal rights activists don't want to read about shooting cows. The 'Haydukes' don't want to think about feminist issues. . . . They seem to want the very party line that I (and I imagine, many others) joined EF! to escape."[22] The inability of the remaining Earth First!ers to be sympathetic to all the causes that the "new" journal publicized led to further instability in the movement and at the paper. In frustration, one Earth

First!er wrote, "Now, Dave & crew are gone; and the new Earth First! marches on with its shining vision. . . . We have advanced so far that we have reached the point where Dave Foreman stood nearly ten years ago: We realize that not everything fits in the journal."[23]

By the close of 1992, under the editorship of Mike Roselle, *Earth First!* had regained its sense of direction. The December 1992 edition reasserted the movement's emphasis on social justice, and its editorial concluded with the following proclamation: "We know the oppression—the loss of the nature, the loss of the wild within and without. This loss cannot be addressed adequately by needlessly separating the social justice crisis from the earth crisis. Earth First! is all the more radical today as a result."[24]

The social justice faction thus established itself as the new Earth First!. In so doing, it adopted a millenarian platform that called for the remaking of society prior to an anticipated biological meltdown. Its editorials encouraged the patience to work for long term change and advocated that individuals "Keep a shovel in one hand and a monkeywrench in the other."[25]

In June 1994, *Earth First!* included a call to "Monkeywrench the Millennium." The author declared that Earth First! should begin again with "The Year One," because for 1,993 years, human beings had "messed up the Earth."[26] The article continued: "Brothers and sisters . . . we have received a sign . . . from the Goddess Mother. She does *not* want us to go forth to the year 2000. She does *not* want us to follow the Solar, Papal, out-of balance destroy the culture of the Earth People Calendar, She is calling for us to Monkeywrench the Millennium."[27] It was up to Earth First!ers to begin again, and "[i]f we're good and conserve our resources wisely, then maybe we'll be lucky enough to see the year . . . *Two*."[28] That article summarized well the "new" Earth First!ers' millenarian belief system. They were charged with transforming human nature and activity in order that in the postmeltdown world, those who remained would live just and ecologically-sensitive lives, thus creating the best possible political community.

Both journals are now doing well. *Wild Earth* began with a relatively small subscription list and a limited budget, but despite its shaky start, its publication has continued. Originally published in Canton, New York, it has now moved to Richmond, Vermont. It is affiliated with

Foreman's new North American Wilderness Recovery Project (also known as the Wildlands Project), which has as its goal "the recovery of whole ecosystems and landscapes in every region of North America."[29] The Wildlands Project is not a new group but rather a means of bringing together conservation biologists and environmental activists and developing a "continental wilderness recovery network."[30] Among those working with him on this project are John Davis, Mitch Friedman, Bill Devall, and Reed Noss.

In the spring of 1995, Foreman (along with David Brower) was elected to the Board of Directors of the Sierra Club, a position that he accepted because he believes that organization reflects the most important of Earth First!'s accomplishments: its emphasis on conservation biology and science-based wilderness reserves. He continues to have misgivings about the nature of the American government, but preserving wilderness remains his primary goal. Foreman and his fellow biocentrists thus continue to fervently pursue the same goals they sought during the early 1980s.

Earth First! is now run by a coalition of editors in Eugene, Oregon, and the movement continues to grow. The current list of Earth First! contacts extends across North America and Europe, to locations as remote as India, Russia, and the Phillipines.[31]

Over time, the hostility that existed between the two factions has lessened; a recent issue of *Earth First!* included two interviews with Foreman.[32] Although the two factions still disagree on many issues, they both share the desire to protect American wilderness, at the same time as they both anticipate a biological meltdown. In that respect they are allies. In the words of Helen Wilson, "Even though we've all sort of split up . . . every time you get together it's like coming home. We don't have to have that title, "Earth First!." That feeling is there, no matter what you call it. No matter what the FBI or anybody else does, that feeling is always there."[33] The two factions are united by their love of the American wilderness but divided in their understanding of human nature, and thus in their interpretations of the postapocalyptic world.

Millenarianism and Earth First!

Millenarian doctrines emerge from a particular set of circumstances and, by their very nature, carry with them important political implications. Earth First! is no exception. The conditions that fostered its development and its factionalization fit well into the pattern of millenarian movements; similarly, the movement's unstable nature, choice of tactics, and ultimate goals are a reflection of its millenarian belief system.

There are three interrelated explanations for the emergence and factionalization of Earth First!. Like most millenarian groups, the Earth First! movement emerged from a situation of relative deprivation. In addition, its origins can be found in what Yonina Talmon terms a postpolitical situation. Finally, its leaders can be interpreted as attempting to found a meaningful community and establish a new political identity.

Earth First! was founded by a group of individuals who worked in the Washington lobbying establishment and were educated members of the middle class. Theories of absolute deprivation would not apply to such a group. If, however, one considers their most central set of expectations as the need to protect wilderness, the movement's founders can be understood to have experienced nonmaterial relative deprivation. For many years, Foreman and his colleagues believed their lobbying efforts were effective at preserving wilderness. After the Roadless Area Review and Evaluation II, however, they believed that changes in the lobbying environment and the goals of government meant that their future success would be limited at best. In this respect, it could be said that their perception of their future ability to realize their expectations had declined dramatically. Seen from this perspective, the creation of Earth First! can be interpreted as a means by which this deprivation could be resolved. It was a way "to overcome the discrepancy between actuality and legitimate aspiration."[34]

Although the concept of deprivation sheds some light on Earth First!'s origins, Talmon's insights concerning postpolitical and societies provide a richer explanation of its genesis and point to its significance.

Talmon's argument that millenarianism frequently emerges in postpolitical states applies to both of Earth First!'s factions. Each of these groups believed that they had no institutionalized way of voicing their political grievances. The first generation of Earth First!ers was largely comprised of individuals who had once believed that the traditional political system could effectively address their concerns; they cherished the myths of the American founding, and many were longtime conservation lobbyists. They were moved to reject those assumptions by "the disaster" that was RARE II. It destroyed their hopes, their faith in the American government, and their "true society." The second group, Earth First!'s millenarian social justice faction, can also be understood in this way. The majority of its adherents felt that the American political system had never, and would never, address their grievances; as a result, they rejected both its symbols and its substance. In their eyes, the Earth First! community constituted an alternative site of political identity and meaning. This aspect of the movement's existence was not, in and of itself, a threat to the American state. Its tactics, however, like those of the biodiversity faction, challenged the political order.

Earth First!'s creators therefore saw the movement as a tactical necessity. More importantly, however, they also felt that the development of the American polity had discouraged meaningful community, and had also encouraged a way of treating the environment that had led to the current crisis. They believed that Earth First! embodied a new way of understanding humankind's relationship to the environment and that that new way of thinking could recreate political community among the movement's adherents. However, those hopes were abandoned by that group when it became clear that Earth First! was not fulfilling them. A substantial minority of its new adherents rejected important elements of the original doctrine, and the movement did not succeed in creating new wilderness preservations or in saving as much wilderness as its founders had hoped.

The resurgence of millenarianism that occurred in the social justice faction directly reflected a desire to re-create meaningful political community and identity. The Earth First!ers in that faction were younger, did not have well-established careers outside the larger social justice movement, and felt alienated from the American political system. Some of them also lacked a sense of family security and understood the Earth First! movement to be their "second" family. Among such individuals, the emergence of a millenarian doctrine might well have been anticipated.

For both factions, wilderness was an alternative standard by which to measure the moral worth of all human activity. During the course of the movement's existence, that belief, coupled with the conviction that a biological meltdown was imminent, led to direct action events, acts of civil disobedience, and the use of monkeywrenching tactics. Earth First!ers understood almost any act, no matter how drastic or illegal, as justifiable if it was committed in order to protect wilderness. That dedication directly challenged the authority and legitimacy of the state, and it resulted in the movement's infiltration by the FBI and the prosecution of a number of Earth First!ers.

The movement's split into apocalyptic and millenarian factions highlights the challenges that such movements pose to traditional political authority, and it also emphasizes the internal problems of millennial groups. Millenarian doctrines are necessarily rigid; they proffer specific predictions and identify the precise activities that must be undertaken by their believers. Such belief systems always suffer difficulties when they encounter the real world, which most often does not conform to their predictions. In such circumstances, adherents become frustrated and/or disillusioned. Both of these situations may lead to internal instability. Like all ideologies, the original Earth First! doctrine purported to encompass the entirety of reality, but it could not. Its adherents' expectations were not met; their lack of absolute success in preserving wilderness, coupled with the movement's growth in size and diversity, led to instability and eventually factionalization.

That split was frustrating for the movement's founders, but it also caused great problems for American law enforcement agencies. While Earth First!ers had been difficult to track while they remained a decentralized but united movement, their activities were more difficult to predict during the movement's periods of instability. Those problems only increased after Earth First!'s final split. The "new" millenarian Earth First!ers remain fairly visible, but their faith in education and social change render them less dangerous to the state than their predecessors. The apocalyptic biodiversity faction, however, poses more of a problem. Its adherents left the movement to pursue their goals independently; they still hope for an imminent apocalypse, and they still believe that their function is to preserve as much wilderness as possible before that event, using whatever tactics they deem necessary. They no longer belong to an identifiable movement, however, and thus are more difficult to track than the "new" Earth First!ers. The belief system of these individuals is also much more extreme: it gives no special status to human life.

Earth First!, however, may also be interpreted in a more positive light. As Anthony Wallace argues, millenarian movements may serve a constructive purpose. Their emergence is indicative of a society under stress, and their existence highlights the problems that are causing that stress. In this way, they may be functional. They encourage a society to deal with challenges to its "mazeway," and they may help it emerge from that experience "revitalized." In part, Earth First! has fulfilled such a role.

Earth First! expanded the range of the environmental debate within the United States, and in this respect, it might be understood as functional. By the extreme nature of its tactics and goals, it made other environmental groups appear moderate, and that comparison allowed them to make greater demands upon the government.[35] Its tactics, moreover, drew media attention to environmental problems, and in that way increased public awareness of those issues. At a time when society's pressures upon the environment are at a premium, those achievements might well be understood as a contribution towards the revitalization of the American political community.

In its origins and in its development, Earth First! thus displayed patterns that are typical of most millenarian movements. It emerged from the confluence of important social and political problems; it was jarred into existence by a disaster; its leaders hoped to remake the world in the image of their vision by threatening private citizens and the state; and when its adherents became frustrated, the movement became unstable.

In its illustration of these patterns, Earth First! further illuminates the phenomenon of millenarian movements; in the substance of its beliefs, it suggests much more. As human civilization puts ever-increasing pressure upon the natural environment, and as state structures cease to be the chief source of meaning for much of the world's population, it is likely that many more environmental millenarian movements will emerge. Even in a technological age, it is the earth that most fundamentally sustains all human life. To envision its demise is to envision the apocalypse.

Appendix
Notes
Bibliography
Index

Appendix

The Basic Principles of Deep Ecology

In their seminal work *Deep Ecology: Living as if Nature Mattered,* Bill Devall and George Sessions summarize the basic tenets of deep ecology as follows:[1]

1. The well-being and flourishing of human and nonhuman Life on Earth have value in themselves (synonyms: intrinsic value, inherent value). These values are independent of the usefulness of the nonhuman world for human purposes.
2. Richness and diversity of life forms contribute to the realization of these values and are also values in themselves.
3. Humans have no right to reduce this richness and diversity except to satisfy *vital* needs.
4. The flourishing of human life and cultures is compatible with a substantial decrease of the human population. The flourishing of nonhuman life requires such a decrease.
5. Present human interference with the nonhuman world is excessive, and the situation is rapidly worsening.
6. Policies must therefore be changed. These policies affect basic economic, technological, and ideological structures. The resulting state of affairs will be deeply different from the present.
7. The ideological change is mainly that of appreciating *life quality* (dwelling in situations of inherent value) rather than adhering to an increasingly higher standard of living. There will be a profound awareness of the difference between big and great.
8. Those who subscribe to the foregoing points have an obligation directly or indirectly to try to implement the necessary changes.

Notes

Preface

1. Hannah Arendt, *The Human Condition* (Chicago: Univ. of Chicago Press, 1958), 2.

1. Millenarianism in the American Context

1. Thomas Jefferson, "Declaration of the Causes and Necessity for taking up Arms," Jefferson's Fair Copy for the Committee in *The Papers of Thomas Jefferson,* vol. 1, ed. Julian Boyd (Princeton, N.J.: Princeton Univ. Press, 1950), 199.

2. Abraham Lincoln, "Address Delivered at the Dedication of the Cemetery at Gettysburg, November 19, 1863," in *Abraham Lincoln: His Speeches and Writings* (New York: Kraus, 1969), 734.

3. John Winthrop, "A Model of Christian Charity," in *Puritan Political Ideas,* ed. Edmund S. Morgan (Indianapolis: Bobbs-Merrill, 1965), 93.

4. George Grant, *Technology and Empire: Perspectives on North America* (Toronto: House of Anansi, 1969), 17.

5. Ibid.

6. Richard Rubenstein, "Religion, Modernization, and Millenarianism," in *The Coming Kingdom,* ed. M. Darrol Bryant and Donald Dayton (New York: New Era, 1983), 240.

7. The word was originally linked to a passage in the New Testament Book of Revelation, which predicts the rise of a chosen people to a thousand year period of glory. Rev. 20:4 (RSV).

8. Norman Cohn, *The Pursuit of the Millennium: Revolutionary Millenarians and Mystical Anarchists of the Middle Ages,* rev. and exp. ed. (New York: Oxford Univ. Press, 1970), 13.

9. Ibid.

10. Ruth Bloch, *Visionary Republic: Millennial Themes in American Thought, 1756–1800* (Cambridge: Cambridge Univ. Press, 1985), xiii.

11. Ernest Tuveson, *Redeemer Nation* (Chicago: Univ. of Chicago Press, 1968), vii–viii.

12. Ibid., 213–14.

13. Catherine Albanese, *Sons of the Fathers: The Civil Religion of the American Revolution* (Philadelphia: Temple Univ. Press, 1976), 4.

14. Ibid., 224–25.

15. Ibid.

16. Grant, 18.

17. Albanese, *Sons of the Fathers,* 222.

18. Catherine Albanese, *Nature Religion in America: From the Algonkian Indians to the New Age* (Chicago: Univ. of Chicago Press, 1990), 50.

19. Ibid., 10. Albanese states that this future Eden is perceived to be a time of peace and harmony and a place where human beings will be "in charge." These characteristics do not apply to Earth First!'s view of the millennium.

20. Grant, 24.

21. Cecelia Tichi, *New World, New Earth: Environmental Reform in American Literature from the Puritans Through Whitman* (New Haven, Conn.: Yale Univ. Press, 1979), viii–ix.

22. David Brower, *For Earth's Sake: The Life and Times of David Brower* (Salt Lake City: Peregrine Smith, 1990), 428.

23. Frederick Jackson Turner, "An Address delivered at the University of Washington, June 17, 1914," cited in Henry Nash Smith, *Virgin Land: The American West as Symbol and Myth* (Cambridge, Mass.: Harvard Univ. Press, 1970), 253.

24. Smith, 2–3.

25. Dave Foreman, interview by author, Tucson, Ariz., Jan. 24, 1992.

26. James Madison [Publius, pseud.], Federalist 14, in Alexander Hamilton, James Madison, and John Jay, *The Federalist Papers* (New York: Mentor, 1961), 99.

27. Thomas Jefferson, "Letter to Thomas Law, Esq., June 13, 1814," in *The Life and Selected Writings of Thomas Jefferson,* ed. Adrienne Koch and William Peden (New York: Modern Library, 1944), 638.

28. Benjamin Barber, *Strong Democracy: Participatory Politics for a New Age* (Berkeley: Univ. of California Press, 1984), 4.

29. Ibid., 20–21.

30. Theodore Lowi, *The End of Liberalism: Ideology, Policy, and the Crisis of Public Authority* (New York: W. W. Norton, 1969), 71.

31. Ibid., 97.

32. Grant, 27.

33. David Clary, *Timber and the Forest Service* (Lawrence: Univ. Press of Kansas, 1986), 25.

34. Ibid., 28, 22. The latter citation is drawn from a letter that Pinchot wrote to himself (over the signature of the Secretary of Agriculture, James Wilson) on February 1, 1905. That letter outlined the responsibilities of the newly-formed Forest Service.

35. Ibid.

36. Ibid., 196.

37. Ibid., 197. See also Clary's discussion of the Roadless Area Review and Evaluation II, 176ff.

38. Ibid., 199. Clary states that the Forest Service "has done well enough by its office on earth."

39. Ibid., 196.

40. Michael Brown and John May, *The Greenpeace Story* (London: Dorling Kindersley, 1989), 9.

41. Ibid., 13.

42. Dave Foreman, *Confessions of an Eco-Warrior* (New York: Harmony, 1991), 204.

43. Victoria Slind-Flor, "Jailed Researcher Claims Shield," *National Law Journal*, Aug. 9, 1993, 3.

44. Rik Scarce, *Eco-Warriors: Understanding the Radical Environmental Movement* (Chicago: Noble, 1990), 4–7.

45. Ibid., 10.

46. Ibid., 13.

47. Ibid., 49.

48. Ibid.

49. Ibid.

50. Ibid., 53.

51. Ibid., 53–54.

52. Ibid., 54.

53. In accord with Greenpeace's Quaker roots, Greenpeacers regard such actions as violent. Disagreement over this issue led to the departure of Paul Watson, one of the group's founding members. Watson later founded another environmental organization, the Sea Shepherd Conservation Society, which "enforces" international whaling laws by sabotaging ships that are engaged in illegal whaling practices. See Brown and May, 51. Scarce also discusses this issue in *Eco-Warriors*, 54.

54. Scarce's focus on action is, however, echoed in David Peerla's paper "The Moral Optic of Earth First!," discussed below.

55. Christopher Manes, *Green Rage: Radical Environmentalism and the Unmaking of Civilization* (Boston: Little, Brown, 1990), xi.

56. Ibid., 22.

57. Arne Naess, "The Shallow and the Deep, Long-Range Ecology Movement. A Summary," *Inquiry* 16 (1973): 95.

58. Manes notes that the term "biocentrism" is a misnomer. Deep ecologists place the entire community of species at the center of their worldview, not the less specific *bios*, or life. Biocentrism has, however, become the popular term for this perspective, although some deep ecologists use the word "ecocentrism" in its place. Manes, *Green Rage*, 144.

59. Ibid.

60. Ibid., 143. See also George Sessions, "Deep Ecology and New Age," *Earth First!* 7, no. 8 (Mabon/Sept. 23, 1987): 27–30.

61. Manes, *Green Rage*, 45–65.

62. Ibid., 9.

63. Ibid., 146.

64. See Christopher Manes [Miss Ann Thropy, pseud.], "Population and AIDS," *Earth First!*, 7, no. 5 (Beltane/May 1, 1987): 32. This article and "Overpopulation and Industrialization" are discussed in detail in Chapter 6 below.

65. Foreman, *Confessions*, 26.

66. Foreman's other publications are not relevant to this discussion. *The Big Outside* (publication data unavailable) was an atlas of roadless areas that Foreman compiled with another Earth First! founder, Howie Wolke. Today, Foreman regards this as his most important book, on the basis of its contribution to conservation biology. *Ecodefense: A Field Guide to Monkeywrenching* (Tucson: Ned Ludd Books, 1973) was a handbook of ecotage or "monkeywrenching" techniques. It was edited by Foreman and Bill Haywood [pseud.] and included detailed instructions on such things as tree-spiking, disabling road construction equipment, and sabotaging engines.

67. The review of *Coyotes and Town Dogs* in *Earth First!* accuses Zakin of treating Foreman "like a near diety." Beverly Cherner, review of *Coyotes and Town Dogs—Earth First! and the Environmental Movement,* by Susan Zakin, *Earth First!* 14, no. 1 (Samhain/ Nov. 1, 1993): 31. As a result, her book has been criticized by a number of individuals in the movement's social justice faction; many of their points are well-taken. See, for example, Mark Davis, "An Open Letter to Susan Zakin, Author of *Coyotes and Town Dogs,*" *Earth First!* 14, no. 1 (Samhain/Nov. 1, 1993): 3, 14–15.

68. See, for example, Zakin's explication of deep ecology, which comprises only two pages of a book of over four hundred pages. Susan Zakin, *Coyotes and Town Dogs: Earth First! and the Radical Environmental Movement* (New York: Viking, 1993), 244–45.

69. See, for example, Judi Bari, cited in Cherner, review of *Coyotes and Town Dogs,* 31.

70. Foreman, interview.

71. Zakin describes Morgan's admittance to Foreman's circle of friends in Washington, D.C., and later states that she "produced" the movement's first newsletter, but she provides no further description of Morgan's character or insight into her contribution to the movement's development. See, for example, Zakin, *Coyotes and Town Dogs,* 85, 145.

72. Mike Roselle, for example, stated that Zakin "ignores major [Earth First!] campaigns that actually changed the course of conservation history." Another Earth First!er, Judi Bari, questioned why Zakin did not find it relevant that California Earth First! had "saved Cahto Wilderness and Headwaters Forest." Cited in Cherner, review of *Coyotes and Town Dogs,* 31.

73. Again, individuals in the movement's social justice faction have complained about her interpretation of the trial. See, for example, Davis, "An Open Letter to Susan Zakin," 14–15.

74. David Peerla, "The Moral Optic of Earth First!" (paper given at the annual meeting of the Canadian Political Science Association, Calgary, Alberta, June 13, 1994), 5.

75. Ibid., 4.

76. Bron Taylor, "The Religion and Politics of Earth First!," *Ecologist* 21, no. 6 (Nov./Dec. 1991): 259.

77. Ibid.

78. Clifford Geertz, "Religion as a Cultural System," reprinted in *Reader in Comparative Religion: An Anthropological Approach,* ed. William Lessa and Evon Vogt, 3rd ed. (New York: Harper and Row, 1972), 168.

79. See, for example, Mary Douglas, *Natural Symbols* (London: Cresset, 1970), and

Peter Berger, *The Sacred Canopy: Elements of a Sociological Theory of Religion* (New York: Anchor, 1969), appendix 1, 175–77.

80. James Wiser, *Political Philosophy: A History of the Search for Order* (Englewood Cliffs, N.J.: Prentice-Hall, 1983), ix.

81. Eric Voegelin, "Reason: The Classic Experience," *Southern Review* 10, no. 2 (Spring 1974): 237–64.

82. Mark Juergensmeyer, *The New Cold War? Religious Nationalism Confronts the Secular State* (Berkeley: Univ. of California Press, 1993), 33.

83. Taylor, 259.

84. Ibid.

85. Amanda Porterfield, "American Indian Spirituality as a Countercultural Movement," in *Religion in Native North America*, ed. Christopher Vecsey (Moscow: Univ. of Idaho Press, 1990), 152.

86. Taylor, 259. Taylor's arguments concerning this issue are most applicable to those who identify themselves with the social justice faction, not to all of the movement's adherents.

87. Ibid., 262.

88. Ibid., 262, 265–66.

89. Edward Abbey, "Foreward!," in *Ecodefense*, ed. Foreman and Haywood, 2nd ed., cited in Taylor, 266n. Taylor uses this quote as part of his explanation of why Earth First!ers consider the American government to be evil and how they justify their illegal activities.

90. Taylor, 263.

91. Ibid., 264.

92. Michael Barkun, *Disaster and the Millennium* (New Haven, Conn.: Yale Univ. Press, 1974), 18.

93. George Draffan, interview by author, Ballard, Wash., Apr. 8, 1991.

94. Bill Devall and George Sessions, *Deep Ecology: Living as if Nature Mattered* (Salt Lake City: Peregrine Smith, 1985), 70.

95. Ibid. The full deep ecology platform is included in appendix 1 of this book.

96. Andrew McLaughlin, *Regarding Nature: Industrialism and Deep Ecology* (Albany: State Univ. of New York Press, 1993), 201–2.

97. Timothy Weber, *Living in the Shadow of the Second Coming: American Premillennialism, 1875–1982,* Enl. ed. (Grand Rapids, Mich.: Academie, 1983), 9.

98. Cohn, 13.

99. See, for example, Barkun, 18, and Yonina Talmon, "Millenarism," in *The International Encyclopedia of the Social Sciences,* vol. 10 (Macmillan, 1968), 351.

100. See, for example, James Rhodes, *The Hitler Movement: A Modern Millenarian Revolution* (Stanford, Calif.: Hoover Institute Press, 1980).

101. Relative deprivation theory is explained in greater detail by Ted Robert Gurr in his seminal work, *Why Men Rebel* (Princeton, N.J.: Princeton Univ. Press, 1970).

102. David Aberle, "A Note on Relative Deprivation Theory as Applied to Millenarian and Other Cult Movements," in *Millennial Dreams in Action: Essays in Comparative Study,* ed. Sylvia Thrupp (The Hague: Mouton, 1962), 209–14.

103. Ibid., 209.

104. Barkun, 35.

105. Aberle, 209. Barkun suggests that it is decremental deprivation, wherein individuals' circumstances do not change but their capability for realizing them in the future declines, that is most likely to produce a millenarian movement. As will be seen, however, decremental deprivation does not appear to be relevant in the case of Earth First!. See Barkun, 35.

106. Aberle, 211.

107. Anthony Wallace, "Revitalization Movements," *American Anthropologist* 58 (1956): 264–81.

108. Anthony Wallace, *Religion: An Anthropological View* (New York: Random House, 1966), 30–31.

109. Ibid., 268–71.

110. Barkun, 39. Barkun also notes that Wallace sometimes relies on physiological data such as heartbeat and adrenal secretions as evidence of societal stress, while at other times he uses forms of societal pathology such as crime and drunkenness.

111. Talmon, 355.

112. Ibid.

113. Martha Lee and Thomas Flanagan, "The Black Muslims and the Fall of America," *Journal of Religious Studies* 16, nos. 1 and 2 (1988): 140–56.

114. Talmon, 355–56.

115. Ibid., 356.

116. Ibid. In "Religion, Modernization and Millenarianism," for example, Rubenstein argues that many of the American protest movements of the 1960s might be classified as postpolitical millenarian movements.

117. Barkun, 50–51. Barkun uses H. B. M. Murphy's definition of the term "true society"; see H. B. M. Murphy, "Social Change and Mental Health," *Milbank Memorial Fund Quarterly* 39 (1961): 385–445. For Murphy, the true society "may consist of face-to-face contacts only, or [a] whole nation, or may even be largely imaginary" (Murphy, 417).

118. Barkun's definition of disaster is drawn from G. Sjoberg, "Disasters and Social Change," in *Man and Society in Disaster,* ed. G. Baker and D. Chapman (New York: Free Press, 1960), 357.

119. Barkun, 52–53.

120. The other two possible responses are apathy and decay, and defensive structuring. Ibid., 77.

121. Ibid., 205–8.

122. Hal Swasser (Forest Service), cited in Michael Lerner, "The FBI vs. the Monkeywrenchers," *Los Angeles Times Magazine,* Apr. 15, 1990, 21.

123. Cohn, 286.

124. Barkun, 211.

125. Eric Voegelin, *The New Science of Politics* (Chicago: Univ. of Chicago Press, 1952).

2. The Founding of a Movement

1. Stephen Crane, "The Black Riders and Other Lines, Number XXXI," reprinted in *Earth First!* 1, no. 1 (Nov. 1, 1980): 1. The complete work can be found in J. C. Levin-

son, ed., *Crane: Prose and Poetry* (New York: Library Classics of the United States, 1984), 1309.

2. Foreman, *Confessions*, 11.

3. David Brower, 328.

4. Ibid., 344.

5. Foreman, *Confessions*, 21.

6. Carol S. Greenwald, *Group Power* (New York: Praeger, 1977), 181.

7. Susan Zakin, "Earth First!," *Smart*, Sept./Oct. 1989, 91. Earth First! activists were not unaware of this connection. In a 1987 Yellowstone action, several pamphlets were signed "The Tucson Eco-Raiders." See James Coates, "Terrorists for Nature Proclaim Earth First!," *Chicago Tribune*, Aug. 2, 1987, sec. 1, 21.

8. Tom Miller, "What is the Sound of One Billboard Falling," *Berkeley Barb*, Nov. 8–14, 1974, 9–12. The Eco-Raiders were arrested in 1973.

9. Edward Abbey, *The Monkey Wrench Gang* (Philadelphia: J. B. Lippincot, 1979), 5.

10. Foreman, interview.

11. Dave Foreman, telephone interview by author, Mar. 9, 1993.

12. Charles Bowden, "Dave Foreman! In the Face of Reality," *Buzzworm*, Mar./Apr. 1990, 49.

13. Dave Foreman, telephone interview by author, Apr. 27, 1992. Foreman claims his speaking style is derived from his early experience in the church.

14. Foreman, interview. Foreman's offenses were numerous but minor, including infractions such as tearing up his identification card. He "did not take orders well."

15. Foreman, telephone interview, Apr. 27, 1992.

16. Ibid.

17. David Petersen, "The Plowboy Interview, Dave Foreman: No Compromise in Defense of Mother Earth," *Mother Earth News*, Jan./Feb. 1985, 17.

18. Ibid.

19. Foreman, *Confessions*, 14–15.

20. Ibid., 13–16.

21. Foreman, interview.

22. Foreman, *Confessions*, 15.

23. Manes, *Green Rage*, 62.

24. Foreman, *Confessions*, 13.

25. Foreman, interview.

26. Foreman's first wife, Debbie Sease, was a lobbyist for the Sierra Club in Washington, a position she continued to hold after their separation and divorce. Foreman, interview. She is now head of the Sierra Club's Washington office.

27. Foreman, *Confessions*, 16.

28. Foreman, interview.

29. Foreman, *Confessions*, 16.

30. During the RARE II process, a printed t-shirt marked "Citizens for Alternative J" was popular among some Washington environmentalists. Alternative J was the token alternative in the RARE II study that designated all roadless areas as wilderness. Foreman, interview.

31. The Yippies were Abbie Hoffman's counterculture organization; the Zippies

were a splinter group formed by a number of individuals who were disillusioned by the "political opportunism" of the original movement. Manes, *Green Rage,* 68–69.

32. Ibid., 65–69, and Scarce, 58–61.

33. It is also worth noting that Mike Roselle was the youngest of the group and the only one who had no significant ties to the Southwest. These facts are significant with respect to the subsequent history of the movement; the factions that formed during the late 1980s were in part rooted in generational differences and geographic concerns.

34. Scarce, 61.

35. Kenneth Brower, "Mr. Monkeywrench," *Harrowsmith,* Sept./Oct. 1988, 40. Susan Zakin clarifies this issue. According to Zakin, Earth First!'s founders stopped in San Luis, Mexico, feasted on seafood, and then spent the remainder of the evening in the city's *Zona Roja* (Red Zone), traveling from whorehouse to whorehouse. In Zakin's account, Earth First!'s founding occurred the next day. Zakin, *Coyotes and Town Dogs,* 130–31.

36. Gordon Solberg, *Dry Country News,* cited in *Earth First!* 2, no. 4 (March 20, 1982): 3.

37. Ibid.

38. Ibid.

39. Albanese, *Nature Religion in America,* 9–10.

40. Dave Foreman, Memorandum on Earth First Statement of Principles and Membership Brochure, Sept. 1, 1980, 2.

41. Aldo Leopold, "The Round River—A Parable," in *Round River: From the Journals of Aldo Leopold,* ed. Luna B. Leopold (New York: Oxford Univ. Press, 1953), 158–65. It was Bart Koehler who chose this reference; see Scarce, 62.

42. Leopold, "Round River," 158.

43. Ibid. Leopold wrote that human beings ride the logs that float down this river, "and by a little judicious 'burling' have learned to guide their direction and speed. . . . The technique of burling is called economics, the remembering of old routes is called history, the selection of new ones is called statesmanship, the conversation about oncoming riffles and rapids is called politics."

44. Scarce, 62.

45. "Earth First!: The First Three Years," *Earth First! Newsletter* 4, no. 1 (Samhain/Nov. 1, 1983): 11.

46. Lord Byron, "Childe Harold's Pilgrimmage," canto 4, stanza 178, cited in *Nature More* 0, no. 0 (July 1980): 1.

47. Foreman, interview.

48. Ibid.

49. In a later issue of the newsletter, this group is revised to include only seven members: Dave Foreman, Bart Koehler, Mike Roselle, Howie Wolke, and Susan Morgan; A. Cosmos Blank, identified as a wildlife photographer from Iowa; and Randall Gloege, a university professor and former Northern Rockies representative of Friends of the Earth. *Earth First! Newsletter* 1, no. 1 (Samhain/Nov. 1, 1980): 5.

The role of women in the Earth First! hierarchy and their representation in various campaigns became an important issue during the late 1980s. These early actions saw women participate and serve as spokespersons for the movement.

50. Ibid.

51. Dave Foreman, *Nature More* 0, no. 0 (July 1980): 2.

52. Foreman, Interview.

53. Dave Foreman, *Nature More* 0, no. 0 (July 1980): 2.

54. Ibid., 1

55. Ibid. Zakin notes that Debbie Sease, Foreman's first wife, attended the first Round River Rendezvous; *Coyotes and Town Dogs,* 146. At the meeting, Foreman asked Sease to become a member of La Manta Mojada. It is unclear at what point she left the group.

56. Interview with Dave Foreman, cited in Scarce, 63.

57. Draffan, interview.

58. Mitch Friedman, interview by author, Bellingham, Wash., Apr. 16, 1991.

59. Naess, 95–100, and Devall and Sessions, 2–3.

60. Warwick Fox, as cited in Devall and Sessions, 66.

61. Paul Shepard, "Ecology and Man—A Viewpoint," in *The Subversive Science,* ed. Paul Shepard and D. McKinley (Boston: Houghton Mifflin, 1969), 2.

62. Devall and Sessions, 67.

63. Ibid., 69.

64. Dave Foreman, memorandum regarding Earth First Statement of Principles and Membership Brochure, Sept. 1, 1980, 1.

65. Howie Wolke and Dave Foreman, memorandum regarding Earth First, Sept. 1980, 1.

66. Foreman, memorandum, 2.

67. Foreman, interview.

68. Speech by Dave Foreman, Santa Fe, N.M., June 25, 1989, cited in Manes, *Green Rage,* 72.

69. Reserve (Reverse) [pseud.], "We've got to do Some Motherin," *Earth First! Newsletter* 1, no. 8 (Halloween/Oct. 31, 1981): 1.

70. Foreman, memorandum, 2–3.

71. Dave Foreman, "The Hounds of Hell are Howling High," *Earth First! Newsletter* 1, no. 6 (June 21, 1981): 1.

72. Greg Winguard, interview by author, Seattle, Wash., Apr. 10, 1991.

73. Foreman, interview.

74. Reserve (Reverse), 1.

75. Manes, *Green Rage,* 25–26.

76. Ibid., 26.

77. Draffan, interview.

78. Letter to Earth First!, *Earth First! Newsletter* 1, no. 3 (Brigid/Feb. 2, 1982): 8.

79. Editorial, *Earth First Newsletter* 1, no. 1 (Samhain/Nov. 1, 1980): 1.

80. "Earth First Platform," *Earth First Newsletter* 1, no. 1 (Samhain/Nov. 1, 1980): 2–4. This first platform also demanded that the moon be granted wilderness designation, noting that it had already suffered outdoor recreational vehicle abuse. As will be discussed below, humor has been an important element of Earth First's "weaponry" since the movement's beginnings.

81. Wolke and Foreman, memorandum, 1.

82. "Earth First Platform," 4.

83. Dave Foreman, speech to the Second Round River Rendezvous, July 1981, reprinted in *Earth First! Newsletter* 1, no. 7 (Lughnasad[*sic*]/Aug. 1981): 1.

84. Tir Eriaur Aldaron [pseud.], "Ele! Mellonkemmi Greetings Earthfriends!" *Earth First! Newsletter* 1, no. 5 (Beltane/May 1, 1981): 5.

85. Manes, *Green Rage*, 5.

3. The Cracking of Glen Canyon Dam

1. Floyd Dominy, *Lake Powell: Jewel of the Colorado*, cited in Manes, *Green Rage*, 5.

2. Bart Koehler [Johnny Sagebrush, pseud.] "Were You There When They Built Glen Canyon Damn?" *Earth First! Newsletter* 1, no. 4 (Spring equinox/Mar. 20, 1981): 4.

3. The composition of this first group of monkeywrenchers paralleled Abbey's characters (Bonnie Abbzug, Seldom Seen Smith, Doc Sarvis and George Washington Hayduke); however, this symbolism was unintentional. Susan Zakin identifies the individuals who participated in the "cracking" as Dave Foreman, Howie Wolke, Louisa Willcox, Tony Moore, and Bart Koehler; see *Coyotes and Town Dogs*, 149.

4. This discussion is drawn from "Were You There When We Cracked Glen Canyon Damn?" *Earth First! Newsletter*, 1–2, and "Earth First! Springs to Life: Organization Urges Dismantling of Glen Canyon Dam," press release, Mar. 21, 1981, copy in Page, Ariz., FBI file, FOIA #344,522/190-71269.

5. "Were You There When We Cracked Glen Canyon Damn?," 2.

6. Ibid.

7. The text of the petition can be found in *Earth First! Newsletter* 2, no. 2 (Yule/Dec. 1981): 3. The petition identified the dam as "the single most destructive project to the environment ever undertaken in the United States" and demanded that Congress pass legislation "directing the breaching of Glen Canyon Dam and the draining of Lake Powell."

8. Johnny Sagebrush was the pseudonym of Bart Koehler, one of the movement's founders.

9. There were also numerous editorials, many of them hostile. The Grand Junction, Colorado, *Daily Sentinel* referred to members of the group as "damn crackers." *Earth First! Newsletter* 1, no. 5 (Beltane/May 1, 1981): 1. The response to this demonstration was so great that it prompted the movement to search for a media coordinator; see *Earth First! Newsletter* 1, no. 4 (Spring equinox/Mar. 20, 1981): 4.

10. Foreman, memorandum, 3.

11. J. Kevin O'Brien (Federal Bureau of Investigation), letter to the author, Feb. 5, 1992

12. The Salt River Project, letter to the director, Federal Bureau of Investigation, Oct. 1, 1981. FBI file, FOIA #344,522/190-71269.

13. Winguard, interview. Winguard added "I don't approve of that because first, I think it's counter productive, and secondly, I don't feel it's effective. At my own personal level, I have moral beliefs about slaughtering human beings. Other than that, I think just about anything's fair game."

14. Dave Foreman, "In Diversity There is Strength," *Earth First! Newsletter* 1, no. 3 (Brigid/Feb. 2, 1981): 2–3.

15. Ibid., 3.

16. The ideological cohesion of the 1981 membership is perhaps best evidenced in its newsletter. While articles from a wide variety of perspectives were published, such differences caused no serious conflicts. Two seemingly unimportant articles, "Some Reflections on a Regional Flower and Creative (Defensive) Littering," *Earth First! Newsletter* 1, no. 3 (Brigid/Feb. 2, 1981): 6, and a want ad for "One dozen attractive, affectionate hard-drinking women" in the March 1981 issue, illustrate this point.

17. Western Slope Public Interest Congress, "Earth First! Will Find Going Tough," *The Daily Sentinel,* reprinted in *Earth First! Newsletter* 1, no. 5 (Beltane/May 1, 1981): 1.

18. "Earth First! Regional Contacts," *Earth First! Newsletter* 1, no. 5 (Beltane/May 1, 1981): 8.

19. By contrast, 1987 issues of *Earth First!* identified local groups and contacts as "contact points" (see, for example, *Earth First!* 8, no. 1 (Mabon/Sept. 1, 1987): 12.). By this point, however, the "Earth First! Directory" had expanded to contain eight national groups, over seventy local groups and contacts, and nine international contacts (in the United Kingdom, Canada, Australia, Spain, Mexico and Japan).

20. In a hastily added, handwritten appeal, the editors asked that funds be sent in cash or money orders, apparently wishing to avoid the clearance period necessary for checks. Such instruments also made it more difficult for interested agencies such as the FBI to trace Earth First!'s supporters.

21. "On the Road Again or The Great Earth First! Road Show," *Earth First! Newsletter* 1, no. 6 (Litha/June 21, 1981): 6–7.

22. Ibid., 6.

23. "The Great Earth First! Road Show Rumbles On . . . ," *Earth First! Newsletter* 1, no. 7 (Lughnasad[sic]/Aug. 1, 1981): 6. Performances were scheduled in California, Oregon, Washington, Montana, Maine, Connecticut, Washington, D.C., Virginia, Tennessee, Texas, New Mexico, Colorado, Utah, and Arizona. It should be noted that the majority of the planned venues in California did not have local organizers or local groups, a fact that highlights the movement's early membership distribution. Californians did not begin to exert significant influence on Earth First!'s ideology until much later in the movement's history.

24. Michael Taft, *Discovering Saskatchewan Folklore* (Edmonton: NeWest, n.d.), 19.

25. The debates concerning formal organizational structures were swiftly decided. They were followed by two more complex arguments: whether Earth First! was a group or a movement, and whether adherents were members or simply Earth First!ers.

26. See, for example, *Earth First! Newsletter* 1, no. 3 (Brigid/Feb. 2, 1981): 4.

27. Helen Wilson, an artist whose work was featured regularly in *Earth First!,* noted that artists contributed to Earth First! in a subtle but meaningful way. She acknowledged that they were not as popular as the musicians but stated that the relative absence of their work in the journal's end days and in *Wild Earth* was immediately noticed and mourned by many Earth First!ers. Helen Wilson, interview by author, Tucson, Ariz., Jan. 26, 1992.

28. Nancy Zierenberg, interview by athor, Tucson, Ariz., Jan. 26, 1992.

29. Darryl Cherney, interview by author, Seattle, Wash., Apr. 11, 1991.

30. Ibid.

31. Friedman, interview.

32. Ibid.

33. Zierenberg, interview. January 26, 1992.

34. Marcy Willow, "Round River Rendezvous Rare Experience," *Earth First!* 5, no. 2 (Yule/Dec. 21, 1984): 9.

35. "200 Celebrate 4th of July with Earth First!," *Earth First! Newsletter* 1, no. 7 (Lughnasad[*sic*]/Aug. 1, 1981): 1.

36. Michelle Miller, "1986 Round River Rendezvous: Reunite in Idaho!," *Earth First!* 6, no. 1 (Samhain/Nov. 1, 1985): 13. The degree of organization evidenced in these later meetings was also necessitated by their growing scope and size. In 1986, for example, the Rendezvous provided daycare services for Earth First! parents.

37. Wilson, interview.

38. Marcy Willow writes that letters to *Earth First!* also indicated that Earth First!ers themselves understood that to be so. Willow, "Round River Rendezvous Rare Experience," 9.

39. "Bob," cited in Willow, "Round River Rendezvous Rare Experience," 9.

40. Ibid.

41. Dave Foreman, "Speech to the Second Round River Rendezvous," cited in *Earth First! Newsletter* 1, no. 7 (Lughnasad[*sic*]/Aug. 1, 1981): 1.

42. In later years, Foreman further developed this parallel. He identified his philosophical loyalties as lying with Thomas Jefferson's vision of the American state and suggested that the intent of the American Revolution had been subverted with the authorization of corporations, "when the business of America [became] business." Foreman, interview.

43. Dave Foreman, cited in Bowden, 49.

44. "200 Celebrate 4th of July with Earth First!," 1, and Dave Foreman, letter to author, Feb. 22, 1995.

45. By the late 1980s, the demographic character of the movement had changed considerably; a significant proportion of Earth First!ers were under thirty, and a number of them preferred to smoke marijuana rather than drink beer. This choice caused tension within the movement, in part because it emphasized the differences between its older "redneck" and younger "hippie" factions. Foreman made a common sense argument against the use of marijuana when he stated that given Earth First!ers' predilection for illegal tactics, it was foolish to invite arrest for something as trivial as the use of illegal drugs for pleasure: "If monkeywrenchers are serious warriors for Earth, they will minimize things that may draw attention to themselves or jeopardize their operations." Foreman, *Confessions*, 166.

46. Friedman, interview.

47. Dave Foreman, "The Reichstag Fire—1981," *Earth First! Newsletter* 1, no. 7 (Lughnasad[*sic*]/Aug. 1, 1981): 7–8.

48. Ibid., 8.

49. Ibid.

50. Ibid.

51. Ibid.

52. "Earth First! Announces "Ecotricks" Contest," *Earth First! Newsletter* 1, no. 7 (Lughnasad[*sic*]/Aug. 1, 1981): 8.

53. Ibid.

54. Howie Wolke, "Thoughtful Radicalism," *Earth First!* 10, no. 2 (Yule/Dec. 21, 1989): 29.

55. Foreman, *Confessions,* 118.

56. Nancy Morton, interview by Christopher Manes, *60 Minutes Transcript,* vol. 22, no. 24, Mar. 4, 1990, 4.

57. The article was reprinted from his book *Ecodefense* and was later printed once more in *Confessions of an Eco-Warrior.* Dave Foreman, "Strategic Monkeywrenching," *Earth First!* 5, no. 6 (Litha/June 21, 1985): 22–23.

58. Ibid., 22.

59. Edward Abbey, *Hayduke Lives!* (Boston: Little, Brown, 1990), 110.

60. Foreman, "Strategic Monkeywrenching," 22–23.

61. Draffan, interview.

62. Wilson, interview.

63. Zierenberg, interview. Ms. Zierenberg added that those individuals who had served time in jail also felt that they were distinguished from the group as a whole.

64. Winguard, interview.

65. Mike Roselle and Darryl Cherney, "Ballad of the Lonesome Tree Spiker," from *They Sure Don't Make Hippies Like They Used To,* home recording; reprinted in Greg King, "Redwood Tree Climbers," *Earth First!* 7, no. 3 (Mabon/Sept. 23, 1987): 6. Earth First!ers referred to Forest Service Officers as "Freddies."

66. Bowden, 48.

67. Industry spokespersons suggest that this might be true. If pressed, they admit that its property damage is far beyond published estimates. Interviews, Washington logging industry. At the same time, however, many Earth First!ers argued that the cost of some forms of monkeywrenching, in terms of public approval, rendered them less than effective. This was particularly true of tree spiking. Draffan, interview.

68. Foreman, interview.

69. See, for example, Jim Robbins, "The Environmental Guerrillas," *Boston Globe Magazine,* Mar. 27, 1988, or Nancy Shute, "Dave Foreman Meets the Feds," *Outside,* Sept. 1989, 15. Also Foreman, interview.

70. Dave Foreman, quoted in Tony De Paul, "Earth First!," *Sunday Journal Magazine* (Rhode Island), Mar. 26, 1989, 8.

71. Foreman, interview.

72. Darryl Cherney, interview by author, Ballard, Wash., Apr. 10, 1991.

73. Foreman, *Confessions,* 146.

74. Ibid.

75. "Show Over, EF! Roadies Unwind," *Earth First! Newsletter* 2, no. 3 (Yule/Dec. 21, 1981): 4, and "Earth First!: The First Three Years," *Earth First!* 4, no. 1 (Samhain/Nov. 1, 1983): 11–12.

76. Dave Foreman, "Earth First!," *The Progressive* 45, no. 10 (Oct. 1981): 39–42.

77. "Earth First!: The First Three Years," 11.

78. Dave Foreman, "Earth First!," reprinted in *Earth First!* 2, no. 3 (Brigid/Feb. 2, 1982): 4–5.

79. Ibid.

80. Those who accuse Foreman of sexism would do well to read the *Progressive* article. Foreman there condemns sexism in the conservation movement (in particular, the Washington offices of the Wilderness Society) and links the oppression of the Earth with the oppression of women. Ibid.

81. Ibid.

82. Later, Foreman distinguished people who "had the wilderness gene" and who would "fight like antibodies and phagocytes for the wild, for the precious native diversity of our planet" from the general population. See Foreman, *Confessions, 57–58.*

83. The largest audience was in Arcata, California, where the Road Show artists performed as guests at an annual fair. "Road Show Progress!," *Earth First! Newsletter* 1, no. 8 (Halloween/Oct. 31, 1981): 3, and "Show Over, EF! Roadies Unwind," 1.

84. By the end of 1981, Earth First!'s merchandise selection included t-shirts, song-books, calendars, and bumper stickers, with messages ranging from "Hayduke Saves" and "Rednecks for Wilderness" to "Damn Watt not Wilderness" and "Malthus was Right." Advertisement, *Earth First! Newsletter* 1, no. 8 (Halloween/Oct. 31, 1981): 9.

85. "You and Earth First!," *Earth First!* 2, no. 5 (Yule/Dec. 21, 1981): 5.

4. The Battle Begins

1. [from Oregon], "Letter to Earth First!," *Earth First! Newsletter* 2, no. 4 (Eostar ritual/Mar. 20, 1982): 2.

2. Morgan remained an active Earth First!er for some time but dropped out as the conflict between its factions escalated. She later joined the environmental group Project Lighthawk. Foreman, interview.

3. See *Earth First! Newsletter* 2, no. 2 (Yule/Dec. 21, 1981): 2, and 2, no. 3 (Brigid/Feb. 2, 1982): 2–3. The sudden increase in letters also reflected the rapid increase in Earth First!'s membership that had occurred at the close of 1981. Foreman's article in *The Progressive* was particularly successful in attracting new members. The February newsletter reprinted many of the responses it had received to that article; most requested membership information.

4. Pete Dustrud, "Recreating," *Earth First! Newsletter* 2, no. 3 (Brigid/Feb. 2, 1982): 6.

5. Dave Foreman, "Earth First! Regional Contacts" reprinted in *Earth First! Newsletter* 2, no. 3 (Brigid/Feb. 2, 1982): 6, and Dave Foreman, "Earth First!," *Earth First! Newsletter* 2, no. 4 (Eostar Ritual/Mar. 20, 1982): 10.

6. Foreman, interview.

7. Ibid.

8. "EF! Contacts," *Earth First! Newsletter* 2, no. 3 (Brigid/Feb. 2, 1982): 1. This front page coverage of the contact list is unique in Earth First! history; it is testament to the importance of the change that Dustrud formalized and to the influx of new Earth First!ers.

9. Ibid.

10. Ibid.

11. Pete Dustrud, "Earth First!er in Eugene," *Earth First! Newsletter* 2, no. 4 (Eostar Ritual/Mar. 20, 1982): 2.

12. The Circle was never formally dissolved, but over time, its role diminished. According to Foreman, the last Circle meeting occurred at the 1986 Round River Rendezvous. "The Circle may be the only ruling body in the history of the world that really did wither away." Foreman, interview. References to the Circle continue as late as 1988, but by that point, the Circle's purpose and membership had changed dramatically. It appears to have become the Rendezvous' major communal meeting. John Davis, "A View of the Vortex," *Earth First!* 8, no. 7 (Lughnasadh/Aug. 1, 1988): 2.

13. Dustrud, "Earth First!er in Eugene," 2. Individuals traveled to the meeting from other locations in Oregon and from California, New Mexico, Nevada, and Montana.

14. Ibid. "Marcy" is Marcy Willow.

15. Ibid.

16. Foreman, interview. Foreman is quoting Aldo Leopold's *A Sand County Almanac* (New York: Oxford Univ. Press, 1949), vii. Foreman misquotes Leopold slightly, substituting "those" for "some."

17. Foreman, *Confessions*, 55–58.

18. Ibid., 58.

19. Wilson, interview. See also Dave Foreman, *Nature More* 0, no. 0 (July 1980): 1.

20. Dave Foreman [Chim Blea, pseud.], "Reducing Population," *Earth First! Newsletter* 3, no. 6 (Lughnasad[sic]/Aug. 1, 1983): 3.

21. Ibid. With respect to immigration, Blea recommended that minor exceptions be made, for example, part-American children in Southeast Asia. In 1987, Edward Abbey initiated another Earth First! debate on immigration with a letter to the *Bloomsbury Review* that also suggested the United States close its borders to all immigrants.

22. Ibid. In an earlier article, "The Question of Babies," Chim Blea presented an emotional account of "her" decision to have an abortion; Blea admitted only a brief regret. It would have been "One more to cause suffering. One more to suffer." Dave Foreman [Chim Blea, pseud.], "The Question of Babies," *Earth First! Newsletter* 2, no. 6 (Litha/June 1982): 3.

23. Draffan, interview.

24. Foreman, interview.

25. Ibid.

26. Draffan, interview.

27. Ibid.

28. Reed Noss, "Deep Ecology, Elitism and Reproduction," *Earth First!* 4, no. 5 (Beltane/May 1, 1984): 16.

29. Ibid.

30. Ibid.

31. Ibid.

32. Ibid.

33. See, for example, Dave Ort, letter to the editor, *Earth First!* 6, no. 5 (Beltane/May 1, 1986): 3.

34. "Klairice," letter to the editor, *Earth First!* 6, no. 4 (Eostar/Mar. 20, 1986): 23.

35. Lynn Jacobs, interview by author, Tucson, Ariz., Jan. 24, 1992.

36. "The Secretary of the Black Committee of the Independent Luddites of Nottinghamshire Division to R. Newcombe and Son, Nov. 11, 1816," cited in George Rude, *Ideology and Popular Protest* (New York: Pantheon, 1980), 152.

37. Edward Abbey, *The Monkey Wrench Gang* (Philadelphia: J. B. Lippincott, 1975), 5.

38. Ibid., 67–68.

39. FBI agents did not immediately grasp this historical allusion. In a 1982 letter to James Watt, an individual identifying himself as "Ned Lud, Rocky Mountain Regional Coordinator, Earth First!" threatened that the group would pursue civil disobedience action if environmentally hazardous activies were not stopped. In the course of investigating this document, the FBI processed the letter through the Documents Section, Laboratory Division, and the Latent Section, Identification Division, where it was compared with the Anonymous Letter File, type checked, and examined for identifiable marks and fingerprints. Despite this detailed and thorough investigation, a report on a letter from "Ned Lad" was filed. Freedom of Information Request No. 344,522. Letter to Assistant U. S. Attorney C. Phillip Miller, Jan. 27, 1983.

40. Dave Foreman, "Violence and Earth First!," *Earth First! Newsletter* 2, no. 4 (Eostar Ritual/Mar. 20, 1982).

41. Ibid.

42. Dave Foreman, "Ludd Readers," *Earth First! Newsletter* 2, no. 4 (Eostar Ritual/Mar. 20, 1982): 11. This book was later published as *Ecodefense: A Field Guide to Monkeywrenching.*

43. Ibid.

44. "Dear Ned Ludd," *Earth First! Newsletter* 2, no. 5 (Beltane/May 1, 1982): 7.

45. Pete Dustrud, "Dear Readers, You now have a New Editor," *Earth First!* 2, no. 7 (Lughnasad[*sic*]/Aug. 1, 1982): 2. Dustrud's identification of the "the few reader responses" was clearly wishful thinking. Monkeywrenching tactics subsequently constituted a significant percentage of "Dear Earth First!" letters.

46. The last official act of the Circle was its acceptance of Pete Dustrud's resignation. Ibid.; Foreman, interview; and Foreman, letter.

47. Dave Foreman, editorial, *Earth First!* 2, no. 7 (Lughnasad[*sic*]/Aug. 1, 1982): 2.

48. Ibid.

49. Ibid.

50. Dave Foreman, "An Environmental Strategy for the '80s," *Earth First!* 2, no. 8 (Mabon/Sept. 21, 1982): 7.

51. Dave Foreman, "Guidelines on Earth First! Wilderness Proposals," *Earth First!* 3, no. 1 (Samhain/Nov. 1, 1982): 11.

52. Ibid.

53. Ibid.

54. Foreman, interview.

55. Dave Foreman [Chim Blea, pseud.], "The Terror of Nuclear War," *Earth First!* 3, no. 1 (Samhain/Nov. 1, 1982): 3. The term "buncombe" or "bunkum" means nonsense or claptrap. It is derived from the rhetorical tendencies of a congressman from Buncombe County in North Carolina during the early 1820s.

56. Ibid.

57. Foreman, interview.

58. Notably, there was no civil disobedience training provided to participants in either the Salt Creek or Bisti protests. Foreman, letter.

59. Bart Koehler, "The Battle of Salt Creek," *Earth First!* 3, no. 2 (Yule/Brigid/Dec. 21, 1982): 1.

60. Foreman, letter.

61. Koehler, "The Battle of Salt Creek," 1.

62. Ibid. See also Joe Kane, "Mother Nature's Army," *Esquire,* Feb. 1987, 101, and Mary Engel, "Earth Man," *Santa Fe Reporter,* Feb. 14–20, 1989, 9.

63. Bart Koehler, "Bisti Mass Tresspass," *Earth First!* 3, no. 2 (Yule/Brigid/Dec. 21, 1982): 11.

64. Ibid.

65. Karen Brown, "Bisti Circus," *Earth First!* 3, no. 3 (Eostar/Mar. 21, 1983): 4. The region is now designated as a Wilderness Area.

66. Tom Galazen, letter to the editor, *Earth First!* 3, no. 2 (Yule/Brigid/Dec. 21, 1982): 5.

67. Dave Foreman, "Around the Campfire," *Earth First!* 3, no. 2 (Yule/Brigid/Dec. 21, 1982): 2.

68. Ibid.

69. "Earth First! Local Groups and Contacts," *Earth First!* 3, no. 2 (Yule/Brigid/Dec. 21, 1982): 8. In early 1983, the paper also began to publish letters from Canadians. See, for example, *Earth First!* 3, no. 3 (Eostar/Mar. 21, 1983): 3.

70. Zakin, *Coyotes and Town Dogs,* 221.

71. Interestingly, the Ghost Shirt Dance was also a millenarian movement.

72. "Cincinnati, Ohio," letter to the editor, *Earth First!* 3, no. 3 (Eostar/Mar. 21, 1983): 3.

73. "Earth First! Foundation," *Earth First!* 3, no. 4 (Beltane/May 1, 1983): 8. In March 1982, the journal had published a brief article noting that steps were underway to create a tax-exempt foundation. "Foundation for EF!," *Earth First!* 2, no. 4 (Eostar/Mar. 20, 1982): 5.

74. Draffan, interview.

75. "Earth First!: The First Three Years," *Earth First!* 4, no. 1 (Samhain/Nov. 1, 1983): 12. See also Mike Roselle [Nagasaki Johnson, pseud.], "Road Show Diary," *Earth First!* 3, no. 3 (Eostar/Mar. 21, 1983): 12.

76. Mike Roselle [Nagasaki Johnson, pseud.], "Road Show Diary," 12.

77. "Blockade Updates," *Earth First!* 3, no. 3 (Eostar/Mar. 12, 1983): 1.

78. For ten years the Sierra Club and other mainstream environmental groups had successfully prevented the completion of this road using traditional tactics such as environmental impact statements, appeals, and lawsuits. See *Earth First!* 3, no. 3 (Eostar/Mar. 21, 1983): 1, 5.

79. Marija Eloheimo, "No G-O Road Arrest," *Earth First!* 3, no. 4 (Beltane/May 1, 1983): 6.

80. "No G-O Road!," *Earth First!* 3, no. 5 (Litha/June 21, 1983): 15.

81. The Gasquet-Orleans protest was coordinated jointly with the Bald Mountain

demonstrations. It was not, however, specifically mentioned in any of the interviews that I conducted, and after its success, it is rarely mentioned in *Earth First!*.

82. Chant Thomas, "Kalmiopsis/Bald Mountain Background," *Earth First!* 3, no. 4 (Beltane/May 1, 1983): 7.

83. Ibid.

84. A list provided in *Earth First!* outlined seventeen of those sales, which totaled over one hundred and twenty million board feet of timber. "Upcoming Timber Sales in Kalmiopsis (From T.S. Map F.Y. 82–85)," *Earth First!* 3, no. 4 (Beltane/May 1, 1983): 7.

85. Dave Foreman, Howie Wolke, and Bart Koehler, "The Earth First! Wilderness Preserve System," *Earth First!* 3, no. 5 (Litha/June 21, 1983): 9.

86. Ibid.

87. Ibid. The Earth First! Wilderness Preserve Plan did, however, make exceptions for indigenous peoples living traditional (pre-1500) ways of life.

88. The area was identified as "the most diverse coniferous forest on Earth . . . [it] runs from nearly Coos Bay in Oregon to Clear Lake in California." Earth First! advocated that it be accessible only by boat, airplane, or foot. Ibid.

89. "Save Bigfoot and the Big Woods, What You Can Do," *Earth First!* 3, no. 4 (Beltane/May 1, 1983): 6.

90. Ibid.

91. Mike Roselle, Steve Marsden, Petro Tama, and Kevin Everhart were the individuals concerned. "Wilderness War in Oregon, Blockaders Assaulted by Bulldozer," *Earth First!* 3, no. 5 (Litha/June 21, 1983): 1.

92. Molly Campbell, "#3 Statements, Personal Accounts," *Earth First!* 3, no. 5 (Litha/June 21, 1983): 7.

93. Peter Swanson, "#3 Statements, Personal Accounts," 7.

94. "Wilderness War in Oregon, Blockaders Assaulted by Bulldozer," 4.

95. "Bald Mountain Road Stopped!!," *Earth First!* 3, no. 6 (Lughnasad[sic]/Aug. 1, 1983): 1.

96. The Oregon Wilderness Act of 1984 effectively negated the court-issued injunction against further development. By 1987, logging was underway at multiple sites in the northern Kalmiopsis, but the Bald Mountain Road was never completed. Scarce, 68.

97. "Round River Rendezvous," *Earth First!* 3, no. 6 (Lughnasad[sic]/Aug. 1, 1983): 1, 4–5.

98. Marcy Willow, "You," from a speech given at the 1983 Round River Rendezvous, reprinted in *Earth First!* 3, no. 6 (Lughnasad[sic]/Aug. 1, 1983): 3.

99. Ibid.

100. "Round River Rendezvous," 4.

101. These story elements were referred to as "The Speech." Friedman, interview.

102. Kenneth Brower, 47.

103. Ibid. Watt was a favorite target. An article in the November 1983 issue of *Earth First!* purports to be his "Last Environmental Statement." Supported by biblical quotes, "Watt" advocates a strengthening of U. S. environmental policy in preparation for the apocalypse. "Jim Watt's Last Environmental Statement," *Earth First!* 4, no. 1 (Samhain/Nov. 1, 1983): 18.

104. "Earth First!: The First Three Years," 11–13.

105. Dave Foreman, "Earth First! and Non Violence, A Discussion," *Earth First!* 3, no. 7 (Mabon/Sept. 23, 1983): 11.

106. Dave Foreman [Chim Blea, pseud.], "Cat Tracks," *Earth First!* 4, no. 2 (Yule/Dec. 22, 1983): 17.

107. Ibid.

108. Ibid. In this argument, Foreman was supported by Howie Wolke, who had earlier asserted that the success of the Kalmiopsis nonviolent direct action could be measured only in terms of its immediate goal, stopping the Bald Mountain Road. Likewise, Wolke argued that "[i]n defense of wilderness, freedom and diversity of life, we must use every available tool and tactic: intellectual, political, legal, illegal, passive, and—violent." Howie Wolke, "The Grizzly Den," *Earth First!* 3, no. 7 (Mabon/Sept. 23, 1983): 12. At this point, Earth First!ers used the terms "direct action" and "civil disobedience" interchangeably, but usually "direct actions" referred to activities that were directly aimed at saving specific wilderness areas, while "civil disobedience" events were those activities directly aimed at raising public awareness of environmental issues. These categories were not mutually exclusive (direct actions often influence public opinion, and civil disobedience events often helped to save wilderness) but this distinction is important later in the movement's history.

109. Dave Foreman, "Around the Campfire," *Earth First!* 4, no. 1 (Samhain/Nov. 1, 1983): 2.

110. Dave Foreman, "Around the Campfire," *Earth First!* 3, no. 7 (Mabon/Sept. 23, 1983): 2.

111. Manes, *Green Rage,* 68–69.

112. Dave Foreman, "Around the Campfire," *Earth First!* 3, no. 6 (Lughnasad/Aug. 1, 1983): 2. Foreman was quoting Ramiro Reynaga Burgoa of the South American Indian Council.

113. Mike Roselle [Nagasaki Johnson, pseud.], "Thou Shalt not Nuke," *Earth First!* 3, no. 7 (Mabon/Sept. 23, 1983): 11.

114. "Sinkyone: Last Battle of the Redwoods?," *Earth First!* 3, no. 7 (Mabon/Sept. 23, 1983): 7.

115. See, for example, Mike Roselle, "Tree-Huggers Save Redwoods," *Earth First!* 4, no. 1 (Samhain/Nov. 1, 1983): 1.

116. Cherney, interview, Apr. 10, 1991.

5. The Eve of the Apocalypse

1. Andrew Bard Schmookler, "Schmookler Replies to Anarchists' Replies to Schmookler's Reply to the Anarchists," *Earth First!* 7, no. 8 (Mabon/Sept. 23, 1987): 26. Schmookler has since written a series of books on social theory. His article was part of a two-year debate on the "best society" that began with a review of his book, *The Parable of the Tribes.* The debate took place in *Earth First!* between May, 1986 and March, 1987, and will be summarized in chapter 6.

2. Draffan, interview.

3. Renee Reed, interview by author, Seattle, Wash., Apr. 19, 1991.

4. Friedman, interview. Friedman was 27 at the time of this interview. He now manages the Greater Ecosystem Alliance in Bellingham, Wash.

5. Bill Pickell (General Manager, Washington Contract Loggers' Association), letter to author, Jan. 7, 1991.

6. Tony VanGessel, interview by author, Apr. 16, 1991, Bellingham, Wash.; Zierenberg, interview; Rod Mondt, interview by author, Jan. 26, 1992, Tucson, Ariz. Zierenberg and Mondt identified this aspect of the movement as part of the cause of the bitterness of its eventual split. Dave Foreman was known affectionately as "Uncle Digger" and his departure was interpreted as a betrayal. Many referred to the split as a "divorce."

7. Kane, 102. Nancy Morton, another Earth First!er, was indirectly subsidizing the movement by providing food and lodging for Foreman and a number of others. Foreman, interview.

8. See, for example, O. Rana (Sweden), letter to the editor, Earth First! 4, no. 4 (Eostar/Mar. 20, 1984): 3, or Australia [pseud.], letter to the editor, Earth First! 4, no. 6 (Litha/June 20, 1984): 3.

9. It is unclear whether or not Earth First! was attracting a substantial international following during this period. Its June 1984 contact list included three international addresses, two of which were affiliated with the Australian Rainforest Campaign (New South Wales, Australia, and the Western Solomon Islands) and one that was offered by a traveling American (in Kyoto, Japan). "Local Earth First! Contacts," Earth First! 4, no. 6 (Litha/June 20, 1984): 8.

10. Mike Roselle, "Burger King Protest Set," Earth First! 4, no. 4 (Eostar/Mar. 20, 1984): 1.

11. Mike Roselle, "Earth First! Protests Rainforest Burgers," Earth First! 4, no. 6 (Litha/June 20, 1984): 11, 12–13.

12. Bill Devall, "The Edge: The Ecology Movement in Australia," Earth First! 4, no. 5 (Beltane/May 1, 1984): 12–13.

13. Coverage of rainforest issues was expanded in 1985, when Earth First! included the Rainforest Action Network News as an irregular insert. The first Rainforest Action and Information Network (RAIN) insert was included in Earth First! 5, no. 6 (Litha/June 21, 1985): 15–18. These inserts also addressed international rainforest issues.

14. See, for example, Rick Davis, "Crime in the Hidaka Mountains: Japan's Grizzly Threatened," Earth First! 5, no. 2 (Yule/Dec. 21, 1984): 10.

15. Kane, 102, and Karen Franklin and Janet Sowell, "The Timber Terrorists," American Forests, Mar./Apr. 1987, 42.

16. "Hardesty Avengers Spike Trees," Earth First! 5, no. 1 (Samhain/Nov. 1, 1984): 1. The journal's report of this tree spiking is unusual; the editors usually avoided directly linking Earth First! to illegal activities.

17. Ibid. Manes cites the name of this organization as "The Bonnie Abbzug Feminist Garden Party" and claims that Mike Roselle was the individual responsible for that tree spiking. The reference to Bonnie Abbzug was an allusion to a character in The Monkey Wrench Gang. Manes, Green Rage, 99–100.

18. Kane, 102. Kane argues that this sudden rise in monkeywrenching was the result of the publication of Foreman's book Ecodefense, but that book was not published until early 1985. The rise in tree spiking was likely related to the publication of a "Tree Spiking" column in "Dear Ned Ludd," the journal's monkeywrenching "how-to" page. William Haywood [pseud.], "Tree Spiking," Earth First! 4, no. 4 (Eostar/Mar. 20, 1984): 14.

19. See, for example, "Forest Service Logs Texas Wilderness," *Earth First!* 5, no. 2 (Yule/Dec. 21, 1984): 1.

20. Jacky Robinson, "Florida Earth First!," *Earth First!* 4, no. 4 (Eostar/Mar. 20, 1984): 7.

21. Peggy Bond, "Montana Earth First! Takes Senator's Office," *Earth First!* 4, no. 8 (Lughnasadh/Aug. 1, 1984): 1.

22. Ibid., 1, 6–7.

23. See, for example, "Mine Threatens Saguaro National Monument," *Earth First!* 4, no. 6 (Litha/June 20, 1984): 6.

24. R. F. Mueller, "Coors Invades Shenandoah Valley," *Earth First!* 4, no. 3 (Brigid/ Feb. 2, 1984): 15.

25. "Coors Boycott!," *Earth First!* 2, no. 4 (Eostar/Mar. 20, 1982): 12. In this article, the company's connections to James Watt, Ann Gorsuch, and Bob Burford, and its funding of the Mountain States Legal Foundation, were cited as the reason for the boycott.

26. "Boycott Coors" and "Boycott Coors 'Beer'" bumperstickers were "Trinkets and Snake Oil" staples. See, for example, "Trinkets and Snake Oil," *Earth First!* 13, no. 6 (Litha/June 21, 1993): 37.

27. Roselle, "Earth First! Protests Rainforest Burgers," 11–13.

28. Ibid., 11.

29. Ibid. Many Burger King franchise owners admitted that they used rainforest beef (because other fast food restaurants used it as well) but promised to discuss the matter with Burger King's head office. The protests also drew media attention to the issue.

30. Kathy Trendler and Don Presley, "Tuolumne," *Earth First!* 4, no. 3 (Brigid/Feb. 2, 1984): 5, and "Save the Tuolumne!," *Earth First!* 4, no. 5 (Beltane/May 1, 1984): 18–19.

31. Dave Foreman, "Around the Campfire," *Earth First!* 5, no. 1 (Samhain/Nov. 1, 1984): 2.

32. See, for example, "Middle Santiam Heats Up," *Earth First!* 4, no. 6 (Litha/June 20, 1984): 1.

33. Draffan, interview.

34. George Draffan, "Cathedral Forest Action Group Fights for Oregon Old Growth," *Earth First!* 4, no. 6 (Litha/June 20, 1984): 4. Draffan's article also includes the group's demands, among them a moratorium on cutting and roadbuilding in old growth ecosystems and a restructuring of the United States Forest Service.

35. Draffan, interview. The "Bonnie Abbzug" spiking, discussed above, was part of the Santiam protest.

36. In his book *Confessions of an Eco-Warrior,* Foreman reflected on the creation of CFAG. He wrote that in cases where an environmental group's diversity hindered its effectiveness, fragmentation was the best solution. He identified the creation of CFAG as the best example of such a situation. The participants had not tried to change Earth First! but instead formed another organization. Foreman, *Confessions,* 173–174.

37. Reed Noss, "Deep Ecology, Elitism and Reproduction," *Earth First!* 4, no. 5 (Beltane/May 1, 1984): 16.

38. Dave Foreman, "Living by the Green Rule," speech to the 1984 Round River Rendezvous, Libby, Mont., July, 1984; reprinted in Petersen, 19.

39. Ibid.

40. Ibid.

41. Jasper Carlton and Gary Lawless, "Carving up the Cabinet Mts Wilderness," *Earth First!* 4, no. 5 (Beltane/May 1, 1984): 1.

42. Ibid.

43. Petersen, 20.

44. (Various), "1984: Wilderness Boom or Bust?," *Earth First!* 5, no. 2 (Yule/Dec. 21, 1984): 18–21.

45. Petersen, 20. Nancy Morton was still providing food and shelter for many of those who worked on the journal.

46. Lance Christie, "Earth First! Foundation," *Earth First!* 5, no. 5 (Beltane/May 1, 1985): 16.

47. "The Articles of Incorporation of the Earth First! Foundation," cited in Christie, "Earth First! Foundation," 16.

48. "Earth First! Foundation Works for YOU," *Earth First!* 6, no. 8 (Mabon/Sept. 23, 1986): 11. It funded over $19,000 worth of research and "grassroots education" projects.

49. Advertisement, *Earth First!* 5, no. 3 (Brigid/Feb. 2, 1985): 23.

50. Dave Foreman, "Around the Campfire," *Earth First!* 5, no. 3 (Brigid/Feb. 2, 1985): 2.

51. Dave Foreman, "Strategic Monkeywrenching" (from *Ecodefense*), reprinted in *Earth First!* 5, no. 6 (Litha/June 21, 1985): 22–23.

52. Roselle, cited in Manes, *Green Rage,* 82.

53. Manes notes that Michael Kerrick, the Willamette National Forest Supervisor, denounced the book at a congressional hearing and threatened to close national forest logging areas to the public if such sabotage occurred. Kerrick later introduced that policy, a fact that Manes cites as evidence that *Ecodefense* "changed forever the way public lands policy was made in this country." *Green Rage,* 92–93.

54. Dave Foreman, "Welcome to Earth First!," *Earth First!* 5, no. 5 (Beltane/May 1, 1985): 16.

55. Ibid.

56. Ibid.

57. Ibid.

58. Mike Roselle, "Oregon Trials," *Earth First!* 5, no. 2 (Yule/Dec. 21, 1984): 6.

59. Manes, *Green Rage,* 100.

60. Ibid. See also, Ron Huber, "Treeclimbing Hero," *Earth First!* 5, no. 6 (Litha/June 21, 1985): 1–4.

61. Protesters usually flew huge banners declaring their cause. At Millennium Grove, Jakubal's banners read "Earth First!" and "Don't Cut Us Down" while Huber's declared "Ecotopia is Rising." Ibid.

62. Ron Huber, "Battle for Millenium [*sic*] Grove," *Earth First!* 5, no. 7 (Lughnasadh/Aug. 1, 1985): 1–6, and Manes, *Green Rage,* 101.

63. Dave Foreman, "Around the Campfire," *Earth First!* 5, no. 6 (Litha/June 21, 1985): 2.

64. Ibid.

65. Dave Foreman, "Around the Campfire," *Earth First!* 5, no. 7 (Lughnasadh/Aug. 1, 1985): 2.

66. Ibid.

67. "Wolke Busted for Alleged Monkeywrenching," *Earth First!* 5, no. 7 (Lughnasadh/Aug. 1, 1985): 22.

68. Howie Wolke, *Wilderness on the Rocks* (Tucson: Ned Ludd Books, 1991), i.

69. Zakin, *Coyotes and Town Dogs,* 279.

70. James Jackson, "Demonstration at the Biological Crossroads," *Earth First!* 5, no. 4 (Eostar/Mar. 20, 1985): 6.

71. Mike Roselle, "Meares Island: Canada's Old Growth Struggle," *Earth First!* 5, no. 3 (Brigid/Feb. 2, 1985): 1.

72. Arthur Dogmeat [pseud.], "The Travesty of Yellowstone Grizzly Management," *Earth First!* 5, no. 4 (Eostar/Mar. 20, 1985): 5.

73. Steve Marsden, "Freddies Attack North Kalmiopsis . . . Again," *Earth First!* 5, no. 3 (Brigid/Feb. 2, 1985): 14.

74. Marcy Willow, "35 States Attend Round River Rendezvous," *Earth First!* 5, no. 7 (Lughnasadh/Aug. 1, 1985): 15.

75. Ibid.

76. Ibid.

77. Dave Foreman, "Around the Campfire," *Earth First!* 6, no. 1 (Samhain/Nov. 1, 1985): 2.

78. Ibid.

79. By November of 1985, there were regional groups across the United States, including Colorado, Idaho, Arkansas, Alaska, Nevada, New Mexico, New Hampshire, Hawaii, Virginia, and Washington, D.C., among others. "Directory," *Earth First!* 6, no. 1 (Samhain/Nov. 1, 1985): 13.

80. Dave Foreman, "Around the Campfire," *Earth First!* 6, no. 3 (Brigid/Feb. 2, 1986): 2.

81. Articles focusing on Earth First! appeared in the *New York Times,* the *Wall Street Journal, U. S. News and World Report,* and *Mother Jones.*

82. Dave Foreman, "Around the Campfire," *Earth First!* 6, no. 5 (Beltane/May 1, 1986): 2.

83. Dave Foreman, "Around the Campfire," *Earth First!* 6, no. 3 (Brigid/Feb. 2, 1986): 2.

84. Ibid.

85. Ibid.

86. Foreman, *Confessions,* 172.

87. Dave Foreman, "Around the Campfire," *Earth First!* 6, no. 4 (Eostar/Mar. 20, 1986): 2.

88. Friedman, interview.

89. Dean Kuipers, "Razing Arizona," *Spin,* Sept. 1989, 34. Foreman claims that these individuals were not Earth First!ers but rather antinuclear activists. Foreman, letter.

90. While Earth First!'s attention was predominantly focused on the protection of wilderness areas, the journal occasionally featured articles on nuclear power and nuclear

weapons. The majority of these articles were written by Mary Davis, using various pseudonyms. Davis's son John later became editor of *Earth First!*.

91. FBI file, FOIA #344,522/190-71269.

92. See, for example, Willow, "35 States Attend Round River Rendezvous," 15.

93. the captain [pseud.], "North Kalmiopsis Under Attack—Again," *Earth First!* 6, no. 6 (Litha/June 21, 1986): 12.

94. George Balu, "Yellowstone Superintendent Says 'Shove It!'," *Earth First!* 6, no. 4 (Eostar/Mar. 20, 1986): 1.

95. Randall T. Restless, "March for the Bears," *Earth First!* 7, no. 1 (Samhain/Nov. 1, 1986): 10.

96. Mike O'Rizay, "Freddies Murder Millennium Grove," *Earth First!* 6, no. 6 (Litha/June 21, 1986): 13.

97. Ibid.

98. Ibid.

99. Christopher Manes [Miss Ann Thropy, pseud.], "Technology and Mortality," *Earth First!* 7, no. 1 (Samhain/Nov. 1, 1986): 18.

100. Ibid.

101. Ibid.

102. Ibid.

103. Ibid.

104. Ibid.

105. Ibid.

106. See, for example, letters to the editor, *Earth First!* 7, no. 2 (Yule/Dec. 21, 1986): 3. One individual supported her argument by stating that "no one would suggest that the world would be better if every one of each salmon's 2 million eggs grew to be a salmon, or every acorn an oak. All living things are fruitful in excess, including humans."

107. During the event, Foreman married Nancy Morton, a longtime Earth First!er whom he had met at an Earth First! Road Show in Chico, California. Ironically, Mike Roselle was his best man. Kane, 102; Michele Miller, "1986 Round River Rendezvous Enters the Ice Age," *Earth First!* 6, no. 7 (Lughnasadh/Aug. 1, 1986): 1, 18; and Zierenberg, interview.

108. Dave Foreman, "Around the Campfire," *Earth First!* 6, no. 7 (Lughnasadh/Aug. 1, 1986): 2.

109. Ibid.

110. Randall T. Restless [pseud.], "The Round River Rendezvous: A Newcomer's Perspective," *Earth First!* 6, no. 7 (Lughnasadh/Aug. 1, 1986): 17.

111. Ibid. See also Kane, 106.

112. In the latter half of 1986, the movement's attention was focused on Forest Service activities in Texas, protests against the World Bank, and support for Paul Watson's Sea Shepherd Conservation Society in its endeavors.

113. Roger Featherstone and Nancy Morton, "An Open Letter to the '87 Rendezvous Committee," *Earth First!* 7, no. 1 (Samhain/Nov. 1, 1986): 17.

114. Dave Foreman, "Around the Campfire," *Earth First!* 7, no. 2 (Yule/Dec. 21, 1986): 2.

6. Misanthropy and Social Justice

1. Dave Foreman, "Whither Earth First!?," *Earth First!* 8, no. 1 (Samhain/Nov. 1, 1987): 20.

2. Cherney, interview, Apr. 10, 1991. Cherney's song refers to his interpretation of a series of comments made by Dave Foreman during 1987. Cherney believed that Foreman had implicitly and explicitly endorsed the spread of AIDS and an end both to American foreign aid and to the United States's acceptance of political refugees from Latin America.

3. Friedman, interview.

4. John Davis [Australopithecus, pseud.], review of *The Parable of the Tribes,* by Andrew Bard Schmookler, *Earth First!* 5, no. 8 (Mabon/Sept. 22, 1985): 24. Andrew Bard Schmookler, *The Parable of the Tribes: the Problem of Power in Social Evolution* (Berkeley: Univ. of California Press, 1984).

5. Andrew Bard Schmookler, "Schmookler Replies to Australopithecus," *Earth First!* 6, no. 1 (Yule/Dec. 21, 1985): 25.

6. Davis, review of *Parable of the Tribes,* 24.

7. Ibid.

8. Ibid.

9. Schmookler, "Schmookler Replies to Australopithecus," 25.

10. Ibid.

11. Andrew Bard Schmookler, "Schmookler on Anarchy," *Earth First!* 6, no. 5 (Beltane/May 1, 1986): 22.

12. See Christopher Manes, "Ascent to Anarchy," *Earth First!* 6, no. 7 (Lughnasadh/Aug. 1, 1986): 21, and Edward Abbey, "A Response to Schmookler on Anarchy," *Earth First!* 6, no. 7 (Lughnasadh/Aug. 1, 1986): 22.

13. Abbey, "A Response to Schmookler on Anarchy," 22.

14. Ibid.

15. Ibid.

16. Ibid.

17. Ibid.

18. Andrew Bard Schmookler, "Schmookler Replies to the Anarchists," *Earth First!* 7, no. 2 (Yule/Dec. 21, 1986): 24–25.

19. Ibid.

20. Jamie Sayen, "'Anarchy' is Baggage," *Earth First!* 7, no. 4 (Eostar/Mar. 20, 1987): 36. Sayen later became the editor of *Glacial Erratic,* a journal sympathetic to Earth First!, which reported on environmental issues in the northern Appalachians. He is currently on the board of directors of the Wildlands Project and editor of *Northern Forest Forum.*

21. Ibid.

22. Ibid.

23. Ibid.

24. "The Continuing Anarchy Debate" included four articles, Andrew Schmookler's "Schmookler Replies to Anarchists' Replies to Schmookler's Reply to the Anarchists" and "Schmookler to Sayen," Robert Goodrich's "Government and Anarchy," and Christoph Manes's "An Anarchist replies to Schmookler's Reply to the Anarchists." All four were published in *Earth First!* 7, no. 8 (Mabon/Sept. 23, 1987): 24–26.

25. Christoph Manes, "An Anarchist Replies to Schmookler's Reply to the Anarchists," 25.

26. Dave Foreman [Chim Blea, pseud.], "Cat Tracks," *Earth First!* 8, no. 1 (Samhain/Nov. 1, 1987): 19.

27. Cherney, interview, Apr. 10, 1991. Cherney remarked that the individuals who were then in charge of the journal, John Davis, Dale Turner, Nancy Zierenberg, and Kris Sommerville, "were not reflective of the Earth First! movement, they [were] reflective of *part* of the Earth First! movement."

28. John Davis, interview by author, Canton, N.Y., Dec. 4, 1991.

29. See, for example, David Barron, "CD Begins Anew in Kalmiopsis," *Earth First!* 7, no. 5 (Beltane/May 1, 1987): 1.

30. The most notable example of the latter was "American Gulag: Leonard Peltier," which appeared in the February issue. It did not contain a single reference to any wilderness issue. Jim VanderWall and Eric Holle, "American Gulag: Leonard Peltier," *Earth First!* 7, no. 3 (Brigid/Feb. 2, 1987): 28–29.

31. Dave Foreman, "Around the Campfire," *Earth First!* 7, no. 6 (Litha/June 21, 1987): 2.

32. Foreman, interview.

33. The journal also published a second article on AIDS: Daniel Conner, "Is AIDS the Answer to an Environmentalist's Prayer?," *Earth First!* 8, no. 2 (Yule/Dec. 22, 1987): 14–16, discussed below.

34. Christopher Manes [Miss Ann Thropy, pseud.], "Overpopulation and Industrialism," *Earth First!* 7, no. 4 (Eostar/Mar. 20, 1987): 29.

35. Ibid.

36. Ibid.

37. Davis, interview.

38. Christopher Manes [Miss Ann Thropy, pseud.], "Population and AIDS," *Earth First!* 7, no. 5 (Beltane/May 1, 1987): 32.

39. Ibid.

40. Ibid.

41. Ibid.

42. Ibid.

43. Dave Foreman, "Around the Campfire," *Earth First!* 7, no. 6 (Litha/June 21, 1987): 2.

44. Ibid.

45. Ibid. Foreman supported his list with slogans so common to the movement that they were encapsulated on the bumperstickers sold in the journal's "Trinkets and Snake Oil" pages, for example, "Resist Much, Obey Little," "Back to the Pleistocene," and "Malthus was Right."

46. Ibid.

47. Ibid.

48. The text of the letter is contained in an article concerning the location and schedule of the 1987 Rendezvous. "8th Annual Round River Rendezvous," *Earth First!* 7, no. 5 (Beltane/May 1, 1987): 18.

49. Dave Foreman, "Around the Campfire," *Earth First!* 7, no. 6 (Litha/June 21, 1987): 2. The majority of those who wrote letters were probably of the movement's social

justice faction. During this period, they were predisposed to find fault with Foreman, and philsophically, they had less antipathy towards domesticated animals.

50. Ibid.

51. Reed, interview.

52. Cherney, interview, Apr. 11, 1991.

53. Chris Bowman, "Earth First!ers' Dare: Tread on Me," *Sacramento Bee,* July 12, 1987, A7.

54. By this point in Earth First!'s history, its annual Rendezvous was attracting individuals from many such marginal groups.

55. Alien Nation described eco-mutualism as a philosophy that recognized that "human society and the natural world are not mutually exclusive." The majority of its newsletter was reprinted in *Earth First!*. Alien Nation, "Dangerous Tendencies in Earth First!," *Earth First!* 8, no. 1 (Samhain/Nov. 1, 1987): 17.

56. Ibid.

57. Ibid.

58. Ibid., 18.

59. Ibid. Foreman described this as a "paranoid reaction to some old-time Earth First!ers partying." Foreman, letter.

60. Ibid. An alternative account of the Alien Nation/Round River Rendezvous Committee confrontation can be found in Peg Millett, letter to the editor, *Earth First!* 8, no. 2 (Yule/Dec. 22, 1987): 3.

61. Murray Bookchin, from a speech to the Greens Conference, Amherst, Mass., July 1987; cited in "An Introduction to Alien Nation," *Earth First!* 8, no. 1 (Samhain/Nov. 1, 1987): 17.

62. Foreman, "Whither Earth First!?," 20.

63. Ibid.

64. Ibid.

65. Ibid., 21.

66. Ibid.

67. Ibid.

68. See, for example, Delores LaChapelle, letter to the editor, *Earth First!* 7, no. 8 (Mabon/Sept. 23, 1987): 3.

69. Foreman, interview. Edward Abbey devoted a chapter of his novel *Hayduke Lives!* to describing the events at this Rendezvous.

70. Ibid.

71. Ibid.

72. Mike Roselle, "Nomadic Action Group," *Earth First!* 7, no. 8 (Mabon/Sept. 23, 1987): 3.

73. Ibid.

74. Ibid. Interestingly, Roselle cited the July 1987 Grand Canyon uranium protest as one of the Nomadic Action Group's successes. He claimed that it was as a result of the group's efforts that Earth First! was "much better prepared for this action than any previous post-RRR action."

75. Dave Foreman, "Around the Campfire," *Earth First!* 8, no. 2 (Yule/Dec. 22, 1987): 2.

76. Ibid.

77. Dave Foreman, "Is Sanctuary the Answer?," *Earth First!* 8, no. 1 (Samhain/Nov. 1, 1987): 22.

78. Ibid.

79. Dave Foreman, "Around the Campfire," *Earth First!* 8, no. 2 (Yule/Dec. 22, 1987): 3. The number of letters was not inconsequential; by this point, *Earth First!* was receiving over fifteen hundred letters to the editor every month.

80. Ibid. As well as the Manes and Conner articles, the journal also published essays of support for Foreman's position from Jamie Sayen (a participant in the anarchy debate), Paul Watson (a founder of Greenpeace as well as the Sea Shepherd Conservation Society), and Bill Devall (one of the authors of *Deep Ecology*).

81. Christopher Manes [Miss Ann Thropy, pseud.], "Miss Ann Thropy Responds to 'Alien Nation'," *Earth First!* 8, no. 2 (Yule/Dec. 22, 1987): 17.

82. Ibid.

83. Ibid.

84. Ibid.

85. Conner, "Is AIDS the Answer to an Environmentalist's Prayer," 14–16.

86. Ibid., 16.

87. "Earth First!," insert in *Earth First!* 8, no. 2 (Yule/Dec. 21, 1987): 1.

88. Ibid.

89. Foreman, memorandum, 1.

90. Ibid.

91. Foreman, *Confessions*, 53.

92. Ibid., 57–58.

93. Zakin highlights this aspect of Roselle's character in her discussion of the movement's founding; she claims that he did not fully participate in the group's adventures in the zona rosa. Zakin, *Coyotes and Town Dogs*, 131–32.

7. A Parting of the Ways

1. Draffan, interview.

2. Dave Foreman, "Around the Campfire," *Earth First!* 8, no. 3 (Brigid/Feb. 2, 1988): 2.

3. Ibid. One column would contain summaries of Earth First! actions, one would provide summaries of international environmental news, and one would focus on rainforest news and events. The February issue put these new editorial policies to good use. It provided some coverage of direct action events, but most of the paper was taken up with wilderness reports and proposals. Davis titled the direct action page "Succinctly Stated Earth First! News Briefs." *Earth First!* 8, no. 3 (Brigid/Feb. 2, 1988): 10–12.

4. Dave Foreman, "Around the Campfire," *Earth First!* 8, no. 3 (Brigid/Feb. 2, 1988): 2.

5. Darryl Cherney later remarked of that period, "All of a sudden . . . if you come to Earth First!, you can't work on any other issues, you can't think about social politics, or if you do, you've got to work on them yourself. Don't put them in the Earth First! Journal!" Cherney, interview, Apr. 11, 1991.

6. Mike Roselle, cited in Zakin, *Coyotes and Town Dogs*, 384.

7. In the March issue, for example, "Trinkets and Snake Oil" took up four full pages. *Earth First!* 8, no. 4 (Eostar/Mar. 20, 1988): 32–35.

8. "Earth First! Foundation Fiscal Report—December 31, 1987," *Earth First!* 8, no. 4 (Eostar/Mar. 20, 1988): 17.

9. At the time of the movement's eventual split, the ownership of these entities became the subject of bitter dispute. Although Foreman had devoted much of his life and energy to Earth First! (and at one time had sold property to support the movement), some Earth First!ers were unhappy with the remuneration he received for his financial support of the paper. Zakin, *Coyotes and Town Dogs*, 410–11, and Cherney, interview, Apr. 10, 1991.

10. Zakin, *Coyotes and Town Dogs*, 410–11.

11. Ibid.

12. Foreman, letter.

13. Along with four colleagues, he draped a banner that declared "We the people say no to acid rain" down the chiseled face of George Washington. Karen Pickett, "Roselle Gets 4 Month Sentence," *Earth First!* 8, no. 4 (Eostar/Mar. 20, 1988): 1.

14. Roselle was originally sentenced to one month in jail, with a three month suspended sentence, but he refused to agree with the conditions of his probation and subsequently had his parole revoked. Ibid., 1, 5.

15. Zakin, *Coyotes and Town Dogs*, 384.

16. Draffan, interview.

17. See, for example, Joseph Mallia, "He's Done it All in the Name of Nature," *Recorder* (Greenfield, Mass.), Feb. 6, 1988, 3; Jamie Sayen, "Voice from the Wilderness," *Coos County Democrat*, Feb. 10, 1988, 2A; and Jim Robbins, "The Environmental Guerrillas," *Boston Globe Magazine*, Mar. 27, 1988. Foreman's tour was also covered in the Illinois and Alaska media.

18. "Earth First!," *Southern Illinoisan*, Mar. 31, 1988, D21.

19. Karen Pickett, "Day of Outrage Shakes Forest Service Nationwide!," *Earth First!* 8, no. 6 (Litha/June 21, 1993): 1.

20. Dave Foreman, "Around the Campfire," *Earth First!* 8, no. 5 (Beltane/May 1, 1988): 2. Pickett married Mike Roselle during the autumn of 1988. John Davis, "A View of the Vortex," *Earth First!* 8, no. 8 (Mabon/Sept. 22, 1988): 2.

21. Foreman's sympathy towards this event probably had much to do with his antipathy towards the United States Forest Service. Although he was usually unwilling to participate in direct action events, he made an exception on this occasion, participating in the Eugene, Oregon, protest. Dave Foreman, "Around the Campfire," *Earth First!* 8, no. 5 (Beltane/May 1, 1988): 2.

22. Pickett, "Day of Outrage Shakes Forest Service Nationwide!," 19.

23. Foreman solicited well-written and succinct contributions from all Earth First!ers. Well aware of the potential for editorial challenges, he was careful to emphasize that there was room for only a select few to be printed. Dave Foreman, "Around the Campfire," *Earth First!* 8, no. 5 (Beltane/May 1, 1988): 2.

24. Dave Foreman, editorial, *Earth First!* 8, no. 6 (Litha/June 21, 1988): 2. Davis, for example, advocated a complete return "to the Pleistocene." He was notorious amongst Tucson Earth First!ers for his regular food scavenging trips. Davis, interview, and Wilson, interview.

25. Dave Foreman, editorial, *Earth First!* 8, no. 6 (Litha/June 21, 1988): 2. Foreman reiterated those sentiments in my interview with him.

26. Dave Foreman, "Around the Campfire," *Earth First!* 8, no. 6 (Litha/June 21, 1988): 32.

27. Ibid.

28. Davis, interview.

29. See, for example, Greg King, "New Battles in Maxxam Campaign," *Earth First!* 8, no. 6 (Litha/June 21, 1988): 5.

30. Zakin refers to Bari as a "pink diaper baby." Her father was a gem cutter, and her mother was the first woman to graduate from Johns Hopkins University with a Ph.D. in mathematics. Zakin, *Coyotes and Town Dogs,* 344.

31. Ibid., 354–55.

32. Ibid, 353.

33. Ibid.

34. Judi Bari, "California Rendezvous," *Earth First!* 9, no. 1 (Samhain/Nov. 1, 1988): 5.

35. Not all Californian Earth First!ers shared Bari's brand of feminism. One such individual wrote a letter to the journal in response to Bari's report; Sequoia accused her of coming to the Rendezvous "determined that the men of Earth First! were controlling all the purse strings and are all sexists." In her opinion, Bari was simply "another victim of the media hype." Sequoia, letter to the editor, *Earth First!* 9, no. 3 (Brigid/Feb. 2, 1989): 3.

36. Wilson, interview.

37. Ibid.

38. See, for example, "Fellow Workers, Meet Earth First!, Earth First!ers Meet the IWW," *Industrial Worker,* May 1988, 5, and Judi Bari, "California Rendezvous," *Earth First!* 9, no. 1 (Samhain/Nov. 1, 1988): 5.

39. Melvyn Dubofsky, *We Shall Be All* (Chicago: Quadrangle, 1969), 105.

40. Ibid., 473.

41. Ibid., 484.

42. Zakin, *Coyotes and Town Dogs,* 361.

43. "Fellow Workers, Meet Earth First!, Earth First!ers, Meet the I.W.W.," 5. The connection between the two groups was also present in a more tangible way: Edward Abbey's father, Paul Revere Abbey, was a member of the IWW until his death. Zakin, *Coyotes and Town Dogs,* 363n.

44. Zakin, *Coyotes and Town Dogs,* 362.

45. John Littman, "Peace, Love . . . and TNT," *California,* Dec. 1990, 89.

46. Kuipers, 36, and John Patterson, "EF! Howls at 1988 Rendezvous," *Earth First!* 8, no. 7 (Lughnasadh/Aug. 1, 1988): 18.

47. Patterson, "EF! Howls at 1988 Rendezvous," 18.

48. Ann Japenga, "Earth First! Comes out of the Shadows," *Spokesman-Review,* July 4, 1988, 6. Notably, none of the journal staff members were involved in planning the Rendezvous, and Foreman almost did not attend it. He and Nancy Morton participated in a few of its workshops and deliberately avoided the post-Rendezvous action. Foreman, letter.

49. Japenga, 6. The article featured a photograph of Ron Frazier dismantling a diesel

engine. Again, somewhat ironically, Earth First!ers later learned that Frazier was a paid informant for the FBI at that time.

50. An FBI agent by the name of Mike Fain attended this Rendezvous. Fain used the pseudonym Mike Tait. He is discussed in greater detail below. Kuipers, 36.

51. Howie Wolke, cited in John Davis, "A View of the Vortex," *Earth First!* 8, no. 7 (Lughnasadh/Aug. 1, 1988): 2.

52. John Davis, "A View of the Vortex," *Earth First!* 8, no. 7 (Lughnasadh/Aug. 1, 1988): 2.

53. Ibid.

54. Jasper Carlton, "From the Garden to the Roundup—6000 Years of Serpentine Persecution," *Earth First!* 8, no. 8 (Mabon/Sept. 22, 1988): 16–19. Carlton does not explain his use of the six thousand year figure, but interestingly, he begins his article with two quotes from the Old Testament, Genesis 3:1 and 3:13–14 (King James).

55. It should be noted that their adoption of "paganism" and "pagan rituals" was neither systematic nor clearly linked to an identifiable pagan doctrine. They were instead a pure celebration of "wildness."

56. Howie Wolke, "The Grizzly Den, " *Earth First!* 9, no. 1 (Samhain/Nov. 1, 1988): 22.

57. Friedman, interview.

58. Its demise was due to its editors' attempts to put their principles into action. In order to be consistent with its anarchist principles, they believed, a journal promoting nihilism and wildness ought not to have an official editorial staff nor attempt to achieve consensus amongst its writers. Such principles, however, were not conducive to the regular publishing of a periodical. Ibid. Ironically, these same problems plagued *Earth First!* after the movement's fragmentation in late 1990.

59. Dave Foreman's first rule for strategic monkeywrenching was that individuals should do so alone or only with "absolutely trusted partners." Such care would ensure that one need not worry about "partners with loose lips, infiltration by informers or agents provocateurs, or betrayal by weak-kneed compatriots trying to save their own skins. . . . *If* they work with others, mature monkeywrenchers work only with those to whom they would entrust their lives." Foreman, *Confessions,* 163.

60. Tait had an unrelenting enthusiasm for committing illegal activities (a characteristic that was usually cause for suspicion among seasoned Earth First!ers). He also lacked an appreciation for basic conservation principles. At one Mount Graham, Arizona, protest, he attempted to plant Scotch pine seedlings and was angered when Earth First!ers prevented him from doing so because the species was not native to the area. Kuipers, 36.

61. Zierenberg, interview.

62. Mark Shaffer, "Ski-resort 'Sabotage' Detailed," *Arizona Republic,* June 21, 1991.

63. Michael Lacey, "Sabotaging the Saboteurs," *New Times,* May 29–June 4, 1991, 8.

64. Mark Shaffer, "Activist Spied on Uranium Mine before Vandalism, Court is Told," *Arizona Republic,* June 22, 1991. Shortly before the Canyon action, power poles were severed at Energy Fuels Nuclear's five uranium mines north of the Grand Canyon. It is unclear whether or not the two actions were linked.

65. Kuipers, 36.

66. Manes, *Green Rage,* 196.

67. Sam Negri, "Earth First! Setup Alleged," *Arizona Republic,* Apr. 25, 1990, B2.

68. John Davis, "A View of the Vortex," *Earth First!* 9, no. 3 (Brigid/Feb. 2, 1989): 2.

69. Ibid.

70. Ibid.

71. El Lobo Solo [pseud.], letter to the editor, *Earth First!* 9, no. 4 (Eostar/Mar. 21, 1989): 3.

72. "EF! Bulletins," *Earth First!* 9, no. 3 (Brigid/Feb. 2, 1989): 19, and Friedman, interview.

73. Mike Roselle and Karen Pickett, "Direct Action Fund: The Year in Review," *Earth First!* 9, no. 4 (Eostar/Mar. 21, 1989): 19.

74. "Earth First! Foundation 1988 Treasurer's Report," *Earth First!* 9, no. 4 (Eostar/ Mar. 21, 1989): 19.

75. Greg King, "Redwood Action Team Report," *Earth First* 9, no. 4 (Eostar/Mar. 21, 1989): 19. As Earth First!'s notoriety grew, it became a fashionable cause to which to donate funds. After the arrest of Foreman, Millett, Davis, Asplund, and Baker, musicians such as Bonnie Raitt, the Grateful Dead, and Don Henley contributed to their defense fund. Foreman, interview.

76. Dave Foreman, "Goodbye Ed," *Earth First!* 9, no. 5 (Beltane/May 1, 1989): insert. Zakin writes that Foreman was "[s]obered by intimations of mortality . . . [and he] decided that his young Frankenstein had outgrown him." *Coyotes and Town Dogs,* 335–36.

77. Foreman, "Goodbye, Ed."

78. Edward Abbey, *Desert Solitaire,* cited in *Edward Abbey—A Tribute, Earth First!* 9, no. 5 (Beltane/May 1, 1989): insert.

79. Foreman, "Goodbye, Ed." Foreman furthered this critique in his later writings. In *Confessions of an Eco-Warrior,* written after the movement's fragmentation, he refers to such individuals as "pompous True Believers." Foreman, *Confessions,* 174.

80. Mary Davis, interview by author, Canton, N.Y., Dec. 4, 1991, and Dale Turner, "Arizona Arrestees Released From Jail!," *Earth First!* 9, no. 7 (Lughnasadh/Aug. 1, 1989): 1.

81. That fact and its implications were not lost on Earth First!ers. See, for example, The Spirit of Tippy [pseud.], letter to the editor, *Earth First!* 9, no. 7 (Lughnasadh/Aug. 1, 1989): 3.

82. Kuipers, 38.

83. They had chosen a tower that marked a curve in the power line; knocking it down would cause the entire line to fall. Ibid., 35.

84. Ibid., and Manes, *Green Rage,* 193–95.

85. Anthony Sommer, "Review Case Against Earth First!, Judge Asked," *Phoenix Gazette,* June 5, 1991, A6.

8. The Resurgence of Millenarianism

1. Judi Bari, cited in "Founder Critical of Leftist Direction of Earth First!," *Arizona Daily Star,* Aug. 14, 1990, D5.

2. Mike Roselle, cited in "Founder Critical of Leftist Direction of Earth First!," 5.

3. That document is unavailable; reference to it appears in "Update on 'Arizona Four' Arrests," *Earth First!* 9, no. 6 (Litha/June 21, 1989): 1–6.

4. A column on the arrests shared the front page with two other stories. Ibid.

5. 'RRR Committee,' "10th Annual Round River Rendezvous," *Earth First!* 9, no. 5 (Beltane/May 1, 1989): 21.

6. Jesse Hardin [Lone Wolf Circles, pseud.], "Workshop Invite," *Earth First!* 9, no. 5 (Beltane/May 1, 1989): 21.

7. Glen Rosales and Jim Herron, "Foreman Won't be Roped In," *Sunday Journal,* June 25, 1989, A1. As has been noted, by this point in the movement's history, the Rendezvous were usually attended by between two and four hundred Earth First!ers.

8. Foolish Coyote [pseud.], letter to the editor, *Earth First!* 9, no. 7 (Lughnasadh/Aug. 1, 1989): 3.

9. Ibid. Darryl Cherney defined "woo-woo" as a "quasi-derogatory" Earth First! term for "people who indulge in crystals, self-healing . . . New Age stuff, who don't apply it to the outer world. They have the attitude that 'I will heal myself first, and in this manner I will heal the world.' " Cherney, interview, Apr. 11, 1991.

10. Wilson, interview.

11. Loose Hip Circles [pseud.; a parody of one of Earth First!'s poets, Lone Wolf Circles], "Riotous Rendezvous Remembered," *Earth First!* 9, no. 7 (Lughnasadh/Aug. 1, 1989): 19. Loose Hip Circles was described as "a sharp-tongued heroine" who had announced her candidacy for Garberville Rodeo Queen. It is likely that the author of this article was Judi Bari.

12. In a later issue of the journal, Mudhead Kachinas were more formally defined as the "ceremonial clowns" of the Pueblo Indians, whose function was to "enforce tribal laws and oversee ceremonial activities." Paul Faulstitch, "Shaman—Ritual—Place," *Earth First!* 9, no. 8 (Mabon/Sept. 22, 1989): 26.

13. Friedman, interview. The Earth First! words to the Marley song were reprinted in the August issue of the journal. Rich Ryan, "RR Reflects on the RRR," *Earth First!* 9, no. 7 (Lughnasadh/Aug. 1, 1989): 18.

14. Friedman, interview.

15. Loose Hip Circles [pseud.], "Riotous Rendezvous Remembered," 19.

16. Ibid. Once out of jail, Foreman continued to fulfil several speaking engagements that he had booked before his arrest. Although these talks were intended to publicize his latest book, *The Big Outside,* they also allowed him to promote the cause of the arrested Earth First!ers.

17. As an example, he cited the development of the Rainforest Action Network, a group founded by Earth First!ers and still led by Earth First!ers, but with a different and distinct goal. John Davis, "A View of the Vortex," *Earth First!* 9, no. 6 (Litha/June 21, 1989): 2.

18. Ibid.

19. Ibid.

20. Ibid.

21. "A Monkeywrencher's Guide to Lawyers and the Law," *Earth First!* 9, no. 6 (Litha/June 21, 1989): 30–32.

22. See, for example, Chaco [pseud.], letter to the editor, *Earth First!* 9, no. 6 (Litha/June 21, 1989): 3.

23. The journal's business manager, Kris Sommerville, moved to Canton to be with her husband, a chemistry professor at St. Lawrence University. The editor, John Davis, had grown up in the Northeast and wanted to return there. The Sommervilles later moved to Colorado. Davis, interview.

24. John Davis, "A View of the Vortex," *Earth First!* 9, no. 7 (Lughnasadh/Aug. 1, 1989): 2.

25. John Davis, "A View of the Vortex," *Earth First!* 9, no. 8 (Mabon/Sept. 22, 1989): 2.

26. The article was subtitled "Living as if the Onto-Ecological Structure of Human Epistemological Self-Consciousness Really Mattered." Wheaton Dedrick La Cont [pseud.], *Earth First!* 9, no. 8 (Mabon/Sept. 22, 1989): 21.

27. The multiple choice quiz contained such questions as "What would be the best way to solve Utah's fiscal crisis?" for which the misanthropic answer was "d. Declare an open season on Mormon school children." H. Misanthropus [pseud.], "The Misanthrope Quiz," *Earth First* 9, no. 8 (Mabon/Sept. 22, 1989): 21.

28. John Davis, "Ramblings," *Earth First!* 10, no. 2 (Yule/Dec. 21, 1989): 2. Davis renamed his editorial column in November 1989, out of respect for the power of Hurricane Hugo, in whose aftermath it seemed "self-indulgent to view our movement as a Vortex." John Davis, "Ramblings," *Earth First!* 10, no. 1 (Samhain/Nov. 1, 1989): 2.

29. John Davis, "Ramblings," *Earth First!* 10, no. 2 (Yule/Dec. 21, 1989): 2.

30. See Mark Shaffer, "Activist Spied on Uranium Mine before Vandalism, Court is Told," *Arizona Republic,* June 22, 1994, and Dale Turner, "Arizona 4 are Now 5," *Earth First!* 10, no. 3 (Brigid/Feb. 2, 1990): 8.

31. Mark Shaffer, "Activist Spied on Uranium Mine."

32. Mark Shaffer, "'Eco-terrorism' Trial Underway," *Arizona Republic,* June 20, 1991, B1.

33. Dave Foreman, cited in Sam Negri, "Earth First! Setup Alleged," *Arizona Republic,* Apr. 25, 1990, B2.

34. Mike Roselle [Nagasaki Johnson, pseud.], "Roadkill," *Earth First!* 10, no. 3 (Brigid/Feb. 2, 1990): 27. Parts of the article were reprinted from *Live Wild or Die,* no. 2.

35. Ibid.

36. Ibid.

37. Ibid.

38. Ibid.

39. Ibid.

40. John Davis, "Ramblings," *Earth First!* 10, no. 4 (Eostar/Mar. 20, 1990): 2. He requested articles on such topics as the Bureau of Land Management's progress in reviewing the wilderness potential of "the land it mismanages."

41. Dale Turner, editorial response to letter from Red Fox [pseud.], *Earth First!* 10, no. 4 (Eostar/Mar. 20, 1990): 3.

42. Darryl Cherney, quoted in *Sixty Minutes Transcripts,* vol. 22, no. 24, Mar. 4, 1990, 3. Zakin records Cherney as referring to Glen Canyon Dam. *Coyotes and Town Dogs,* 378. That reference makes logical sense, but it is not what is recorded in the program's transcripts, or in other sources. See, for example, Littman, 88.

43. John Davis, "On the Triune Nature of Earth First!," *Earth First! Journal* 10, no. 5 (May 1, 1990): 2.

44. Scarce, 83.

45. Ibid., and Foreman, letter.

46. Foreman, interview.

47. Davis, "On the Triune Nature of Earth First!," 3.

48. Ibid., 5.

49. Ibid.

50. Dale Turner, "Changing Times, Changing Names," *Earth First! Journal* 10, no. 5 (May 1, 1990): 2.

51. Ibid.

52. Davis, "The Triune Nature of Earth First!," 5.

53. The pagan subheadings might also have been a result of Foreman's very brief flirtation with goddess religion. They were never part of a coherent or systematic use of pagan symbols. Foreman, interview. See, for example, *Earth First* 1, no. 1 (Samhain/Nov. 1, 1980): 1.

54. Davis, "On the Triune Nature of Earth First!," 5.

55. "Index to Gratuitously Offensive Remarks," *Earth First! Journal* 10, no. 5 (May 1, 1990): 2.

56. Littman, 89.

57. Zierenberg, interview.

58. Mike Roselle, cited in Zakin, *Coyotes and Town Dogs,* 385. It should be noted that in her review of *Coyotes and Town Dogs,* Beverly Cherner argues that the Redwood Summer activists had no choice but to focus on private forests because "there are few coastal redwoods in California's public forests." Cherner makes no comment on Roselle's apparent hesitancy.

59. In the early morning of April 22, 1990 (Earth Day), for example, someone toppled a transmission pole outside Watsonville, California, an action that cut electrical power to over ninety-two thousand people. Later, another pole was toppled, which cut the area's power for rest of the day. Littman, 89.

60. Ibid., 128.

61. Bari engaged a former Chicago Bears linebacker in a shouting match, inspired by his apparent threat to rape the clinic's director. She and Cherney wrote and performed a parody of "Will the Circle Be Unbroken" that included the following stanza: "Reverend Boyles hated abortion / And for a peaceful end he search / He said 'He'd never bomb our clinic' / We said 'We'll never bomb your church.'" Zakin, *Coyotes and Town Dogs,* 372–74, and Littman, 88.

62. Scarce, 84.

63. Ibid.

64. Judi Bari, "For FBI, Back to Political Sabotage?," *New York Times,* Aug. 23, 1990.

65. Among the suspects in the case are antiabortion activists, the author of an anonymous death threat ("The Lord's Avenger"), and Bari's ex-husband. Some Earth First!ers, including Bari and Cherney, suspect that the FBI may have planted the bomb. Littman, 87. See also Robert A. Jones, "Here come the '60s, With the FBI in Tow," *Los Angeles Times,* June 26, 1990.

66. Judi Bari, "The Bombing Story—Part 1: The Set-Up," *Earth First!* 14, no. 3 (Brigid/Feb. 2, 1994): 14.

67. Karen Pickett and Woody Joe [pseud.], "Redwood Summer Goes On!," *Earth First! Journal* 10, no. 6 (June 21, 1990): 1.

68. Trip Gabriel, "If a Tree Falls in the Forest, They Hear it," *New York Times Magazine,* Nov. 4, 1990, 62.

69. Ibid.

70. Jake Krelick [Jake Jagoff, pseud.], cited in "1990 Round River Rendezvous," *Earth First!* 10, no. 4 (Eostar/Mar. 20, 1990): 25.

71. Ibid.

72. Phil Knight, "RRR Rocks and Rolls in Montana," *Earth First! Journal* 10, no. 7 (Aug. 1, 1990): 19.

73. Ibid.

74. Dennis Fritzinger, "The RRR EF! Journal Meeting—A Watershed," *Earth First! Journal* 10, no. 7 (Aug. 1, 1990): 2.

75. Ibid.

76. Ibid., 4. After the Rendezvous, John Davis, Rod Mondt, Kris Sommerville, and Nancy Zierenberg joined Dave Foreman and Nancy Morton at Yellowstone National Park. They apparently discussed starting a new group and publication, an endeavor that Foreman had wanted to engage in for over two years. Foreman, letter.

77. Friedman, interview.

78. Cherney, interview, Apr. 10, 1991.

79. Friedman, interview.

80. John Davis, "Editor's Note," *Earth First! Journal* 10, no. 7 (Aug. 1, 1990): 2.

81. Also noteworthy in this issue was the new heading for the "Letters to the Editor" page. Mike Roselle had withdrawn his permission for the journal to use his cartoon graphic, which had been used for years; in its absence, the page was retitled "Dear shit fer brains." That phrase had long been the page's subtitle, but its leap to prominence in August 1990 may have had much to do with Davis's growing resentment of those who challenged his authority.

82. The trial of the Arizona Five will be discussed further in chapter 9.

83. Mike Geniella, "Leadership dispute splits Earth First!," *Press Democrat,* Aug. 12, 1990, A1.

84. Ibid., A14.

85. John Davis, "Editor's Note," Kris Sommerville, "Renunciation," Nancy Zierenberg, "Time to Move On," and Dale Turner, "Regrets and Relief," *Earth First! Journal* 10, no. 8 (Autumn equinox/Sept. 22, 1990): 2–3.

86. Sommerville, "Renunciation," 2.

87. The poem began, "The Journal is boring / haven't read it in a year / each issue gets worse / God, I need another beer." Gina Trott, "A Report from the Journal Advisory Committee," *Earth First! Journal* 10, no. 8 (Sept. 22, 1990): 4.

9. Conclusion

1. Aldo Leopold, *A Sand County Almanac, and Sketches Here and There,* Special Commemorative Ed. (New York: Oxford Univ. Press, 1949), vii.

2. Karen Pickett, "Breaking Up or Breaking Apart?," *Earth First! Journal* 11, no. 1 (Nov. 1, 1990): 2. The journal's pagan subheadings were not restored in this issue.

3. Ibid.

4. Ibid., 3. Charles Hurwitz was the chief executive officer of Maxxam, a Texas corporation that bought out Pacific Lumber (PL), a small family-owned logging company in northern California. PL had practiced conservative cutting policies so that in that purchase, Maxxam acquired more untouched redwood forest than any other company operating in California. Zakin, *Coyotes and Town Dogs,* 345.

5. John Davis, "editor's note [sic]," *Earth First! Journal* 11, no. 1 (Nov. 1, 1990): 2.

6. John Davis, "The Successors of EF!J," *Earth First! Journal* 11, no. 2 (Dec. 21, 1990): 2.

7. As noted above, Earth First! does not make that information available.

8. In 1990, for example, that option cost four hundred dollars.

9. Zierenberg, interview.

10. In the first issue of *Earth First,* Foreman had written: "Not only does EARTH FIRST support wilderness designation for *all* Forest Service RARE II areas and BLM roadless areas, we also believe . . . it is time to *recreate* wilderness: identify key areas, close roads, remove developments, and reintroduce extirpated wildlife." Dave Foreman, *Earth First* 1, no. 1 (Samhain/Nov. 1, 1980): 1.

11. Its short range goals were listed as follows: "1) Protect all remaining roadless areas in North America, 2) Establish Wilderness Recovery Areas on roaded but other wise undeveloped public lands, 3) Begin human population reduction through lowered birth rates, 4) Add to the federal or state Wilderness preservation systems large, presently-private undeveloped tracts in all bioregions, and 5) Terminate commodity extraction on all undeveloped public lands and protect these lands as Wilderness or Wilderness Recovery Areas; reintroduce extirpated species as habitat permits." "Statement of Purpose," *Wild Earth* 1, no. 1, (Spring 1991): ii.

12. Foreman, *Confessions,* 50.

13. According to Susan Zakin, the plea bargain was based on a deal which saw the defendants plead guilty to the 1987 sabotage of the Snow Bowl ski resort, an incident that occurred before stringent federal guidelines went into effect. *Coyotes and Town Dogs,* 439.

14. Their sentences were of varying lengths: one month for Asplund, six months for Baker, three years for Millett, and six years for Davis. As of November 1993, only Davis remained in jail. Beverly Cherner, "Editor's Note" to "An Open Letter to Susan Zakin, Author of *Coyotes and Town Dogs,*" *Earth First!* 14, no. 1 (Samhain/Nov. 1, 1993): 3.

15. Mark Shaffer, "'Eco-terrorism' Trial Underway," *Arizona Republic,* June 20, 1991, B1. As discussed in chapter 8, FBI agent Mike Fain had, on tape, identified Foreman as "the guy we need to pop to send a message."

16. At the end of that time, Foreman's felony charge will be reduced to a misdemeanor. Beverly Cherner, "Editor's Note" to "An Open Letter to Susan Zakin, Author of *Coyotes and Town Dogs,*" 3.

17. Zakin, *Coyotes and Town Dogs,* 442.

18. "How We Work," *Earth First!* 11, no. 4 (Ostara/Mar. 20, 1991): 2. All members of the "editorial collective" were paid two hundred dollars per month.

19. Ibid.

20. Robert Marten, "A Hunting We Will Go," *Earth First!* 12, no. 1 (Samhain/Nov. 1, 1994): 26–27.

21. "The cattle were semi-guilty participants in a policy of destroying the Earth by eating it." A. Nony Moose [pseud.], "Shooting Cows: A Novel Idea," *Earth First!* 11, no. 8 (Mabon/Sept. 23, 1991): 10.

22. Allison Slater, "The Party Line," *Earth First!* 12, no. 2 (Yule/Dec. 1, 1991): 2.

23. Matthew, letter to the editor, *Earth First!* 13, no. 6 (Litha/June 21, 1993): 3.

24. Tim Ballard, Jacob Bear, Lara Mattson, and Don Smith, "Earth First! and Social Justice," *Earth First!* 13, no. 2 (Yule/Dec. 21, 1992): 2.

25. Karen Wood, "Getting Back to Our (Grass) Roots," *Earth First!* 14, no. 6 (Litha/June 21, 1994): 2.

26. Reverend Rabbi [pseud.], "Monkeywrench the Millennium, Published on the 13th Day of the 7th Moon, Year One," *Earth First!* 14, no. 6 (Litha/June 21, 1994): 15.

27. Ibid.

28. Ibid.

29. Dave Foreman, John Davis, et al., "The Wildlands Project Mission Statement," *Wild Earth,* Special Issue, 1992, 3.

30. Dave Foreman, "Around the Campfire," *Wild Earth* 3, no. 2 (Summer, 1993): i.

31. "Earth First Directory," *Earth First!* 14, no. 6 (Litha/June 21, 1994): 39.

32. "Two Interviews with Dave Foreman," *Earth First!* 13, no. 6 (Litha/June 21, 1993): 25.

33. Wilson, interview.

34. Aberle, 211.

35. See, for example, Brock Evans, Vice President for National Issues of the Audubon Society, cited in Michael Lerner, "The FBI vs. the Monkeywrenchers," *Los Angeles Times Magazine,* Apr. 15, 1990, 21.

Appendix

1. Devall and Sessions, 70.

Bibliography

Books

Abbey, Edward. *Desert Solitaire: A Season in the Wilderness.* New York: Ballantine, 1968.

———. *Hayduke Lives!* Boston: Little, Brown, 1990.

———. *The Monkey Wrench Gang.* Philadelphia: J. B. Lippincot, 1979.

Aberle, David. "A Note on Relative Deprivation Theory as Applied to Millenarian and Other Cult Movements." In *Millennial Dreams in Action: Essays in Comparative Study,* edited by Sylvia Thrupp, 209–14. Comparative Studies in Society and History. The Hague: Mouton, 1962.

Albanese, Catherine. *Nature Religion in America: From the Algonkian Indians to the New Age.* Chicago History of American Religion. Chicago: Univ. of Chicago Press, 1990.

———. *Sons of the Fathers: The Civil Religion of the American Revolution.* Philadelphia: Temple Univ. Press, 1976.

Arendt, Hannah. *The Human Condition.* Chicago: Univ. of Chicago Press, 1958.

Barber, Benjamin. *Strong Democracy: Participatory Politics for a New Age.* Berkeley: Univ. of California Press, 1984.

Barkun, Michael. *Disaster and the Millennium.* New Haven: Yale Univ. Press, 1974.

Berger, Peter. *The Sacred Canopy: Elements of a Sociological Theory of Religion.* New York: Anchor, 1969.

Bloch, Ruth. *Visionary Republic: Millennial Themes in American Thought, 1756–1800.* Cambridge: Cambridge Univ. Press, 1985.

Brower, David. *For Earth's Sake: The Life and Times of David Brower.* Salt Lake City: Peregrine Smith, 1990.

Brown, Michael, and John, May. *The Greenpeace Story.* London: Dorling Kindersley, 1989.

Clary, David. *Timber and the Forest Service.* Development of Western Resources series. Lawrence: Univ. Press of Kansas, 1986.

193

Cohn, Norman. *The Pursuit of the Millennium: Revolutionary Millenarians and Mystical Anarchists of the Middle Ages*. Rev. and exp. ed. New York: Oxford Univ. Press, 1970.

Crane, Stephen. *Crane: Prose and Poetry*. Edited by J. C. Levinson. New York: Library Classics of the United States, 1984.

Devall, Bill, and George Sessions. *Deep Ecology: Living as if Nature Mattered*. Salt Lake City: Peregrine Smith, 1985.

Douglas, Mary. *Natural Symbols*. London: Cresset, 1970.

Dubofsky, Melvyn. *We Shall Be All: A History of the Industrial Workers of the World*. Chicago: Quadrangle, 1969.

Foreman, Dave. *Confessions of an Eco-Warrior*. New York: Harmony, 1991.

Foreman, Dave and Bill Haywood [pseud.], eds. *Ecodefense: A Field Guide to Monkeywrenching*. Tucson: Ned Ludd Books, 1973.

Geertz, Clifford. "Religion as a Cultural System." In *Reader in Comparative Religion: An Anthropological Approach,* 3rd Ed., edited by William Lessa and Evon Vogt, 78–89. New York: Harper and Row, 1972.

Grant, George. *Technology and Empire: Perspectives on North America*. Toronto: House of Anansi, 1969.

Greenwald, Carol. *Group Power*. New York: Praeger, 1977.

Gurr, Ted Robert. *Why Men Rebel*. Princeton: Princeton Univ. Press, 1970.

Hamilton, Alexander, James Madison, and John Jay. *The Federalist Papers*. New York: Mentor, 1961.

Jefferson, Thomas. "Declaration of the Causes and Necessity for taking up Arms." In *The Papers of Thomas Jefferson,* vol. 1, edited by Julian Boyd, 193–219. Princeton, N.J.: Princeton Univ. Press, 1950.

———. "Letter to Thomas Law, Esq.," June 13, 1814. In *The Life and Selected Writings of Thomas Jefferson,* edited by Adrienne Koch and William Peden, 636–40. New York: Modern Library, 1944.

Juergensmeyer, Mark. *The New Cold War? Religious Nationalism Confronts the Secular State*. Berkeley: Univ. of California Press, 1993.

Leopold, Aldo. *Round River: From the Journals of Aldo Leopold*. Edited by Luna B. Leopold. New York: Oxford Univ. Press, 1953.

———. *A Sand County Almanac and Sketches Here and There*. New York: Oxford Univ. Press, 1949.

Lincoln, Abraham. "Address Delivered at the Dedication of the Cemetery at Gettysburg, November 19, 1863." In *Abraham Lincoln: His Speeches and Writings,* 734–35. New York: Kraus, 1969.

Lowi, Theodore. *The End of Liberalism: Ideology, Policy, and the Crisis of Public Authority*. New York: W. W. Norton, 1969.

Manes, Christopher. *Green Rage: Radical Environmentalism and the Unmaking of Civilization*. Boston: Little, Brown, 1990.

McLaughlin, Andrew. *Regarding Nature: Industrialism and Deep Ecology.* Albany: State Univ. of New York Press, 1993.

Porterfield, Amanda. "American Indian Spirituality as a Countercultural Movement." In *Religion in Native North America,* edited by Christopher Vecsey, 152–64. Moscow: Univ. of Idaho Press, 1990.

Rhodes, James. *The Hitler Movement: A Modern Millenarian Revolution.* Stanford, Calif.: Hoover Institute Press, 1980.

Rubenstein, Richard. "Religion, Modernization, and Millenarianism." In *The Coming Kingdom,* edited by M. Darrol Bryant and Donald Dayton, 223–46. New York: New Era, 1983.

Rude, George. *Ideology and Popular Protest.* New York: Pantheon, 1980.

Scarce, Rik. *Eco-Warriors: Understanding the Radical Environmental Movement.* Chicago: Noble, 1990.

Schmookler, Andrew Bard. *The Parable of the Tribes.* Berkeley: Univ. of California Press, 1984.

Shepard, Paul. "Ecology and Man—A Viewpoint." In *The Subversive Science: Essays Towards an Ecology of Man,* edited by Paul Shepard and Daniel McKinley, 1–10. Boston: Houghton Mifflin, 1969.

Sjoberg, G. "Disasters and Social Change." In *Man and Society in Disaster,* edited by G. Baker and D. Chapman, 356–84. New York: Free Press, 1960.

Smith, Henry Nash. *Virgin Land: The American West as Symbol and Myth.* Cambridge, Mass.: Harvard Univ. Press, 1970.

Taft, Michael. *Discovering Saskatchewan Folklore.* Edmonton: NuWest, n.d.

Talmon, Yonina. "Millenarism." *International Encyclopedia of the Social Sciences.* Volume 10. New York: Macmillan, 1968.

Tichi, Cecelia. *New World, New Earth: Environmental Reform in American Literature from the Puritans Through Whitman.* New Haven, Conn.: Yale Univ. Press, 1979.

Tuveson, Ernest. *Redeemer Nation.* Chicago: Univ. of Chicago Press, 1968.

Voegelin, Eric. *The New Science of Politics.* Chicago: Univ. of Chicago Press, 1952.

Wallace, Anthony. *Religion: An Anthropological View.* New York: Random House, 1966.

Weber, Timothy. *Living in the Shadow of the Second Coming: American Premillennialism, 1875–1982.* Enlarged ed. Grand Rapids, Mich.: Academie, 1980.

Winthrop, John. "A Model of Christian Charity." In *Puritan Political Ideas, 1558–1794,* edited by Edmund Morgan, 75–93. Indianapolis: Bobbs-Merrill, 1965.

Wiser, James. *Political Philosophy: A History of the Search for Order.* Englewood Cliffs, N.J.: Prentice-Hall, 1983.

Wolke, Howie. *Wilderness on the Rocks.* Tucson: Ned Ludd Books, 1991.

Zakin, Susan. *Coyotes and Town Dogs: Earth First! and the Radical Environmental Movement.* New York: Viking, 1993.

Journal Articles and Conference Papers

Foreman, Dave. "Earth First!" *The Progressive* 45, no. 10 (Oct. 1981): 39–42.

Lee, Martha, and Thomas Flanagan. "The Black Muslims and the Fall of America." *Journal of Religious Studies* 16, nos. 1 and 2 (1988): 140–56.

Murphy, H. B. M. "Social Change and Mental Health." *Milbank Memorial Fund Quarterly* 39 (1961): 385–445.

Naess, Arne. "The Shallow and the Deep, Long-Range Ecology Movement. A Summary." *Inquiry* 16 (1973): 95–100.

Peerla, David. "The Moral Optic of Earth First!." Paper given at the annual meeting of the Canadian Political Science Association, Calgary, Alberta, June 13, 1994.

Taylor, Bron. "The Religion and Politics of Earth First!." *Ecologist* 21, no. 6 (Nov./Dec. 1991): 258–66.

Voegelin, Eric. "Reason: The Classic Experience." *Southern Review* 10, no. 2 (Spring 1974): 237–64.

Wallace, Anthony. "Revitalization Movements." *American Anthropologist* 58 (1956): 264–81.

Newspapers, Periodicals, and Miscellaneous Materials

Bari, Judi. "For F.B.I., Back to Political Sabotage?" *New York Times,* Aug. 23, 1990.

Bowden, Charles. "Dave Foreman! In the Face of Reality." *Buzzworm,* Mar./Apr. 1990, 46–51.

Bowman, Chris. "Earth First!ers Dare: Tread on Me." *Sacramento Bee,* July 12, 1987, A7.

Bradley, Ed. "Earth First!." *Sixty Minutes Transcript,* vol. 22, no. 24, Mar. 4, 1990.

Brower, Kenneth. "Mr. Monkeywrench." *Harrowsmith,* Sept./Oct. 1988, 40–51.

Coates, James. "Terrorists for Nature Proclaim Earth First!." *Chicago Tribune,* Aug. 2, 1987. sec. 1, 21.

De Paul, Tony. "Earth First!." *Sunday Journal Magazine* (Rhode Island), Mar. 26, 1989.

"Earth First!." *Southern Illinoisan,* Mar. 31, 1988, D21.

Federal Bureau of Investigation file, F.O.I. #344,522/190-71269. Washington, D.C.: FBI.

"Fellow Workers, Meet Earth First!, Earth First!ers Meet the IWW." *Industrial Worker,* May 1988, 5.

Foreman, Dave. Letter to author, Feb. 22, 1995.

"Founder Critical of Leftist Direction of Earth First!." *Arizona Daily Star,* Aug. 14, 1990, D5.

Franklin, Karen, and Janet Sowell. "The Timber Terrorists." *American Forests,* Mar./Apr. 1987, 41–42.

Gabriel, Trip. "If a Tree Falls in the Forest, They Hear It." *New York Times Magazine,* Nov. 4, 1990.

Geniella, Mike. "Leadership Dispute Splits Earth First!." *Press Democrat,* Aug. 12, 1990, A1.

Japenga, Ann. "Earth First! Comes out of the Shadows." *Spokesman-Review,* July 4, 1988, 6.

Jones, Robert A. "Here Come the '60s, With the FBI in Tow." *Los Angeles Times,* June 26, 1990.

Kane, Joe. "Mother Nature's Army." *Esquire,* Feb. 1987, 98–106.

Kuipers, Dean. "Razing Arizona." *Spin,* Sept. 1989, 33–38.

Lacey, Michael. "Sabotaging the Saboteurs." *New Times,* May 29–June 4, 1991, 8–10.

Lerner, Michael. "The FBI vs. the Monkeywrenchers." *Los Angeles Times Magazine,* Apr. 15, 1990, 10–21.

Littman, John. "Peace, Love . . . and TNT." *California,* Dec. 1990, 82–128.

Mallia, Joseph. "He's Done it All in the Name of Nature." *Recorder,* (Greenfield, Mass.), Feb. 7, 1988, 3.

Miller, Tom. "What is the Sound of One Billboard Falling?" *Berkeley Barb,* Nov. 8–14, 1974, 9–12.

Negri, Sam. "Earth First! Setup Alleged." *Arizona Republic,* Apr. 25, 1990, B2.

Petersen, David. "The Playboy Interview, Dave Foreman: No Compromise in Defense of Mother Earth." *Mother Earth News,* Jan./Feb. 1985, 17–22.

Pickell, Bill (General Manager, Washington Contract Loggers' Association). Letter to author, Jan. 7, 1991.

Robbins, Jim. "The Environmental Guerrillas." *Boston Globe Magazine,* Mar. 27, 1988.

Rosales, Glen, and Jim Herron. "Foreman Won't be Roped In." *Sunday Journal,* June 25, 1989, A1.

Roselle, Mike, and Darryl Cherney. "Ballad of the Lonesome Tree Spiker." *They Sure Don't Make Hippies Like They Used To,* home recording.

Sayen, Jamie. "Voice from the Wilderness." *Coos County Democrat,* Feb. 10, 1988, 2A.

Shaffer, Mark. "Activist Spied on Uranium Mine before Vandalism, Court is Told." *Arizona Republic,* June 22, 1991.

———. "'Eco-terrorism' Trial Underway." *Arizona Republic,* June 20, 1991, B1.
———. "Ski-resort 'Sabotage' Detailed." *Arizona Republic,* June 21, 1991.
Shute, Nancy. "Dave Foreman Meets the Feds." *Outside,* Sept. 1989.
Slind-Flor, Victoria. "Jailed Researcher Claims Shield." *National Law Journal,* Aug. 9, 1993, 3.
Sommer, Anthony. "Review Case Against Earth First!, Judge Asked." *Phoenix Gazette,* June 5, 1991, A6.
Zakin, Susan. "Earth First!." *Smart,* Sept./Oct. 1989, 88–94.

Earth First! and Related Publications

Appalachian Earth First!. Brigid/Feb. 2, 1989–Dec. 1990.
Chase, Steve, ed. *Defending the Earth: A Dialogue Between Murray Bookchin and Dave Foreman.* Boston: South End, 1991.
Davis, John, ed. *The Earth First! Reader: Ten Years of Radical Environmentalism.* Salt Lake City: Peregrine Smith, 1991.
Earth First. 1, no. 1 (Samhain/Nov. 1, 1980).
Earth First! (photocopied newsletter). 1, no. 2 (Yule/Dec. 21, 1980)–1, no. 8 (Halloween/Oct. 31, 1981).
Earth First!. 2, no. 7 (Lughnasad/Aug. 1, 1982)–10, no. 4 (Eostar/Mar. 20, 1990), and 11, no. 3 (Brigid/Feb. 2, 1991)–14, no. 6 (Litha/June 21, 1994).
Earth First! Journal. 10, no. 5 (May 1, 1990)–11, no. 2 (Dec. 21, 1990).
Earth First! Newsletter. 2, no. 2 (Yule/Dec. 21, 1981)–2, no. 6 (Summer Solstice/June 21, 1982).
"Earth First! Springs to Life: Organization Urges Dismantling of Glen Canyon Dam." Press release. Mar. 20, 1981.
Foreman, Dave and Howie Wolke. Memorandum Regarding Earth First. Sept. 1980.
Foreman, Dave. Memorandum on Earth First Statement of Principles and Membership Brochure. Sept. 1, 1980.
Glacial Erratic. 1, no. 4 (Winter 1989), and 2, no. 1 (Spring 1990)–2, no. 4 (Winter 1990).
Live Wild or Die. Two issues, undated.
Nature More. 0, no. 0 (July 1980).
Washington Earth First! Newsletter. June 1986–April 1991.
Wild Earth. 1, no. 1 (Spring 1991)–4, no. 3 (Summer 1994).

Selected Earth First! Interviews

All interviews were conducted by the author.

Cherney, Darryl. Ballard, Wash. Apr. 10, 1991.
Cherney, Darryl. Seattle, Wash. Apr. 11, 1991.

Davis, John. Canton, N.Y. Dec. 4, 1991.
Davis, Mary. Canton, N.Y. Dec. 4, 1991.
Draffan, George. Ballard, Wash. Apr. 8, 1991.
Foreman, Dave. Tucson, Ariz. Jan. 24, 1992.
———. Telephone Interviews. Apr. 27, 1992; Mar. 9, 1993.
Friedman, Mitch. Bellingham, Wash. Apr. 16, 1991.
Jacobs, Lynn. Tucson, Ariz. Jan. 24, 1992.
Mondt, Rod. Tucson, Ariz. Jan. 26, 1992.
Reed, Renee. Seattle, Wash. Apr. 19, 1991.
VanGessell, Tony. Bellingham, Wash. Apr. 16, 1991.
Wilson, Helen. Tucson, Ariz. Jan. 26, 1992.
Winguard, Greg. Seattle, Wash. Apr. 10, 1991.
Zierenberg, Nancy. Tucson, Ariz. Jan. 26, 1992.

Other Interviews

Stark, Tamara (Media Director, Greenpeace Canada). Telephone Interview. May 26, 1993.

I also interviewed representatives of the Washington logging industry on the condition that they remain anonymous. The date and location of these interviews would provide significant clues as to the identity of these subjects, and so cannot be provided here. All of these interviews took place in the Pacific Northwest.

Index

201